Towards a New Poverty Agenda in Asia

Towards a New Poverty Agenda in Asia

Social Policies and Economic Transformation

Arjan de Haan

SAGE
www.sagepublications.com
Los Angeles • London • New Delhi • Singapore • Washington DC

First published in 2010 by

SAGE Publications India Pvt Ltd
B1/I-1 Mohan Cooperative Industrial Area
Mathura Road, New Delhi 110 044, India
www.sagepub.in

SAGE Publications Inc
2455 Teller Road
Thousand Oaks, Califo.nia 91320, USA

SAGE Publications Ltd
1 Oliver's Yard
55 City Road
London EC1Y 1SP, United Kingdom

SAGE Publications Asia-Pacific Pte Ltd
33 Pekin Street
#02-01 Far East Square
Singapore 048763

Published by Vivek Mehra for SAGE Publications India Pvt Ltd, typeset in 10/12 pt Adobe Garamond by Star Compugraphics Private Limited, Delhi and printed at Chaman Enterprises, New Delhi.

Library of Congress Cataloging-in-Publication Data

Haan, Arjan de.
Towards a new poverty agenda in Asia: social policies and economic transformation/Arjan De Haan.
p. cm.
Includes bibliographical references and index.
1. Social policy. 2. Economic development. 3. Poverty. 4. Asia—Social policy. 5. Developing countries—Social policy. I. Title.
HN18.3.H333 320.609172'4—dc22 2010 2010028615

ISBN: 978-81-321-0504-6 (HB)

The SAGE Team: Elina Majumdar, Aniruddha De and Deepti Saxena

Contents

List of Tables and Graphs

Tables

Graphs

List of Boxes

Preface

Since the 1990s, poverty has become the overarching theme of international development debates. And even inequality has entered, or returned to, the mainstream of development publications like the *Human Development Report* and *World Development Report*. Around the turn of the century, a growing strand of literature also started to pay attention to the role of social policy, based on the critique of the residual nature in which social policy or development has been framed during the period of structural adjustment, and liberal and neo-liberal paradigms of economic analysis and public policy making.

Building on this new strand of social policy research—manifested by Bob Deacon, United Nations Research Institute for Social Development (UNRISD), the University of Bath, Morales-Gómez, and others—I published my own contribution (de Haan, 2007b) as a development practitioner working at one of the older and larger international development agencies, the Department for International Development (DFID). Around the time, there were signs that a more proactive and developmental notion of social policy was starting to be adopted. But various trends appear to continue to work against this. There is a continued tension between a focus on poverty and emphasis on targeting, and a broader developmental approach that UNRISD and others have emphasized. Another important constraint to the debate has been the emphasis on achieving impact, tangible results visible to stakeholders and taxpayers, and "aid effectiveness"—while desirable in itself, this continues to stymie the thinking about the long-term project of enhancing capacities of development states. The entry of the new "vertical" initiatives, the many new and private agencies like the Gates Foundation, and perhaps even the recent emphasis on "social protection" and cash transfer can have a similar impact, taking the attention away—though by no means intentionally—from the wide range of public policy capacity that is required for development in the broad sense. And increasing attention has focused on the role of the international community in fragile states, where the conditions for developmental public policies are thought to be absent.

So, the global debate and practices continue to throw up sufficient questions to justify continued analysis of social policy ideas and practices across the globe. This book focuses on these issues in Asia, and I am aware that "limiting" oneself from a global scope to one that covers over 3 billion people, more than 900 million of whom live under the poverty line as redefined by the World Bank in 2008, in itself is hardly convincing for those who rightly emphasize the need to understand development in specific national and historical context. I saw three sets of reasons to further develop the arguments regarding the role of social policy in an Asian context. First, the international debate matters across Asia: it influences the public debate, for example, in Vietnam which has been quick to adopt and try out different approaches; it matters in China where experimenting using national and international knowledge has been a key part of its reform approach since 1978; and it is important in India even though the debate tends to be one of contestation rather than of (mutual) learning.

Second, as I hope to illustrate in this book, making comparisons across Asia appear to be particularly fruitful, and largely unexplored. Countries at similar levels of economic development have very different outcomes in terms of poverty and human development indicators, and they have very different social policy approaches that are, at least partly, responsible for these different outcomes. There is a great deal of path dependence in social policy approaches, but they are not unchanging, and learning occurs, through experience and through international exchange. Comparison of social policy "regimes" and their relevance for enhancing well-being, as heuristic device, can contribute to international academic and policy learning.

Third, this book is written at a time when the impacts of a new phase of globalization—where emerging economies like China and India are reversing earlier globalization trends, and are (re)positioning themselves as major economic power houses—are only starting to become visible in Asia. The role of social policy is rapidly changing in the context of the more successful economies, partly as a Polanyian reaction to the more negative consequences of past growth patterns, partly because of the perceived complementary role of social policy in economic growth, and partly because of on-going projects of nation-state building—perhaps particularly a concern in the large countries with a federal administration. The impact of the 2008–09 financial crisis which ended a short decade of stability and growth is as yet unclear, though there is no doubt that the crisis that started in the United States (US) with the bankruptcy of the Lehman Brothers, once again, highlighted the extent of global interconnectedness, but also with a strong commitment—unlike after the 1929 crisis, for example—to ensure global policy coordination and avoid protectionism. On top of these challenges, climate change is likely to have an enormous impact, often in the countries which have little capacity to deal with even "normal" development problems (and with the least responsibility for causing it), and for India and China because of their global roles, as the Copenhagen Summit in December 2009 demonstrated. While this book does not discuss the impact of climate change, the challenges and additional strains caused by increased droughts and flooding, and falling agricultural productivity, provide additional reasons to consider the cross-sectoral capacity for policy making.

This book draws on different academic disciplines, and takes sides in theoretical debates, particularly around the separation of economic from social policy analysis. The project also implies a call for development agencies to come out of its silos of sectoral polices, and for social development to have a stronger focus on policy reform, including because social policy can be as regressive as other forms of public policies. Finally, the book emphasizes improved understanding of the deeply political nature of social policy and development policies more broadly. This makes it a hugely challenging project, which is by no means finished, but I hope this book will make a small contribution to this important debate, at a time when it is clear that current social policy responses are insufficient to deal with new realities.

Acknowledgements

The motivation to develop my earlier work in an Asian context came from what to me still appears as rather odd travels across the world, and my intellectual debts—and I hope friendships—are firmly grounded in those paths. After a period of leave in which I wrote *Reclaiming Social Policy*, in good civil service tradition I was sent to a place I probably knew least about, China. The process of learning during my short period of two to three years has been an amazing experience, which will continue for years to come. In the DFID office in Beijing, I learnt to re-evaluate what I knew about the nature of international development, appreciate why many Chinese think the rest of the world does not understand China, including why many senior officials did not manage to smile during Beijing Olympics events (on this I still think they got it wrong, and feel I have millions of Chinese on my side), and of course, most importantly, they taught me much about a country whose diversity and language make even the hardest working scholar a beginner for many years. So, thank you, in particular, Qiao Jianrong, Sun Xuebing, Hao Aimin, Liu Yang, Martin Taylor, John Warburton, Holger Grundel, and Elizabeth Wilson within DFID, and Zhang Xiulan, Li Xiaoyun, Wang Xiaoyi, Li Shi, Sarah Cook, Jennifer Holdaway, and many colleagues and friends at the International Poverty Reduction Center in China (IPRCC) and the State Council Leading Group Office for Poverty Alleviation and Development (LGOP) offices.

Other people in DFID who gave encouragement for my continued explorations and supported the extra-curricular activities as much as they could include Ellen Wratten, Jillian Popkins, and Charlotte Heath. Gerard Howe, Bridget Dillon, Pat Holden, Paul Healey, and Judy Walker have all motivated me to continue my explorations of social policy issues. I have benefited greatly from the collaboration, earlier on, with colleagues in and outside the DFID India office, particularly Dennis Pain, Shalini Bahuguna, Gita Ṣabharwal, Aruna Bagchee, Sarojini Thakur, Shan Mitra, Amaresh Dubey, Harsh Mander, and S.K. Thorat.

The social policy research community has provided constant inspiration for my work over the years. Bob Deacon, Ian Gough, and Armando Barrientos have always been a great source of inspiration as well as encouragement, and I draw liberally on their work. The team at UNRISD has been very important for my motivation to write on social policy, particularly Thandika Mkandawire, Huck-ju Kwon, and Katja Hujo. It has been a great pleasure and privilege to be working with Anis Dani, who developed the social policy framework to strengthen commitment within the World Bank to the 1995 Copenhagen Summit commitments. Colleagues at my new academic home, the Institute of Social Studies, particularly Ashwani Saith and Mahmood Messkoub, have provided inspiration to revisit the debates on universalization, and my students continue to motivate me to better explain the importance of social policy analysis.

At SAGE Publications, I would like to thank Sugata Ghosh and Elina Majumdar for the encouragement to write this book, and their patience and support. I have also greatly benefited from the thoughtful comments of an anonymous referee.

Finally, as always, my family deserves most credit, for putting up with yet another writing project. My children are starting to understand that their Dad's name on a book comes after many hours of the time they rightly think is theirs. Paramjit has been my main source of support, and constant reminder that the world is much bigger than my explorations in "development" suggest.

Introduction

This book explores the role of social policy in enhancing well-being and combating exclusion, and in shaping the conditions for market forces and economic growth. It looks at the ways in which social policies are formulated and implemented, particularly in Asia, and in the context in which globalizing forces affect people's livelihoods as well as the opportunities for national public policies. It does so at a time when a global financial crisis is affecting livelihoods and well-being of people all around the world, following a period of unprecedented economic growth, which contained both rising inequalities and the causes of that financial crisis.

This exploration is driven by an interest in the capacities for policy making to protect groups from becoming excluded, and to promote inclusion, particularly through universal approaches to service provision, while simultaneously being supportive of economic policies. The international development literature pays much attention to indicators of well-being, and increasingly in its multidimensional forms, following in particular Amartya Sen's (1982) emphasis on capabilities to perform functions. But too little attention, in my view, is given to the policies and institutional preconditions for promoting well-being, and to explore the directions set out in the volume edited by Ahmad et al. (1991) to explore public actions that address deprivation and vulnerability. An exploration of existing policies, even at a time where globalization and structural adjustment has led to policy convergence in many areas, shows very different ways in which policy making is being practiced and indeed conceptualized across Asia.

Social policy needs to be understood in a broad sense. This is not merely a matter of definition, but has political overtones, and social policy is seen here as an expression of principles of solidarity and inclusion. The notion of social policy applied here takes sides in debates between strands of theories that have deep ideological and political roots, particularly the way in which analysis of economic policies has been separated from, and given priority over that of other public policies.

Social policy complements economic policies, and does not just deal with the unintended consequences of economic trends like globalization or crises. Social policy is broader than social protection or social security, and is used in this book in a way to promote cross-sectoral analysis and policy making. The need for such a broad view is evident during economic crises because of the nature of fiscal stimulus packages. However, such an understanding was absent—or perhaps, even discouraged—during the period of "adjustment" in Africa in particular, which is one reason why this book discusses the African experience. In adopting this approach, the book engages with different academic disciplines, of course the social policy literature, but also debates on globalization, growth, and poverty reduction, because of its influence on the broader development debate, and the governance literature that has become increasingly important alongside a focus on poverty reduction. In the way this book uses the concept social policy, the political dynamics are put up-front rather than the more technical focus that characterizes much development analysis.

National social policy—as an element of broader public policy—is more, not less as commonly argued, important in a globalized world, and in more open economies and societies. The current crisis makes this increasingly evident, but the argument does not only apply to crisis responses. The book therefore emphasizes the need for strengthened analysis of social policies, and its role in shaping of well-being across nations. It documents this in a comparative way, with a focus on the varied contexts of the Asian continent, ranging, for example, from the more disparate and civil society-driven articulation of social policies in Bangladesh, toward the strongly centralized state-driven policy evolution with relatively large degrees of local autonomy in implementation and experimentation in China, and the politicized form of social policies defined by and shaping extensive social churning.

The development paths in, and some of the intellectual history of, Asia stand out from most of the rest of the world, as shown in Graph I.1 and Table I.1. By the year 2000, China's rise had become evident, following the reforms started in 1978, and with the events of 1989 that had solidified political control. Vietnam followed China's path to a great extent, and now "ticks all the boxes for the Millennium Development Goals" alongside economic policies that have brought the country "halfway from rags to riches" (*Economist*, 2008a: 3–16). Table I.1 illustrates the drastic transformations in Asia, which, as we will see later, contrast sharply with those of other parts of the world. In these relatively successful countries, new social policy challenges have rapidly emerged, including rising inequalities and ageing populations (with some countries growing old before they grow rich).

Graph I.1 Poverty Trends: Regional Differences

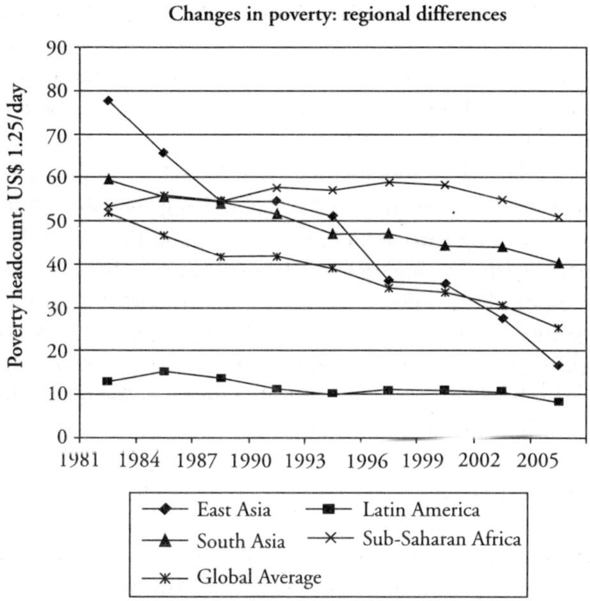

Source: Based on World Bank data (World Bank, 2008).

Table I.1 Asian Transformation

	GDP per capita (PPP US$)	*Annual growth*	*Urbanization % urban population*		*Demographic shift total fertility rate*	
	2005	*1970–2005*	*1975*	*2005*	*1970–75*	*2000–05*
Bangladesh	2,053	2.0	10	25	6.2	3.3
Cambodia	2,727	n.a.	10	20	5.5	4.1
China	6,757	8.4	17	40	4.9	1.7
India	3,452	3.4	21	29	5.4	3.1
Indonesia	3,843	3.9	19	48	5.2	2.4
Korea	22,029	6.0	48	81	4.3	1.2
Malaysia	10,882	3.9	38	67	5.2	2.9
Pakistan	2,370	2.5	26	35	6.6	4.3
Sri Lanka	4,595	3.2	20	15	4.1	2.0
Thailand	8,677	4.9	24	32	5.0	1.9
Vietnam	3,071	5.2	19	26	6.7	2.3

Sources: Gross domestic product (GDP) and urbanization figures are World Bank data; demographic data from Gubhaju (2007), based on data from *World Population Prospects: The 2004 Revision*, United Nations Population Division.

Both countries also felt the impact of the 2008 financial crisis and preceding economic downturn relatively quickly and severely. Indonesia, too, saw exceptionally high rates of economic growth at least till the 1997 financial crisis. India experienced decades of sustained economic growth and improving standards of living, and Bangladesh, too, has been relatively successful, over a somewhat shorter period.

The economic developments in Asia reflected in Table I.1 took place under varying political regimes and social and cultural fabrics (with, as described later, a strong patriarchy in both South and East Asia). The growth was associated with opening up to global markets, but the economic policies that were responsible for this success were "unorthodox"; a story—or rather series of stories—that, by and large, has continued to escape the mainstream debate, and it is unlikely that other parts of the world can emulate this success, at least not in the near future. Finally, these changes have taken place under a most dramatic demographic shift, as the fertility rates presented in the table indicate, providing an economic boost, while being part of changing family and gender relations, but simultaneously presenting a new challenge of rapidly ageing population.

The question which we are interested in, for this book, is how social policies are constituted in this modernizing and globalizing world, with a focus on Asia, and the way this has been integrated and becomes a core feature of global markets. An underlying concern relates to the capacity for policy making required to protect groups from becoming excluded, and promote inclusion across the various dimensions of well-being and opportunities. A focus on Asia will help understand the conditions under which these relative successes can be achieved, and highlight the challenges for other parts of the world. While there are no direct "lessons for" the rest of the world from Asia's development path (de Haan, Zhang, and Fan, 2010: 171–83), this book does argue that a comparative approach can help in understanding conditions for success, as argued next.

Comparisons

There are various reasons to adopt a comparative approach. First, scholars and policy makers compare anyway. Studies use comparative frameworks, implicitly more often than explicitly. It is therefore of crucial importance to clarify the basics for comparisons. In the development studies literature, comparisons are often implicit, and often unreflective. Social policy studies in the development literature have dismissed notions of social policy as irrelevant for contexts in the South. This resistance has some good reasons, but runs the risk of throwing out the baby with the bath water, and is often based on implicit models from one particular context, thus neglecting the diversity of policy "regimes" that exist in Organization for Economic Co-operation and Development (OECD) contexts too. It is important to ensure lessons from northern and emerging economies' social policy are documented, contextualized, and appropriately used in other contexts.

Second, national policy makers learn from experience elsewhere,[1] and for understanding national policy, it is of great relevance to trace genealogies of ideas and how ideas are mediated within specific political contexts. In aid-dependent countries, donor and, thus, northern influence on practices is immediately recognizable. In India, while not aid-dependent, in the health sector, for example, the 1943 Bhore Committee led to the introduction of western ideas, unsurprisingly, but the new National Rural Health Mission launched in 2005 also carried much external influence. In the case of China, comparisons have become a central feature of official policy (of course, international exchange was crucially important pre-1979 as well), and in Vietnam, there is a clear interest of learning from China. As China is opening up, learning from and experimenting with models from elsewhere is core to policy innovation. And as China is becoming a world power, its model of development has attracted a great deal of attention, particularly in developing countries, and it is actively promoting the exchange of knowledge and culture. Comparative research can provide a stronger grounding for such comparisons.

An idea of policy "regimes" can facilitate learning and comparative research. A notion of welfare regime as developed by Esping-Andersen (1990, 1999), used and extended by Gough and Wood (2004), Abu Sharkh and Gough (2008), and others for social policy research in a non-OECD context, focuses on the interdependent way welfare is produced, through market, state, family, and the voluntary sector. The idea of regimes is based in the observation that these patterns of welfare provisions differ systematically across OECD countries, often related to historical patterns of political mobilization. Esping-Andersen originally identified three regimes or approaches to solidarity,[2] which are described in more detail later in the book. Development of such a regimes approach is of relevance outside the

[1] According to Pierson (2004: 15), welfare states that developed later than the classic ones in western Europe "have always been strongly influenced both by the example of developed welfare states elsewhere (with an evident debt to both Bismarck and Beveridge) as well as the prompting of international agencies." The classic study on the welfare state by Mommsen (1981) was an explicit attempt to compare German and British experience.

[2] Silver (1994) emphasizes that welfare state solidarity has differed systematically across OECD countries, and the context specific and historically determined nature of patterns of social integration and exclusion, and policy responses.

OECD context, including in the poorest parts of the world, as it highlights the varying ways in which social policies evolve, and, for example, universalization is or is not achieved (and this can indeed be in many different ways, as experience in the OECD also suggests).[3]

A descriptive scan of social policy constellations—and comparison between South Asia and East Asia in particular—does suggest that patterns can be discerned. As suggested in de Haan (2007b), one can usefully describe "principles of solidarity." In different contexts, different notions of solidarity and social integration, and in some contexts, extending to notion of citizenship can be distinguished. As in OECD contexts, these appear to have degrees of path dependence, and in the South, often colonial origins. But also, there are traces of regional similarities, and with influences of regional and global lesson learning.

Such regimes are by no means static. They are path dependent in the sense that traditions and differences continue to influence configurations of social policies. But of course, these configurations are dynamic, influenced by—often interacting—factors like globalization, immigration, economic crises, and political or social pressure, including public debate which notably in India is a key element of evolving social policy, or fears of "social unrest" which is a much stronger driver of change in China.

Following the emphasis on politics of social policies, the framework proposed here, thus, also implies a comparison of political and administrative systems. Amartya Sen (1999) famously showed a clear link between democratization and well-being in his assertion that no famine had ever taken place in a functioning democracy, though democracies like India's had a less impressive record in dealing with endemic hunger. The comparison of social policy regimes here further develops this argument, with reference, for example, to continued deep deprivation in parts of India and the circumstances under which poverty reduced so rapidly in China, and the ways in which the implementation of social policies itself shapes political and institutional dynamics.

In a recent paper, Ian Gough (2008) demonstrates that even though the conditions in the global North and South vary a great deal, there are "analytical" lessons from the OECD literature on welfare states. First, social policies show a certain amount of path dependency, a tendency of changes

---

[3] The universalization of socio-economic security in the South Asian context was the subject of a special issue of the *Indian Journal of Human Development* (January–June 2008); see in particular articles by Ashwani Saith (2008b) and Guy Standing (2008) for strong arguments in favor of universalization and egalitarianism.

to occur in directions depending on its own past. Second, and related, patterns of social policy are constituted through a combination of "5 Is," of industrialization (or structural change), interests, institutions, ideas, and international influence. The matrix given in Table I.2 summarizes how this can be used, with reference to China and India, and this book uses this framework in a loose way also to compare Asian experiences with Latin American and African countries' social policy histories. The details do not need to concern the reader at this stage, as they will be described in detail in the second part of this book. The key point here is that it is possible to make comparisons of social policies in different contexts, and that a framework like the one proposed here can help to understand similarities and differences.

At the same time, it should be stressed that using a framework like this sets out a large research agenda. Such an agenda would involve, on the one hand, deeper context-specific analysis and description of national social policies, and on the other hand, more formal testing of hypothesis about the relevance and impact of policy regimes. This book highlights the potential of comparison evolvement of social policy across Asia, and to some extent, in comparison with Africa and Latin America, with its different histories and levels of economic development.

Structure of this Book

To promote such an understanding of social policy, this book proceeds as follows. The first part of the book focuses on the global trends and debates, and the second on the comparative narratives of national social policy experiences. Chapter 1 sets the context for the discussion and concepts used in this book, describing the various approaches to social policy, how they have evolved over time, and why; despite important critiques, I believe a social policy concept is of relevance for understanding social policy in the South. The chapter discusses how the notion of social policy relates to other strands of development debates, and how it can be used in a comparative way. It briefly describes how approaches to social policy have evolved, from a more proactive notion during the 1950s and 1960s, via a residual fashion from the 1970s onward, to a re-evaluation under influence of the increased attention to poverty and rise of a governance agenda in the second half of the 1990s.

A key question around the concept of social policies is how they relate to economic growth and macroeconomic policies. Are social policies concerned merely with correcting malfunctions in the operation of society and

Table I.2 Comparing Social Policy: China and India

	Industrialization	*Interests*	*Institutions*	*Ideas ("welfare regimes")*	*International influence*
China	Great transition Privatization Demography: one-child policy, ageing	Political power contingent on growth and "social harmony"	Congruence economic–social Gradual and decentralized reform, extensive use pilots	"Harmonious society"	Open and proactive lesson learning "Responsible global actor" (reinforced through 2008 financial crisis)
India	Continued rurality/Informality	Electoral cycles Trade unions Scheduled Castes (SC)/Scheduled Tribes (ST)/Other Backward Classes (OBC) frameworks	Patch work of programs and institutions Colonial legacy Federalism, with centralized welfare programs	Universalism along welfarist/residual principles	Colonial legacies Global social science research networks

Source: Based on de Haan and Sabharwal (2008), using the framework developed by Ian Gough (2008).

economy, or are they proactive interventions shaping those institutions? The period of adjustment has given prominence to the first, residual definition of social policy; however, the key hypothesis is that social policies do—intentionally or unintentionally, and as shown convincingly in the gendered analyses of economic policies and budgets—play a constitutive role in creating patterns of inclusion and exclusion, and directly and indirectly shape the conditions for market functioning. Chapter 1 analyzes the ways in which social policies impact economic growth: the negative impact of expanding state finances and the moral hazard caused by state transfers; the importance of health, nutrition, and education policies for economic growth; the importance of policies related to redistribution and social inclusion for economic growth, and difficulties posed by sharp social divisions for the possibility of carrying out economic reforms; and the importance of social security in helping to address adverse long-term consequences of economic shocks, and for allowing people to take risks.

Chapter 2 sets the scene for understanding the need for and challenges faced by social policies, by describing trends of global well-being and inequality. Economic growth, where it has been achieved, and opening up of economies usually have benefited countries and often, most people within those. But these gains have not come automatically, and in most if not all countries, groups and regions have fallen behind and, where they have governments, often have responded with poverty alleviation programs rather than policies that enable these areas to participate in mainstream development (China being a partial exception). The analysis in this book focuses on the interaction between globalizing and national forces and processes—which will be illustrated later in the book referring to policy changes in India during the 1990s and China since 1978 in particular—and contrasted with cases of globalization where the policy agenda was more strongly determined by external forces, notably in Africa.

Processes of economic opening up are generally not, and should not, be accompanied by less state intervention. The financial crisis has demonstrated that not only better regulation of the financial sector is needed but also to be better prepared to protect populations from the effects of crises. Countries with more integrated markets, including during periods of adjustment, do not spend less, but often more on social sectors—ideas about "demise of the nation states," thus, appear misplaced, as Chapter 3 will discuss. Higher social spending may be related to the need to mitigate the risks associated with more open economies. Proactive social policies are required to help prepare populations for more competitive markets, as particularly the East Asian experience indicates. Regulation and international agreements related to labor conditions become key when service provisions are privatized and opened up to international markets. Thus, open economies tend to have more proactive social policies, to mitigate risks, prepare for competition, and improve quality of regulation.

Chapter 4 describes recent trends in international development strategies for poverty reduction. It discusses the theoretical approach of the post-Washington Consensus, the progress that this entails in terms of broad-based and comprehensive approaches to development and poverty reduction, and attention to institutions in reform debates even though the consensus remained optimistic about the possibilities of markets. This chapter critically appraises two development approaches that gained popularity during the 1990s: sector-wide approaches developed to improve policy making and services, particularly in health and education; and the Poverty Reduction Strategy Papers developed for heavily indebted poor countries (HIPC) to combine debt relief with a focus on poverty reduction in the development strategies. While progress has been made toward more integrated strategies for poverty reduction, the evidence suggests that development practices still fall short in strengthening cross-sectoral capacity for social policy formulation, and integrating an understanding of the political nature of public policies. While poverty reduction strategies have managed to bring deprivation to the core of the international development agenda, perspectives need to be broadened beyond the confines of addressing "poverty," so as to facilitate better understanding of the political economy that underlies policy making for the poor and also, the non-poor, and positioning itself strategically in terms of inclusive social policies.

Chapter 4 further discusses the contested theme of "residual" social policies, targeted safety nets, and social funds, which have dominated the social policy debate since the 1980s. The chapter explores the role of the poverty analyses that have formed the intellectual basis for such residual approaches to social policy making. The dominant poverty approaches, with a focus on "outcomes," have reinforced residual approaches. Social funds are an example of such a residual approach to social policy. With the rise of structural adjustment policies, and the need to provide these with a "human face," donors experimented with instruments to ameliorate the worst effects of crises and adjustment. While these social funds have evolved substantially, they have not sufficiently contributed to strengthening mainstream policy making for social and economic development. The chapter also describes approaches to social protection, rapidly gaining in popularity after crises like East Asia's in 1997 (when international institutions came under heavy critique because of their advice to countries like Indonesia and Thailand), and the recent emphasis on conditional and unconditional cash transfers, asking whether these social policies are associated merely with mechanisms to deal with the unintended consequences of economic change and crises, and thus may reinforce the marginalization of social policy.

Building on the writings of Esping-Andersen, Ian Gough, and Hilary Silver, the second part of this book applies typologies of "social policy regimes," as heuristic tools, and emphasizing principles of solidarity. Chapters 5–8 look at national social policies from an historical perspective, which is essential to understand the ways in which social policies come into being—including specific forms of private–public mix, statutory or community-based approaches, and social insurance or security versus national service approaches—and the political dynamics behind the policies. This includes a quantitative overview of public expenditure, as an indication of the differences in state intervention across countries and their commitment to social and human development, but also highlighting that this "social" spending can reinforce inequalities.

Chapter 5 discusses Latin American social policies, which historically were characterized as state "corporatist." In this social policy regime, during most of the last century, pressure group bargaining rather than rights of citizens dominated the policy-making process. This has contributed not only to the large inequalities that have marked the continent for a long time but also to the institutions responsible for shaping social policy. Approaches moved toward a more liberal regime during the period of adjustment, though more recently (and perhaps under influence of the frequent crisis that marked the continent during the 1990s), countries like Chile and Brazil appear to be moving toward more inclusive policies, and in Bolivia, for example, the politics of indigenous groups provide new social policy directions.

With roots in the late colonial period, and shaped during the post-colonial period of inward-oriented economic development, social policies in many countries obtained a strongly "dualistic" nature, with inclusive social policies for a small section of the population and targeted projects for the large majority of poor people. While Africa—or at least many countries in it—is generally regarded as uniformly poor, with failed development policy, the early history after independence was marked by proactive developmental policy, with various degrees of success. Proactive social policies were a key component of this, accompanying nation building. Social policies were dramatically reshaped under adjustment, with much international influence, as Chapter 6 describes. While the notion of social policy is generally regarded as irrelevant for Africa, this book instead argues—building on recent writings at the African Union and Adésínà (2007), for example—that more attention needs to be paid to creating the preconditions for creating developmental social policies.

Chapter 7 describes how East Asian policies have been productivist oriented and inclusive. The states have been important for its economic success, including in the proactive policies of privatization (avoiding a Soviet-style implosion). But social transfers have remained consciously small, within conservative fiscal policies, and an emphasis on individuals' and households' own responsibilities and "Confucian values." Principles of universalism have been combined with an emphasis on people's, households', or communities' own contribution, and targetted approaches such as the anti-poverty programs in China, emphasizing integration into economic growth and mainstream development. Nation building has been a prime driver of its social policies, and many of the nation-state building exercises have taken place under one-party and authoritarian regimes, with the East Asia crisis of 1997 impacting both implementation of social policies and the politics in which these are embedded.

As in Africa, social policies in South Asia, described in Chapter 8, have retained a strong dualistic character, with the (temporary) exception of Sri Lanka and the Indian state of Kerala. Social policies have evolved alongside an impressive but less deep economic and social transformation as the one witnessed in East Asia. Colonial traditions continue to influence approaches to social welfare, primarily by the state in India, and much more strongly determined by the large non-governmental organizations (NGOs) in Bangladesh. Political democracy and the way this emerged from the colonial period gave a particular shape to the implementation of the social policy model in India, including in the dualism between modern (organized) and informal (unorganized) sectors, its many "centrally-sponsored" schemes, and notably, through the "reservation" policies for marginalized groups.

The book's conclusion tries to bridge the analytical framework proposed here with a practical framework for supporting social policy making. The framework has a normative and rights-based element, departing from international agreements, particularly the declaration of the Social Summit. It suggests a framework for assessing cross-sectoral social policies, on the basis of access, quality and relevance, and participation. It emphasizes the path-dependent character of social policy making, the ways social policies shape patterns of provision and of exclusion and inclusion, and the context-dependent ways in which international agreements are and can be translated into welfare outcomes. This emphasizes a strengthened analysis of social policy in the development of poverty reduction strategies and in responses to the current crisis, and incorporating an understanding of safety nets and social protection into wider analysis of national policy making, including their politicized nature.

SOCIAL POLICY IN AN AGE OF GLOBALIZATION

PART ONE

Since the golden, post-war period came to an end in the early 1970s, the state has been under pressure. Accompanying political changes, neo-liberal policies that emphasize reduced state intervention became mainstream in OECD countries, and structural adjustment came to dominate the Global South. Social policies have been particularly under stress, with an emphasis on reducing budget deficits—even in contexts where such deficits were not particularly marked, as in East Asia during the 1997–98 crisis—and increasing the targeting of publicly provided benefits.

Poverty reduction has now become core to much of the international development debate. Around the turn of the century, following political changes in OECD countries, the critique of structural adjustment, and the global pressure toward debt relief, poverty became the agreed overarching objective. Even inequality reappeared on the agenda (Nel, 2006; United Nations Development Program [UNDP], 2005; World Bank, 2005). Since 2000, increased aid financing has been committed, and the trend in aid flows indeed went upwards, at least for a few years, but they remain small compared to private flows like investments and migrants' remittances. At the same time, global inequalities continued to rise, and there are major questions regarding development efforts in parts of the world where economic stagnation followed adjustment, and in other parts where groups and regions have remained excluded from economic success, and unprotected against the severe crisis of food, fuel, and finance that marked 2008.

The main interest of this book is to analyze the policies that can reverse the trends toward marginalization that many economic growth experiences have entailed, even if economic growth is good for "the poor." This first part of the book will describe the most important global trends: of globalization, rising inequalities, and the ways in which states have responded to these. This is followed by a description of responses in the international development community, which has been one of the instruments through which globalization has proceeded, has been the carrier of neo-liberal ideologies, but also contains diversity and has evolved responding to pressure in both North and South. But we first try to define social policy somewhat more precisely.

1

Why Social Policy Matters

The role of social policies in the shaping of well-being, combating exclusion, and responding to economic crises is the key theme of this book. The term social policy is used in an ambitious sense, in at least three respects. In the first place, this book considers social policy as an essential complement to economic policies. To define social policy in a "residual" fashion—as the interventions that deal with the unintended consequences of economic trends and policies, a definition that has dominated under structural adjustment and under liberal ideologies—in the perspective of this book misses the critical point of the constitutive role of public policies in shaping market processes as well as well-being.

Second, the perspective is cross-sectoral, arguing that public policies and international development debates need to be based in a better understanding of the interrelated nature of sectoral policies (and the cross-sectoral impact of policies). The field of analysis, thus, is broader than that of social protection, which has received much more attention in recent studies, particularly as response for the world's poorest people (Barrientos and Hulme, 2008), and after the crises of 1997–98 and 2008–09. In the perspective adopted in this book, it is argued that the social protection approach in the international development debate tends to underestimate the importance of strengthening of broader public policies.

Third, the social policy perspective promoted here highlights the political dynamics of public policies, the fact that interest groups and political projects drive social policy formulation, implementation, and often, even monitoring. These political dynamics, inevitably, imply trade-offs in term of well-being and impacts on poverty—for example, regarding political support of powerful interest groups versus the promotion of universal approaches—which is why social policy analysis should have politics at its core.

This chapter elaborates on the role of national social policies, and its importance in reducing poverty reduction and enhancing well-being. It provides a working definition of social policy. It highlights the changes in social policy approaches with the advent of structural adjustment, and how the role of social policy has changed under globalization and economic integration. It discusses the way social policy has been dealt with in the development studies literature, and whether a notion of social policy, which emphasizes national path dependence and principles of social integration, can be usefully applied to the very different contexts in the North and the South.

Definitions: OECD and Development Contexts

Different people have different understandings of social policies, as do governments and international agencies, and these differences are typically deeply rooted. Social policy analysis in the European tradition suffers from a "dependent variable problem," and definitions and measurements have varied considerably (Gough, 2008), probably ever since the start of the study of social policy, in Germany in 1873. The term "social policy" has been used for the public policies of government, the way societies promote welfare of society's members, and also, for the study of these policies. Drawing on my earlier work (de Haan, 2007a), this section discusses some of the key questions in these debates, proposing a working definition relevant for countries outside the OECD context.

To start with, social policies are a sub-set of public policies. But the nature of public policies and how they are understood are not undisputed. Much depends on disciplines and ideological backgrounds. Economists tend to focus on the role of the state in the provision of goods and services that are in the public interest but not provided through markets, and as creator of enabling environments for and regulator of these markets. Political scientists tend to focus on public policies as outcomes of political struggles, in the broad sense of the term, and the result of differences in interest. There are almost as many definitions of social policy as there are institutions that study it. At the London School of Economics (LSE), social policy is introduced as

> an interdisciplinary and applied subject concerned with the analysis of societies' responses to social need...focused on those aspects of the economy, society and

polity that are necessary to human existence and the means by which they can be provided…The study of Social Policy is designed to reflect on the ways in which different societies have developed ways of meeting these needs, or have failed to do so. Some societies rely on informal or family institutions, some on private markets and individual actions, some on governmental actions through what is often termed the welfare state.[1]

In this view, social policy is broader than a notion of the welfare state, relevant in most OECD countries. The idea of welfare states has at least four common elements (Cox, 1998).[2] First, welfare has been conceived of as an entitlement, based on citizenship, a main theme in T.H. Marshall's work of 1950, and a question that continues to be relevant and deeply contested in both South and East Asian contexts. Second, income maintenance was the core of the welfare state, which developed mainly in a period of economic growth with full employment. Third, central planning and coordination was a key mechanism of welfare state operations. Finally, the approach was based on an assumption that the welfare state would bring out the best in human nature. Such a definition of welfare state is much more restricted than what is to be understood as social policy that is relevant for conditions in the South—but this does not make the lessons of that context irrelevant.

The definition of social policy is thus also wider than that of, and incorporates, social security, as defined, for example, by the International Labor Organization (ILO), which highlights social security and protection as fundamental human rights: "the protection that a society provides to individuals and households to ensure access to health care and to guarantee income security, particularly in cases of old age, unemployment, sickness, invalidity, work injury, maternity or loss of a breadwinner."[3] While notions of the "public management of social risks" (Esping-Andersen, 1999: 36) and social protection are part of social policies, and the approach here is in line with the way the volume edited by Ahmad et al. (1991) on approaches to social security in the broad sense to address deprivation and vulnerabilities, the focus in this book is on a cross-sectoral view of public policies.

[1] Department of Social Policy, LSE, available online at http://www.lse.ac.uk/collection/socialPolicy/introduction.htm (accessed in May 2010).

[2] In its recent report on the welfare state, the Dutch *Wetenschappelijke Raad voor het Regeringsbeleid* (2006) emphasizes its four main functions: to care, to insure, to educate and improve, and inclusion.

[3] See www.ilo.org. Moreover, the International Social Security Association has the mandate to promote social security worldwide; a recent project was designed to assess the "coverage gap" (van Ginneken, 2010).

The research program on social policy in the South at the University of Bath adopted a similar broad definition, highlighting four elements (2004: 26). First, social policy is a "policy," an intentional action within the public sphere to achieve certain goals. Second, it is oriented to welfare goals. Third, it operates through a wide variety of policy instruments and sectors, such as land reform, work programs, food subsidies, tax expenditures, health, education, and social protection. Finally—and consistent with Esping-Andersen's (1999) emphasis on the combined, interdependent way in which welfare is produced and allocated between state, market, family, and the non-profit sector—it is formulated and implemented by various collective actors, not confined to the nation state, but includes regions, localities, associations, and transnational and global actors. In the research program, the concept of "welfare regimes" was used and expanded as a way of helping to understand the complexity of social policy arrangements, the leading principles of solidarity that determine public policy interventions, emphasizing countries' histories and ideologies.[4] This research program, too, continued to struggle with terminology, particularly the critique that notions of welfare states and social policy are derived from northern debates and hence of limited analytical value in the South. Nevertheless, the broader definition is, in my view, more suitable than the definition used in the related research program at the Institute of Development Studies (IDS), Sussex, which defined social policy as concerned with the public provision of (public or private) goods and services to meet human need, thus stressing the role of the state.

As described by Hill (1996), for whom social policy is simply about "the role of the state in relation to the welfare of its citizens," there are questions whether social policy should be "merely concerned with the correction of malfunctions in the operation of society (and particularly of the economy) or involve some overall and logically prior concern with welfare in society, and about the extent to which welfare should be regarded as a key state responsibility." One of the key thinkers in the British tradition, Titmuss, favored a narrow definition: "the study of a range of social needs and functioning, in conditions of scarcity, of human organisation, traditionally called social welfare systems, to meet those needs," and focused on the social services, lying "outside or on the fringes of the so-called free market" (Lavalette and Pratt, 1997: 2). The comparative work on the impacts of liberalization

[4] As described in de Haan (2007a), and further in Part II of this book, I prefer a social policy regime terminology rather than welfare regimes.

led by Lance Taylor similarly defined social policy as, "an important tool that can in principle be used by governments to cushion some of the adverse effects of external liberalization" (Taylor, 2001: 7). Similar differences continue to inform debates around, for example, labor markets and whether the state should merely manage the "market failures," or play an active role in shaping the working and outcomes of labor markets. And again, after the 2008 crisis, where there has been much emphasis on regulating the financial sector after its collapse, many economists tend to see the role of social policy or social protection as merely an important addition, whereas arguably, for example, in the Chinese context, the social policy response can be seen as a turning point in China's development model, and in this case, one of global significance as well (see Box 1.1). More broadly, the position taken in this book is that a social policy focus includes core welfare responsibilities in a way that includes a concept of interrelationship with markets processes, striving to move away from a "ghettoization" of social policy. Social policies

Box 1.1 China's Stimulus Package after the Financial Crisis—Turning Point in its Development Model?

There is probably no country outside the OECD where the global economic crisis hit harder and sooner than in China. But it has been weathering the crisis very well, and this has been attributed to a large economic stimulus package, worth more than 10 percent of GDP, and enabled by the reserves China has built up particularly since the East Asia crisis of 1997–98. It is during crises that the complementarity of economic and social policies becomes clearer than ever.

The stimulus package has a strong emphasis on building infrastructure, which has an immediate economic impact. But it also envisages improvement in access to social services, particularly in the health sector which was neglected during the early reform period but which has seen a careful establishment of a new health insurance system over the last few years, as part also of the government's efforts to build a "harmonious society."

Social spending was kept continuously low in China, as we will see later in the book, and the high personal savings rates were a key and increasingly criticized feature of the Chinese development model (as well as indirectly the global system, as China's savings funded the United States' borrowing). The intention of the stimulus package is simultaneously to improve access to health care and reduce national inequalities, thus reduce the need for personal savings for health costs, and thus enhance consumption of the consumer goods which China previously produced for the world market.

Source: de Haan (2010a).

are seen as constitutive complements to economic policies, and as creating conditions for market functioning.[5]

The question whether social policy analysis should be concerned with the welfare and poverty impacts of other macro policies has been central to poverty concerns around adjustment programs, particularly in Africa. For example, there has been much debate about the impact of trade liberalization or devaluation, of infrastructure projects or fuel subsidies, and other projects or policies without an apparent direct relation to poverty.[6] This is a critical concern, but a discussion of this would expand the scope of the book too much. This book focuses on specific policy instruments, the policies and actors that directly shape well-being and processes of inclusion, while emphasizing the interrelationships between social policy instruments and other types of policies and market processes.

The emphasis on deliberate action in the approach to social policy implies a focus not on the policy "outcomes" but on policies to achieve these outcomes.[7] This leads, first, to a consideration of policy "space." In the African context, the fragmentation of social policy formulation is critically important. For example, Ghana "continues to lack a unified or well-articulated social policy [though] social programmes have existed in a variety of sectors since Independence" (Aryeetey and Goldstein, 2000: 284). More broadly, as emphasized in Dani and de Haan (2008a), in many countries attempts have been made to put social policies in place even though strong governance structures were absent, and the ability to raise taxes limited. Here lies a primary difference with many of the Asian countries, which have experienced much more "space" to design their own policies, albeit of course in very different ways.

---

[5] Peden (1991) stresses the need to study economic and social policy in their interrelationships in the context of Britain, from Victorian ideas till the Thatcher period. It was a central theme of the UNRiSD research program (Mkandawire, 2000, 2004), and *World Development Report 2006* (World Bank, 2005) makes a similar argument about the potential complementarity of policies for efficiency and for equity.

[6] The International Financial Institutions have developed the analytical instruments of Poverty and Social Impact Analysis. See also "New Frontiers of Social Policy," which emphasized "putting the social back in public policy" (Dani and de Haan, 2008b: Preface).

[7] Kanbur (2007) in a discussion of economic and social policies distinguishes outcome/objectives, policies, and mechanisms. He questions whether there is a separate field of social policies, which underlines the argument in this book that the instruments of social policies have received insufficient attention. See also Cook and White (2001) on approaches to welfare policy analysis (new institutional economics, politics, and political economy).

Second, the book has an institutional approach, and concentrates on "actual" policies as much as policy intentions and the constraints on the scope of institutions and actors as much as policy objectives. Such constraints include formal and informal rules (for example, in India constraints imposed by caste "rules and norms"), commitment as well as capacity to deliver policies (a particular strength in China, including in experimenting with new approaches), and the unintended outcomes of public policies (for example, reinforcement of caste identities as a result of affirmative action). Policies, including social policies and social protection, thus, are shaped by politics (Hickey, 2008; Moore, 2000), and this book tries to contribute to the strand of literature that tries to "put the politics back into development" (Hickey, 2005), and particularly to emphasize the political nature of social policies, as described further below.

A further question regarding a social policy definition relates to its coverage of sectors. This book argues it is essential to define social policy wider than social protection, or safety nets (and, conversely, it is important to avoid a temptation to define social protection too broadly). It should also not be restricted to the area of "poverty alleviation": targeted programs for poverty reduction do have a place in the field of social policy, but universal principles are central even in situations of fiscal constraints, including because of public pressure, in the shaping of solidarity and national identity (and can be more effective than targeted approaches). The working definition of social policy used in this book relates to the policies related to enhancement of human development, health, and education; preferential policies such as "reservation" in India; the range of poverty alleviation schemes such as integrated development projects and microfinance; and social protection instruments such as employment schemes and welfare transfers to the poorest unable to create their own livelihood.

The approach to social policy adopted in this book builds on the seminal work by Drèze and Sen (1989), which argues that the provision of social security in developing countries needs to be viewed from a broad perspective, and as an objective to be pursued through public means rather than as a narrowly defined set of particular strategies. It also builds on—but cuts across—their distinction between "growth-meditated security" and "support-led security" (Drèze and Sen, 1989, 1991): while their framework focuses on whether countries have waited to grow rich before extending large-scale public support, or provided social services at low levels of GDP (like Sri Lanka and Kerala in India), this book emphasizes different ways in which solidarities can be articulated. But it goes beyond the conclusion by Atkinson and Hills (1991)—who argue that while there are many lessons from comparative research about the methods of social policy analysis, there are few lessons concerning policy recommendations—and the framework proposed here is directly relevant for policy analysis and advice.

In particular, this book builds on the definition of social policy provided by Aina (1999: 73), which focuses on the

> systematic and deliberate interventions in the social life of a country to ensure the satisfaction of the basic needs and the well being of the majority of its citizens. This is seen as an expression of socially desirable goals through legislation, institutions, and administrative programs and practices...[and] is thus a broader concept than...social work and social welfare.

Similarly, the broad definition adopted by the Social Policy Research Center at the Chinese Academy of Social Sciences is important for the arguments made in this book, with its state-centered focus, of course, pertinent for the Chinese context, it highlights the: "laws and regulations to solve social problems, to promote social order, social environment and social welfare through government legislation and interference" (Yang Tuan, 2003: Preface).

Recent literature on social policy in the international research and policy community has strongly advocated for a broad social policy definition. For example, a United Nations Department of Economic and Social Affairs (UNDESA, 2007) policy note stresses:

> Social policy is an instrument applied by governments to regulate and supplement market institutions and social structures. Social policy is often defined as social services such as education, health, employment, and social security... [but] social policy is also about redistribution, protection and social justice. Social policy is about bringing people into the centre of policy-making...by mainstreaming their needs and voice across sectors, generating stability and social cohesion. Social policy is also instrumental in that governments use it pragmatically to secure the political support of citizens, and to promote positive economic outcomes by enhancing human capital and productive employment.

The commitments made at the Copenhagen Summit for Social Development,[8] which contains until today the most important international agreements with respect to social policies, underlie the defining of scope and objectives of social policy. The Copenhagen Summit conclusions—broader than the Millennium Development Goals' (MDGs) framework that was derived from the Summit—are key to the way this book studies social

---

[8] The Copenhagen Declaration and Programme of Action was ratified by heads of state and governments at the UN Summit on Social Development in 1995.

policies, as well as the public policies through which these objectives are to be achieved. This crucially includes the aim regarding social integration. The interest in social policy is not merely around achieving material outcomes, like "halving poverty," "reducing maternal mortality," or "education for all," but equally about the social and institutional processes responsible for such outcomes, different as these are across the world.

The social policy approach advocated in this book highlights the interconnections between economic and social policies. "Integration" of social and economic policies was subject of discussion in the early 1970s through publications of UNDESA in 1971. The idea disappeared from the radar screen with the advent of structural adjustment, but has more recently reappeared, for example, in the articulation of mutually reinforcing social and economic policies as priority of the "Concertación" government in Chile, and in the Copenhagen Programme of Action. Economic crises, including the 2008–09 financial crisis, highlight the importance of an integrated view. In response to crises, national governments have the choice to reduce, maintain, or increase government spending (the latter being the choice of China—with large financial reserves—toward the end of 2008 when the impact of the crisis started to be felt, while, for example, for Pakistan, a new period of austerity and International Monetary Fund [IMF] packages seemed a likely outcome). This book describes the various ways in which economic and social policies have been articulated across the Global South, and the political conditions that shaped this articulation, as social policy is an intensely political project, as described next.

Social Policy, too, is Political

It is important to state from the outset that many social policies have not been equitable, or participatory. Just because policies are called social does not mean they are just, in intention or outcome. In Europe, social policies expanded under authoritarian rule. Social policy was a cornerstone of Africa's Apartheid regime. In Rwanda, affirmative action was part of the extremely violent inter-ethnic strife (Mamdani, 2001). Social policy is often biased toward elites or urban populations. The Prime Minister of colonial Southern Rhodesia promised to "do all I can do to develop the native if I am allowed to protect my own race in our own areas and, if I am not, I will not do anything" (Osei-Hwedie and Bar-on, 1999: 92). The resulting dualism in provision of social services and rights, partly reinforced by the post-colonial modernization projects, still strongly influences many of the social policies across the South, as this book will document for South Asia and Africa. The socialist public policies like in China and Vietnam, too, created sharp dualism, between those working in state enterprises and those outside, and between urban and rural inhabitants.

Karl Polanyi's classic study of early 20th century political economy is a central starting point for the way policies and the role of the state is understood in this book, similar to the way it informs discussions on the links between economic and social policies (Mehrotra and Delamonica, 2007). Polanyi emphasized the "clash of the organizing principles of economic liberalism and social protection which led to a deep-seated institutional strain," interacting with the conflict of classes which turned this crisis into a catastrophe.[9] His framework focused on the interaction between expansion of market forces and social institutions trying to steer these markets, and the way policies are embedded in institutional contexts. Against the deep social and economic crisis of the 1930s, which ended with the Second World War, Polanyi emphasized the central role of the state in organizing the market, as an institution, and the shaping of nation states through the extension of citizens' social rights. As Esping-Andersen (1999: 11) put it, the state functioned as "an alternative to the supposedly disembodied treatment of economic life typical of mainstream economics."[10] The market is a political and social construct, and neatly separable domains of a "market" free from "politics" or "social concerns" do not exist (Chang, 2003, 2004). The interactions between social and economic policies are of key importance for the framework presented in this book, as is the diversity of actors and institutional areas, and interactions of state, market, communities, and households.

As social policy, too, is political, and the outcomes of social policies are not necessarily equitable, it is therefore critically important to emphasize a normative and "rights-based" approach to social policy, which we come back to in the concluding chapter. Social rights has been central to northern social policy debate, particularly in Marshall's (1950) writings after the Second World War, who highlighted the recognition of citizens' social rights,

[9] Polanyi (1968: 134) emphasizes the pressure by a wide variety of people for social protection, understood in a broad sense, with reference to the social fabric. The comparison of the liberalization period of the 1980s/1990s with the 19th century period of liberalism (for example, Stewart, 2006) seems overstated, as this recent period simultaneously saw an increase in pressure to address global poverty problems (de Haan, 2009c).

[10] For Esping-Andersen "social policy" is a broad concept regarding the "public management of social risks" (1999: 36), while "welfare states" are the particular form of public policies that emerged after the Second World War.

alongside promises to bridge class divisions (Esping-Andersen, 1999: 34). Even though institutional and economic conditions for social policy are different, this notion of social rights is critical, I believe, to the normative framework in the context of the South too. The normative social rights' framework is combined with a focus on the path- and context-dependent nature of social policies, thus highlighting historical differences in which rights and state–citizen relations are defined in different countries.

For this purpose, to combine a rights framework with analytical emphasis on path dependence, this book employs a notion of principles of solidarity (de Haan, 2007b), as these are enshrined within the delivery of national policies. Social policy making is not a technocratic exercise, but embedded in political economy. Social policy is "an intensely political project…in which competing ideologies can clash" (Lavalette and Pratt, 1997), and the following box (Box 1.2) on health systems in OECD countries illustrates this. It results from the struggles of interest groups and working classes. While in the OECD literature the political nature of social policies has been amply studied,[11] this tends to be underemphasized in the development literature. However, social policies, including celebrated social protection instruments, in the South of course follow from, for example, elite's attempts to diffuse power struggles and reduce political tension (as the Social Fund, Program of Actions to Mitigate the Social Costs of Adjustment (PAMSCAD), in Ghana aimed to); to establish a harmonious society (as in China, reinforced after the 2008 crisis); attempts to reduce rural–urban migration (Maharashtra's Employment Guarantee Scheme); or aims to create a productive labor force (a predominant aim of East Asian policies).

The interaction between, on the one hand, political developments like democratization and decentralization, and on the other hand, the formulation and implementation of social policies is necessarily a central part of a social policy analysis. The New Deal established by President Roosevelt led to radical changes in the fiscal relations between federal and local government.[12] Lindert's (2004) history of OECD social policy highlights the simultaneous evolvement of public social spending and both economic growth and the extension of democracy or political voice—with a conclusion that the welfare state did not compromise economic growth, but also pointing at a paradox

[11] As highlighted, for example, by Fraser (1973) for the origins of the welfare state in Britain, and Piven and Cloward (1972) for the US in the 1930s and 1960s.

[12] Mitchener (2009). Even though the New Deal might not have been responsible for ending the Great Depression (most historians seem to agree it was the Second World War), the new economic and social policies did create an institutional legacy that is still visible in the US.

Box 1.2 Ideologies behind Health System and Reforms across the OECD

The debates on health reforms under the Obama administration brought to the fore the very different ideologies behind preferences for health systems, well beyond the question what the most efficient way of organizing health care might be. President Obama's plans for health care reform, focusing on bringing the tens of millions of US citizen under health insurance, were proving to be extremely hard to get accepted, just as President Clinton found this a major stumbling block. The views on what the US health care system should look like were extremely strong, and international comparisons were frequently invoked to convince political supporters. According to Ian Dunt, on the website, http://www.politics.co.uk, in August 2009, who witnessed the health reform debate in the US,

> Adverts have been prominently shown making the [UK National Health Service] out to be some sort of death factory, casually condemning people if they fail to meet certain age criteria...And town hall meeting after town hall meeting...have seen irate American right-wingers harangue speakers as they describe any move (and Obama's moves are very tentative) to universal healthcare as a Communist coup against the republic.

The Canadian health care system—universal in a slightly different way—is similarly held up as far inferior, with, for example, Canadian citizens stating in advertisements that they would have died if they had not been able to access (private) health care in the US.

Health care systems are organized fundamentally differently across OECD countries, and the quotes above serve to illustrate how strong the views can be, and how far politicians are willing to go to politicize the organization of social services. Less extreme but still strongly held views can be found when health systems are compared in Europe, with the left in Britain strongly advocating for the universal National Health System (NHS), and objections to privatization or health insurance systems—while many continental Europeans feel strongly that their systems, which are more mixed, and use social health insurance and citizens' contributions are at least as good if not superior. A social policy framework, as proposed in this book, emphasizes the need to understand these differences, looking beyond technical comparisons and analyzing the political and historical reasons that determine systems of health (and other) services, and the ideologies that drive these histories and current debates.

Source: Dunt (2009).

that social spending is least likely to happen where it is most required. Analysis of the nature of policy processes in post-communist countries shows responsive states are nurtured by increasing wealth (Johanssen and Pedersen, 2008). This should not lead to deterministic conclusions, but the key point here is to emphasize—against the more technocratic analysis that characterizes much of the international development literature—the interplay of social policy formulation and forms of political contestation and representation, which will be described in this book for non-contributory pension schemes in Brazil and South Africa, and anti-poverty schemes like the Maharashtra Employment Guarantee Scheme and the new National Rural Employment Guarantee Scheme in India which are outcomes of political negotiation and, in turn, can be grounds for advocacy on behalf of poor people (Joshi, 2005).

Understanding the tax or other funding bases is, of course, essential to understanding the formulation and implementation of social (and other public) policies; yet, it has remained relatively understudied with the notable exception of recent work at UNRISD (Hujo, 2008). There are large differences in levels of taxation and public funding across the OECD context. The tax base of poorer countries is often low, did not increase with the expansion of public finances in the 1960s, and raising tax revenue is usually seen as a technical problem rather than as part of the development of a social contract. Moreover, donors have tended to fund large part of countries' social spending, even though critique of adjustment has highlighted restrictions in social spending, and an opposing critique has emphasized the neglect of infrastructure and agriculture. The result of these combined forces has been low levels of accountability, as the budgeting and thus broader policy process continues to be strongly driven by external actors.

The interest in taxation for the social policy analysis proposed here is, thus, not from a technical perspective, but seen as an important and oft-neglected entry point for analysis of the underlying social contract. This has two components. First, with independence, states generally received international legitimacy without underlying pressures of war and inter-state competition that were decisive in European nation-building processes (Herbst, 2000). The international system, thus, provided legitimacy to a large number of nation states which historically had a very weak basis and, in comparison with European state formation, took away the necessity to raise taxes and strengthen a social contract with its citizens. Second, aid dependency and the international debate with the large impact of international financial institutions and global civil society has greatly influenced the social contract, generally by reducing the need for taxation as well as accountability in terms of service provision. New aid modalities that emerged in the late 1990s—as described in Chapter 4—implicitly or explicitly tried to address this, but the complex forces that drive development practices make this a continuing challenge (de Haan, 2009c).

Development Studies Literature and Social Policy

Social policy has remained understudied in mainstream development studies. The reasons for this are complex. As discussed more extensively in de Haan (2007b) and briefly described here, a social policy analysis is a critical but, by and large, neglected complement to, for example, the literature on public expenditure management and governance, the project-oriented social development literature, and critical analysis of globalization.[13]

First, the analysis here builds on the literature that has emphasized the importance of institutions for economic growth. As Nick Stern (2002) has stressed, the neglect of the importance of institutions and governance during the 1980s and the 1990s has come with hard lessons. Even now, there is evidence that adjustment lending can privilege fiscal adjustment over strengthening institutions, and that institutions like the World Bank engage predominantly with finance ministries and departments neglecting other policy institutions, or more broadly that developing countries' advice continue to "kick away the ladder" (Chang, 2007). But at least the analyses that emphasize the importance of institutions for economic growth (Rodrik, 2003) and recent analyses on the role of public spending for growth (Baldacci et al., 2008; Moreno-Dodson, 2008) have broadened the debates on growth and distribution, and the social policy notion used here builds on this, particularly looking at the deliberate policies that have tried to alter patterns of inequality, while considering the importance of these social policies for overall growth patterns.

While it is important to continue to emphasize the different institutional preconditions in the South compared to the OECD contexts, the development of social policy is a central component of countries' continued institutional transitions (as the New Deal was in the US), including the writing of social contracts (as defined by Franklin D. Roosevelt during the Great Depression with his statement, "I place the security of men, women, and

[13] Over the last decade, conflicts and post-conflict reconstruction, and the role of social contracts in this, has become an increasingly important strand of the international development literature and practices; this aspect is not covered in detail in the current book even though the issues are of equal relevance as in the more stable states this book concentrates on.

children of the nation first"). This book will emphasize the connections between models of economic growth, the specific social policy instruments, and the commitments these imply between states and citizens, and the newly created or reform of institutions that follow from such political projects. The social contracts not only shape, and are essential part of, state–citizens relations (and as such defined differently in different countries and at different periods of time), but also have a big impact on the relationships between citizens.

Further, the analysis in this book presents a social development perspective on the public expenditure management literature, which has had a predominantly technical focus (for example, Kaul and Conceição, 2006). The literature on public expenditure management has a strong focus on the technical and procedural aspects of the budget processes and reforms. Over time, following introduction of results-based management practices, there is increasing emphasis on how systems deliver result, including for enhancing well-being and poverty reduction. Also, advocacy-oriented literature has emphasized the need to broaden the space for public debate on budget issues (Norton and Elson, 2002). But even this literature has tended to neglect the question how important state interventions should be, norms regarding relative importance of sectors, and the political context and contestation that drives public spending and taxation. It is important to improve our understanding of the "stories behind" budget allocations, and to broaden the debate beyond the need for higher budget allocations and the emphasis on the lack of a link between expenditure and "results." This book provides guidance regarding how public policies and policy reform can be shaped to attain welfare goals, while highlighting the political and path-dependent nature of public policy making, and the interrelated or cross-sectoral linkages which determine long-term well-being outcomes.

Many of the studies on links between growth and economic policies on the one hand, and poverty reduction and inequality on the other, have been in the form of statistical regression. These studies, as all studies, have methodological limitations.[14] More important from the social policy perspective presented here is that such quantitative analyses cannot substitute for understanding public policy making, and understanding the various ways in which policies impact processes of human development or poverty reduction, or even economic growth. Regression analyses, by their nature, are limited in

[14] Forbes (2000). Jomo and von Arnim (2008) provide a critique of General Equilibrium Models in the analysis of liberalization. See also Ravallion (2004).

providing understanding of the "stories behind" trends and correlations, and particularly of the reasons why public policies came into being. Therefore, and notwithstanding their popularity, they are limited in the extent to which they can guide the formulation of policy alternatives.

At the other side of the spectrum of the development studies debate, the social development literature, by and large, has not tried to relate to the macro-level analysis of poverty, nor the literature on reform and public expenditure management. Very important path-breaking work has been undertaken from a gender perspective, with analysis of the gender implications of macro policies (Elson, 2004; Elson and Çagatay, 2000, 2003), and the budget analysis that has aimed to challenge macroeconomic theories and policy making (Budlender, 2000, 2003). By and large, in development agencies, engagement with macro-policy issues from a social development perspective has remained limited, despite intentions to move "upstream." Studies on social policy have focused on social protection, and on operational inputs to processes of Poverty Reduction Strategy Papers (PRSPs). At the World Bank, social development specialists have limited engagement with social policy issues, as the 2004 Social Development Strategy and the efforts to promote the project New Frontiers of Social Policy illustrate.[15] The social development literature has continued to focus on project approaches, often not distinguishing sufficiently the social "dimensions" of development from social "policy."

Much poverty research, globally and in many Asian countries, has tended to concentrate on "outcomes," and has remained based in an individualistic theoretical framework. It has focused on numbers and proportions of people in poverty, and poverty "profiles," the measurement of characteristics of the poor. Studies that have focused on the human development or similar indices (including Amartya Sen's capabilities approach) have broken through the barriers of the "money-metric" approach. But these too have remained concentrated on measuring outcomes. A huge gap remains between the understanding of characteristics of the poor, the causes behind characteristics and

[15] See the discussion in the "Forum" of *Global Social Policy* (2006); also Hall (2007). The "new frontiers" for the World Bank related to the transformation of subjects into citizens, fostering accountable states, and strengthening countries' capacity for revenue mobilization. While this project did not appear to find much resonance within the World Bank itself, most of the external commentators expressed skepticism about the extent to which this would be a new departure for the Bank. The lack of macro-policy engagement by social development specialists is related to a continued focus on safeguards for World Bank projects, and a lack of coordination of social development inputs with the Bank's own human development agenda, which includes work on social funds.

trends, and particularly, of the public policies that influence well-being. The social policy notion used in this book emphasizes the social relations and institutions that lie beneath measured outcome indicators, building on conceptualization of poverty that emphasize context-dependent ideologies and practices of "social exclusion" and "inclusion" (de Haan, 1998, 2009a; Silver, 1994).

The literature on participation also has not closed the gap between understanding poverty and understanding public policies. A main contribution of participatory poverty studies has been to complement quantitative studies with different and "subjective" perceptions and interpretation of poverty, but usually has not been linked to analyses of policy-making processes. Debates on quantitative versus qualitative approaches to poverty (Kanbur, 2003) center on differences in approaches to poverty analysis, and not on policy making. Cornwall and Gaventa (2000) make an effort to link debates around participation and social policy, and importantly highlight how decentralization, privatization of provisioning, and globalization challenge traditional approaches to participation in social policy. They emphasize, "social policy must see citizens not only as users or choosers, but as active participants in shaping and implementing social policy and social provisioning." Work on participation also has focused on "new democratic spaces" (Cornwall, 2004), the ways and reasons participatory processes are invited into, and become part of mainstream public policies, but with optimistic assumptions about the ability of the poor to access joint decision-making processes. As Brett (2003) notes, and illustrated in this book, policy development often does not derive from participatory principles, or follows participatory structures. In any case, a large agenda remains to link studies of bottom-up approaches and grassroots initiatives to understanding of how macro policy is shaped and can be influenced, for example, the conditions under which structural inequalities are starting to be addressed (Bebbington et al., 2008). This book builds on the literature on participatory budgets and on democratic spaces, and tries to integrate this in a wider view of public policy making.

The literature on globalization, which is, of course, voluminous, has again grown rapidly after the 2008 financial crisis, and much of this has a focus on economics and economic policy making (see Chapter 2). Inevitably, a review of social policy over the last decades puts public policy in the context of globalizing economies and societies.[16] The literature on public

[16] Taylor (2001) discusses impacts of liberalization and the varied social policy responses across nine case studies.

policies has had a strong focus on global institutions (Nayyar, 2002). It emphasizes the relationship with globalization processes such as access to the World Trade Organization (WTO) (Zhou, 2008), and on the global dimensions of social policy, including the emergence of hegemonic neo-liberal global policies and weakening of national entitlements and rights.[17] Complementing this, the current book reasserts the importance of national public policy: public finance data show that states have remained important; country narratives and comparisons indicate the importance of national histories of social integration, and hence, the nation state maintains the key arena for the realization of rights of citizens.

Against the theme of globalization and the increasing volatility of the economy as experienced during the late 1990s crises in East Asia and Latin America since the 1980s (Krugman, 2009), and increasingly at the time of the writing of this book following the "triple-F" crisis of food, fuel, and finance, development policy and literature have devoted much attention to the theme and concept of social protection.[18] This book, while drawing on strands of work in this field, distinguishes itself by emphasizing a wider definition of social policy and the interrelationship between different aspects or sectors of public policy. Similarly, the approach advocated here aims to be wider but build on the ILO work on social security, particularly related to new forms of universalistic social protection and the seminal work on social security in developing countries (Ahmad et al., 1991).

In developing this broader understanding of social policy in the context of globalization, the book draws on publications that have made national policy processes central in the aim to understand the processes leading to inclusion and exclusion.[19] Studies in the publication edited by Taylor have already been mentioned. Further, the International Development Research Center (IDRC) funded project in the late 1990s on transnational social policy, as published by Morales-Gómez (1999), provided a range of national perspectives on the evolution of social policy approaches. The UNRISD research program on Social Policy in a Development Context has been the most explicit recent attempt to bring a policy perspective into the social and human development debate, aiming to "move (thinking) away from

[17] Deacon (1997). Yeates (2001) shows that different frameworks have been proposed for the integration of a global perspective in social policy analysis.

[18] Perspectives of various agencies documented earlier in Conway, de Haan, and Norton (2000); see websites of various development agencies, for example, www.socialprotectionasia.org, www.epri.org.za; Cichon et al. (2004); DFID (2005); Ravallion (2003b), Barrientos and Hulme (2008).

[19] Mackintosh and Tibandebage (2004: 144) conclude that "the health policy and development literature lacks an overarching theory of policy," and that policy analysis needs a more analytical approach and "thicker methodologies."

social policy as a safety net...towards a conception of active social policy as a powerful instrument for development working in tandem with economic policy."[20] Central to conceptualizing the approach was Thandika Mkandawire (2000, 2004), who incorporated lessons from the "late industrializers" among current OECD countries for understanding the importance of social policy, taking issue with views regarding the primacy of economic policy over social policy, and helping to move the debate away from a residual social policy approach that had dominated debates under structural adjustment.

The Legacy of Structural Adjustment

Colonialism involved a highly exploitative integration of the South into the global economy. The social policies that emerged during the colonial period, with large differences between countries and colonial powers, showed very narrow interpretations of social welfare, largely determined by colonial objectives. In this context, while a narrow definition is often justified with reference to low levels of development that make extensive social policy infeasible, colonialism did alter social networks and informal support, and taxation policies contributed to commercialization of the economy, in turn creating demands on social policy interventions.

Social policy in the colonial world was designed and implemented by colonial officials, volunteer agencies, missionaries, foreign economic interests, and various local groups. Policies were selective and discriminatory (Aina, 1999; Osei-Hwedie and Bar-on, 1999). They benefited elites and focused on security of colonial officials, were spatially restrictive and urban biased, and provided only minimum services to the majority of the population. They often closely followed colonial interests, such as the education in India for the purpose of creating an administrative elite. Health provisions often related to the need for healthy workers, defined in utilitarian terms, and with a focus on cities with their larger working population concentration and more intense public health risks. In the late colonial period, and often under international pressure, protective legislation and limited social policies were introduced for workers in the large, usually export-oriented manufacturing and mining enterprises.[21]

---

[20] This research project resulted in a range of UNRISD Working Papers (www.unrisd.org), an international conference in 2001, and a series of publications by Palgrave. See UNRISD (2006) for a summary of lessons.

[21] The authors that contributed to the edited volume, de Haan and Sen (1999), describe such dynamics for the jute industry in eastern India.

The nationalist governments that came into power with independence in Asia and Africa brought great expectations and promises regarding provision of services to the entire population under a social contract to end the injustice of colonialism. Even in the absence of formal colonization, like in China, the post-war development strategies were ideologically stimulated by promises of nation building and a new era for its population. Optimism was fueled by the growing world economy of the 1960s, including growing demand for primary commodities, and in the early 1970s, by the financial measures that helped to weaken the impact of the 1973 oil crisis, and the often generous international support under the influence of the Cold War.

Socialism dominated as an ideology in many parts of Africa, China of course, and even in India, under the democratic Gandhi–Nehru compromise. The ideology led to nationalization of means of production, justified by promises that this would benefit the entire population, and to increasing employment provided in the civil service and public sector enterprises—with some benefits to the rural populations through remittances. In Kenya, even in the late 1980s, public sector employment formed 50 percent of total formal sector employment (Kulunde Manda, 2003: 153). Donors were supportive of state investment in social sectors (Manji, 2000: 12), with visible benefits to populations. The impact that the social contracts have had on the population can still be traced, for example, in India where research shows that poor people turn out in large numbers to vote, and expect services to be provided by the state—and not NGOs, for example—and even in contexts such as southern Orissa where decades of promises have had little positive impacts (de Haan, 2008; Kumar, 2001). Even though the administrative bases and international contexts differ, understanding social policy in the South, similar to the shaping of welfare states in the North where social provisions and nation building went hand in hand, implies recognition of intertwining of ideologies of nationalism and entitlements to state-provided services.

In the immediate post-war period, the approach to social policy was proactive, rather than reactive (Adésínà, 2007). Though now often forgotten, particularly in the debates on Africa, human development indicators showed remarkable improvements, for a short period of less than two decades. Social security provisions remained limited to civil service and some other "formal sector" employees, but governments very rapidly expanded provisions. Many of the social policies introduced during Tanzanian and Chinese experiments with socialism have been of lasting importance: in terms of nation building and national unity, and in the case of China also, as precondition for its subsequent economic miracle. Latin America since the 1930s was marked by expansion of social policy, in many cases prompted by massive rural–urban migrations: though stratification of services was dominant, in principle, labor and education, health, and other social policies were universalistic.

Across the world, in the North and the South, the economic crisis and subsequent reforms from the 1970s have been seen as a breakpoint for social policies as had prevailed since the Second World War and independence. The year 1973 was probably the key turning point in this history, though the impact was not realized until later, and perhaps masked by the fact that, for example, the World Bank was intensifying its interest in poverty reduction. A number of factors contributed to the reversal. The fall of Allende in Chile led to the advent of the "Chicago Boys" neo-liberal structural adjustment, and the 1980s was the period in which adjustment predominated. The collapse of the Soviet Union contributed to a perceived triumph of liberalism and "Washington Consenus" well into the 1990s, while the rise of China and its global impact was escaping attention throughout the 1990s.

The expansion of infrastructure for social services had proceeded fast in Africa and with much optimism regarding the possibility to build in accountability to the system. Many nationalist leaders considered policy and resources as elements of patronage. Much of the expansion was donor funded, and in a project mode, which tended to neglect the wider policy environment (de Haan, 2009c). The financial and economic crisis from the early 1970s onward forced many countries to adjust their public funding.

The impact of adjustment and the types of social policies that emerged, their merits and shortcomings, have been much debated. The following elements stand out. First, fiscal constraints have dominated the social policy debate—for example, in discussions on pensions, unemployment benefits, and user fees in Africa—in which affordability and efficiency became central concerns. However, there has been limited debate about the need to enhance fiscal resources, except for continued calls for increasing aid. Related to this, an instrumentalist vision of human development came to the fore, emphasizing its contribution to economic growth, with less emphasis on entitlements and the intrinsic value pertaining to development of people's capabilities.

Second, globalization, of course, has been seen as a driving force behind adjustment. Globalization is not historically unique, and may be reversed (Brawley, 2003: 195), but "from the standpoint of the welfare state the financial openness of economies is an entirely new and significant development" (Mishra, 1999: 5). This has been considered as a threat to the functioning of the economic models of the welfare state, the fiscal and monetary policies of Keynesianism, and interventions to achieve full employment, mass education, and industrial relations. In the South, the fiscal constraints were accompanied by increasing influence of international organizations, which stressed approaches to social policy mirroring the concerns in the North.

Third, social policy approaches became embedded in radically different approaches to public policy: "the past two decades have been a watershed of policy and institutional reform in many developing countries" (Grindle, 2002). The early period after independence had a strong focus on, and faith in, state control, production, and provision of public goods. Newer approaches emphasize decentralization, partnerships ("public–private"), participation, and involvement of civil society in at least the implementation of public policies. The new "governance" agenda also came to emphasize the performance of the public sector, and ways of measuring this (the MDGs framework is an example of this). Good governance is now generally recognized as precondition for economic growth and poverty reduction.

The new governance agenda is embedded in a "post-Washington Consensus," which suggests new approaches to economic policies, with, again, a wider role for public policies. This stresses the complementary role of the state vis-à-vis the market, economic growth as precondition for poverty reduction, and the role of the private sector and trade. It further stresses that national ownership of the development agenda is crucial, and empowerment of people, basic health, and education are seen as essential ingredients for development and poverty reduction. This new consensus puts governance and institutions at the center of attention (Stern, 2002). Chile, once more, seems to have symbolized the shift, with a return to democracy and emphasis on inclusive development, while maintaining macroeconomic focus on stability and global markets (Taylor, 2006), and new forms of social dialogue emerged after economic crises in South Korea and Argentina.

Fourth, driven by economic crises and the re-emergence of conservative ideologies in the North, social policy became increasingly focused on alleviating the impacts of crises and shocks, particularly on poor people. The "social funds" as developed by the development banks, and the lack of linkages with sectors or ministries of human development within those agencies, illustrate how social policy approached turned "residual." Directly related, social policy debates since structural adjustment obtained a strong focus on targeting.[22] This has been both a means of reducing public

[22] Countries' political and ideological histories also influence the extent of targeting, as shown in much higher percentages of targeted social assistance in Australia and New Zealand, compared, for example, to Ireland, Canada, and particularly Germany (Esping-Andersen, 1999: 75).

expenditure and of ensuring that benefits reach the most-needy people. Examples of this can be found in the analyses that accompanied structural adjustment programs, in India, for example, in the reform of the public distribution system to a Targeted Public Distribution System, as well as in most OECD countries. Deacon (2005) highlighted evidence that within international organizations, universal approaches to social welfare have been becoming more popular again, though I am less convinced that these approaches are widely accepted in these agencies (de Haan, 2007b).

Thus, approaches to public policy have moved from the optimism of the period immediately after independence, via the markets approach of the 1980s, to a renewed emphasis on the importance of public intervention, in terms of enhancing welfare as well as correcting "market failures" more generally, and perhaps more universalistic approaches. At least until 1997, countries in Asia did not experience equally severe crises and drastic responses as other countries in the South. Nevertheless, pressure came to bear on public policies in India during the 1990s, even though they did not experience economic or similarly severe fiscal crises. And China, of course, initiated possibly the most drastic reversal of public policies, in 1978, but much more as a result of internal pressures like the aftermath of the Cultural Revolution and concerns about severe poverty and political changes than external pressure. While convergence in terms of openness and public policies characterizes Asian development paths as much as in the rest of the world, the incentives and national space for setting out the path were radically different.

Why Social Policy is Important in the South

While a renewed focus on social policy is thus consistent with recent development thinking regarding, for example, the importance of institutions for economic growth and its link to human development, its notion is far from generally accepted as useful in the South, and particularly during a period of globalization. Many academics and practitioners have actively argued against the application of a notion of social policy—the UNRISD research initiated by Thandika Mkandawire about five years ago has provided the main exception. This section briefly reviews some of these critiques and argues that these have tended to throw the baby out with the bath water, and that at least the method of social policy analysis can be of great help to enhance understanding of how well-being is shaped by public policy, even in situations where the reach of public policy remains limited.

It has been argued that western social policy experiences and concepts are irrelevant for the South. For example, during the Arusha social policy conference in December 2005, in a debate on the experiences of Self-Employed Women's Association (SEWA), a participant stressed that western experience does no help in understanding the Indian context. Wood (2003: 90), reflecting on the research program, "Social Policy in Development Contexts," stressed that "colleagues at Bath were, early on, accused in effect of contextual ignorance and intellectual imperialism by poor country specialists." Baltodano (1999) emphasized that concepts of social policy are intimately linked to the historical evolution of western societies, to the evolution of sovereign states, and the creation of social order, and thus make the concept less useful in a period of globalization. Building on this, Kabeer (2004) explains how the IDS research program on social policy chose to use a sustainable livelihoods framework to address the conditions in poorer southern countries and the institutional configuration of social provisioning which prevailed in different contexts. Departing from an emphasis on limitations of state-driven welfare systems, this emphasized the need to recognize that policy goals are shared by a wide range of institutional actors, of families, social networks, private sector, and civil society organizations, as well as the international development agencies.

Further, it is commonly asserted that social policy agendas have been set by international agencies, as part of an agenda of global neo-liberalism. As argued by Aina (1999), for example, state-lead social provisioning became a victim of World Bank and IMF solutions to economic crises, who regarded social policy as wasteful and negative, contributing little to economic growth or national revenue. Poku (2002) argues that African governments capitulated to the will of World Bank and IMF in their formulation of social policy. This was accompanied by a decline of influence of the United Nations (UN) specialized agencies like World Health Organization (WHO) and ILO (Poku and Whiteside, 2002). Partly because of this dominance in agenda setting, subsequent social policies and inventions have often not been considered as proper substitutes but as a continuation of this external imposition. International agencies' attempts to develop international social policy have often been perceived to imply new conditionalities (Deacon, 2003). These perceptions may not square entirely with the practices of policy making, for example, social sector funding has not been reduced as severely as often argued, and in India, the targeting of the public distribution system was as much a home-grown process as imposed under World Bank pressure. But the perceptions matter, and the concerns over external imposition are real—even in China, debates on price reforms, for example, explicitly referred to and criticized the advice given by the World Bank (Luo Xiaopeng, 2007)—and appear to have intensified as information has become more widely available globally.

The concerns over transfer of concepts are valid. However, the critique has inadvertently widened the gap in the understanding of the policies that do impact populations' well-being, the reasons for failures of such policies, and how these policies are shaped. Northern concerns anyway are mirrored in development debates. The critique often shows little awareness of the diverse histories of development and crises of OECD welfare states, and the social policies that existed before the modern form of welfare states emerged.[23] Colonial traditions continue to exert influence on the way public policies are structured, as this book will show when discussing traditions of solidarity. The emphasis on residual social policy and approaches to decentralization and participation became increasingly popular in both North and South, and it is critical to understand the international transfer of ideas, a process that cannot be simply attributed to projects of global domination. The role of international agencies needs to be better understood, including how the opposing international ideas and debate—and aid flows—have limited the space for many countries to develop their own social policy traditions.[24]

By rejecting the lessons from the social policy literature, the research lost an opportunity for serious assessment of existing policies, their histories, politics, and impacts. For example, there is no doubt that non-state actors are less important in most contexts outside OECD countries (of course, with exceptions like China), but this diversity and interaction between them is of great relevance in itself. In Bangladesh, a welfare regime approach needs to take account of the strong NGOs and international influence. Christiansen and Whyte's (2008) study of government and NGOs social security support for children in Uganda highlights the interactions between formal and informal spheres, and how norms can influence and conflict with each other. Processes of "decommodification"—the key concept in Esping-Andersen's categorization of welfare regimes in OECD countries—and the interaction between states, markets, and households are different in

[23] For example, the old Poor Law that was in operation in England before 1834 has been described as a "developmental institution," facilitating economic growth and, for example, reducing destitute migration (Smith, 2008).

[24] Deacon (2005) believes "the international epistemic community of social policy analysts" has played an important role in promoting a recent shift back to universalistic approaches to social welfare.

countries with, for example, large agricultural populations. But in all cases, welfare is constituted in the interaction between these spheres.

Development studies' neglect of labor market issues is relevant for the discussion here, as the limited size of the formal labor market and further "informalization" are thought have made classic social policy concerns irrelevant. However, what constitutes "informal," and the conditions in that sector, are directly shaped by the labor market policies that influence the formal sector and particularly how it defines what is formal and which criteria and entitlements apply. The case of SEWA, discussed in Chapter 8, illustrates this direct interaction, as the social policies and trade union actions that structures the labor market in the Indian context, is central to SEWA's advocacy efforts, including the mere fact that SEWA had to lobby for years to be recognized as trade union.

The critiques have raised important objections against simplified transfers of notions of social policy. They rightly emphasize the gap between rhetoric and reality of state-led policies in the South, and the low coverage of social policy and social security provisions, and focus on formal labor markets that exclude the large majority of people in many countries, particularly women. The state as core social policy actor, as described by Esping-Andersen, is indeed of less relevance in the South, and both international and national community-level institutions and informal arrangements need to be more central to the analysis. As argued in Dani and de Haan (2008a), analysis of social policy in the South needs to take account both of the weaker public policy institutions and the structural inequalities that mark many post-colonial societies. Nevertheless, following the lead of UNRISD and University of Bath research programs, a focus on the public policies that constitute welfare, and how these are shaped in interaction of, say, formal and informal spheres of welfare provision, and as an outcome and constituent element of political settlements, is critical for understanding how welfare is shaped globally.

Social policy considerations are important in the context of the South, and in poorer and unequal countries. As we will see, in many poor countries, public spending, including on social services as proportion of GDP, is far from insignificant. Some African countries, including South Africa, Kenya, and Zimbabwe, have public spending as high or higher than the average for high-income countries, with Asian countries having lower levels of public spending (though data comparisons are difficult, particularly for the large federal countries). There is little evidence that these proportions have been declining during adjustment or globalization, and social spending often is and remains a high proportion of overall spending. Finally, as in OECD countries, the variation in public and social spending across countries is very large, crying out for better explanations than we have at present. The diversity in social spending is illustrated in Graph 1.1, based on data for about 70 middle- and low-income countries, from the Human Development Report (UNDP, 2009b), which shows that countries with high Human Development Indices (HDIs) have a very large variety in social spending, and at low levels of spending one can see a high diversity in HDI.

As forcefully argued by many, particularly since the 1987 book on the "human face of adjustment" (Cornia, Jolly, and Stewart, 1987), state intervention, including for social services, is more and not less urgent at lower levels of economic development. With considerable variation, state intervention tends to expand with economic growth, but the state has a crucial role to play in social policy areas like the provision of basic education, public health, and famine relief, as well as economic areas of agricultural research, infrastructure, and regulation, as precondition for economic and human development. Much government intervention is inefficient and inequitable, as Graph 1.1 also suggests, but this makes public policy an area for study, rather than being an argument for academic neglect.

With globalization, and with the global crisis of 2008–09, this argument is as important as before, because of increased demands for basic provisions for skills of the global economy, and the need to compensate those who

Graph 1.1 Human Development Index and Social Spending

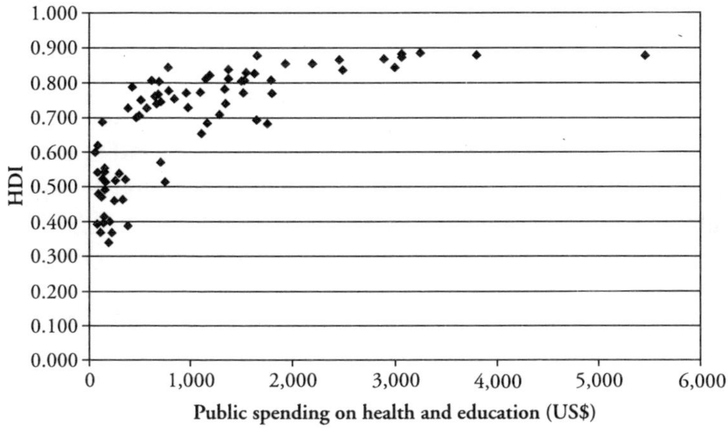

Source: UNDP (2009b).

lose out in economic reforms. With the economy opening up, states' possibilities for taxation are challenged. Capacities for taxation in poor countries were never well developed, and aid dependence has reinforced the problem. Increased capital mobility has reduced options for fiscal policies. Post-war ways of regulating production, labor conditions, and redistribution have become increasingly unpopular. The emergence of a global market in health, education, and social insurance may contribute to undermining welfare provisions within countries. Even before the financial crisis hit in 2008, it was evident that the search for social policy approaches was an urgent priority.

This book therefore emphasizes a broad and proactive definition of social policy, partly in response to the narrow definition of social policy adopted in both liberal academic and policy thinking, and the related dominant approach during the 1970s. A broad concept of social policy is justified on the basis that it is important to conceptualize public policy making across sectors, to emphasize the interaction between social and economic policies (a point that has tended to receive too little attention in the liberal or neo-liberal paradigm), the cross-sectoral impact of policies (of, for example, pensions which are used for grandchildren's education), and to allow a better understanding of traditions and politics of social policies and how these influence particular models of service delivery. Part II of this book will show how such a framework can help in analyzing countries policy trajectories; we now turn to an overview of recent trends in economic growth and patterns of exclusion and inequalities.

2

Globalization

All Boats Rising or Growing Divides?

The period since the mid-1950s has witnessed both unprecedented increases in global wealth and rapidly rising disparities. The 1950s and 1960s was a period of general optimism and economic growth, even though at the end of the period development economists like Chenery argued for more attention to poverty reduction and inequality. The 1970s and 1980s came to be known as the lost development decades, but at the same time saw the East Asian success stories, including the rise of China, which became the single most important driver of global poverty and inequality trends, followed by the sustained high growth in India. Finally, recent years have seen economic growth return to Africa, though the earlier decades of crises have created enormous disparities within the Global South, particularly with Asia. As Table 2.1 indicates, substantial shifts are taking place in regions' shares of global GDP, with particularly Europe's becoming smaller, and Asia's rising, while the share of sub-Saharan Africa has become ever smaller even though its recent economic performance has been better than the OECD's average.

The 1970s was a global turning point in the development strategies, from inward-oriented development with a central role of the state, toward export-oriented mode of development, an emphasis on reducing state intervention, and increasing interconnectedness of economic, political, and social–cultural processes. But the conditions under which liberalization occurred differed markedly. In the North, it was directly related to the

Table 2.1 Real 2005 GDP Shares (in Percent) of the World's Regions

	1970	*1980*	*1990*	*2000*	*2009*
World (Less US)	72.74	73.82	73.24	71.69	73.34
North America	29.86	28.90	29.41	31.02	29.26
Latin America	5.41	6.85	5.92	6.16	6.40
Europe	40.36	38.02	35.63	33.67	30.62
Former Soviet Union	4.27	4.09	3.84	1.89	2.48
Asia	13.54	15.31	18.75	20.60	23.71
East Asia	11.47	12.99	15.78	16.85	18.79
Southeast Asia	0.89	1.21	1.54	1.94	2.26
South Asia	1.18	1.12	1.43	1.82	2.66
Middle East	2.26	2.70	2.53	2.77	3.16
Africa	2.47	2.44	2.24	2.09	2.51
Sub-Saharan Africa	1.99	1.87	1.64	1.43	1.72

Source: International Macroeconomic Data Set; available at http://www.ers.usda.gov/Data/Macroeconomics (accessed in December 2009).

political changes, notably the rise to political power of Ronald Reagan and Margaret Thatcher. In much of the South, liberalization of economies has been experienced as imposed, typically through the structural adjustment and reforms imposed by World Bank and IMF, and as informed by northern countries' own economic interest rather than a concern for improving welfare in the South. China and India followed different paths, but here, too, policy formulation was and continues to be concerned with external imposition of ideas.

This chapter, building on de Haan (2007b), describes inequality trends between and within countries, and how these relate to economic growth, and processes of liberalization and globalization, thus providing a basis for assessing and understanding social policies in the rest of the book. This shows that the increases in wealth over the last decades have not been shared equally, and that both globally and nationally increasing inequalities pose new challenges to public policies. The chapter discusses the role of globalization, structural adjustment, and economic opening up for economic growth and welfare. It concludes that generalizations are unlikely to stand test of scrutiny, and that better context-specific understanding of such processes, countries' starting positions, and policies is required. However, processes of globalization do make increasingly urgent and challenging demands on public policies, as the one-sided growth policies in China and the welfarist approaches in India, described in Part II of this book, demonstrate.

For the purpose of social policy analysis, it is important to go beyond descriptions of poverty and human development indicators and focus also on inequalities. While the international development debates have focused on absolute measures of well-being, a description of inequalities forms an essential starting point for understanding socio-economic relations between and exclusion of groups and people. Moreover, perceptions of inequalities are at least as relevant for citizens' actions and public policy responses as the "actual" inequality and poverty trends. The concept of social policy that this book proposes departs from a notion that principles of solidarity and inclusion are critically important for the shape that social policy obtains in particular contexts.

From the outset, however, it is important to stress how much views on inequality, its trends, and causes differ. Few topics in the development studies literature have been more controversial than the questions whether global inequality has been rising during globalization, whether it has reduced or increased poverty, and for what reasons. Similar differences, of course, exist at national levels, and in many cases, there are very different assumptions of justice underlying these differences and importance attached to "facts." For example, a study showed that in Scandinavia, popular assessment regarded a top-and-bottom income ratio of 4:1 as just, compared to 12:1 in the US (Esping-Andersen, 1999: 7), while in China, increasing inequalities were seen as an essential and justifiable (though always contested) element of the post-1978 economic reforms.

In the debates on inequality, many economists have pointed at the positive benefits of globalization, and how successful those economies have been that have integrated themselves into world markets. Sachs (2005), for example, while acknowledging the importance of the anti-globalization protests, argues that it would be wrong to blame globalization for many problems of poverty in the South. Like Sachs, Bhagwati (2005) refutes claims of anti-globalization movements regarding disastrous impacts of globalization, and argues that outward economic policies—like China's—have created enormous benefits for its population. The IMF (2000) stresses that outward-oriented policies have benefited East Asia while inward-oriented policies have harmed Latin America and Africa.

On the other hand, there is a large contingent of analysts and activists stressing the negative impacts of globalization. For example, Munck (2005) emphasizes how globalization deepens inequities and social exclusion, and Stiglitz (2002) stresses that "globalization today is not working…for many of the world's poor." In response to Sachs, Vandana Shiva (2005) highlights the modernist assumptions in his analysis, ignoring the links between accumulation of wealth in the North and underdevelopment in the South under colonialism. Taylor (2001) concluded that social impacts of globalization and liberalization were unfavorable in eight of 11 case studies.

Also, there is evidence of "real public unease about...the pace of globalization," perhaps more so in the North than in the South.[1] According to Robert Reich (2008: 7), "supercapitalism" was marked by the gradual loss of the institutions that "had negotiated to spread the wealth and protect what citizens valued in common" during the period of "democratic capitalism" of the decades since the Second World War, particularly in the US. Of course, the forces against globalization do not come only or even mainly from the academic side, but are fueled by, for example, workers who perceive they may be losing jobs or experiencing wage cuts because of increasing international competition.

It will be important to observe how the 2008–09 financial crisis will reshape this debate; important not only from a theoretical point of view but also because these ideas have the potential to influence, no doubt, the growing protectionist sentiments. There has been much debate about the return of the interventionist ideas of the post-war period, and of course, countries around the world have put in place packages to revive the economy. There is also much discussion about better regulation, particularly in the financial sector of course. But it is far from clear whether the opposing views will converge. The opponents of globalization do feel vindicated by the crisis. The defenders of liberalization now concede that there was a failure of regulation, but it does not seem to be the case that this has fundamentally shattered the belief in markets and the potentials from globalization that follows from this.

The theoretical reasons for such differences in views on globalization and the associated ideas about markets are manifold. Globalization is a complex process, and attributing changes in poverty or inequality to globalization is difficult, as described in the next section. There is a range of technical questions on how to measure inequality, even more so than poverty which now has fairly commonly accepted ways of international measurement.[2] The technical details matter a great deal, as we will see later. Further, partly technical but also intensely political, there are differences whether we should be concerned about inequalities in outcomes or with

[1] According to a global poll held by GlobeScan; available at http://www.globalpolicy.org/globaliz/econ/indexgen.htm#poll (accessed on February 7, 2008).

[2] Ravallion (2004) shows how within the fairly narrow domain of "money-metric" poverty analysis results depend on the indicators and units of analysis chosen, and describes competing concepts of absolute versus relative inequality; vertical versus horizontal inequality; and interpersonal versus inter-country inequality.

inequalities in opportunities: the former is a traditional social–democratic concern and also found in some welfarist approaches to social policy, while the latter dominates in neo-liberal approaches, for example, emphasized in the *World Development Report 2006* (World Bank, 2005), but also in the productivity-oriented approaches of social policies in East Asia. There are differences in whether policy should address inequality as a concern in itself, or because of its impact on other areas, such as limiting productivity and access to markets (again, a concern that dominates in *World Development Report 2006*), and the potential impact on social stability (a main concern in China). Further, normative differences inform and sometimes confuse the debate on inequality. Analysts and policy makers differ in views regarding how much inequalities should matter in our concerns, with the *Financial Times* journalist, Martin Wolf—one of the most vocal supporters of globalization[3]—for example, arguing that the increases in well-being are more important that rising inequalities. Finally, there are differences in views on whether governments are primarily responsible for addressing inequalities, or whether this should be left to private and charitable agencies.

Clearly, there is no simple answer to questions about regarding inequality trends and what causes it. Kanbur's (2001) assessment that the debate is often split between different camps that make few efforts to understand each other still seems pertinent. With respect to the globalization debate, Basu (2001) stresses, perhaps slightly naively: the "curious feature about the debate on globalization...that those who favor it see no negative fallout from globalization and those who oppose it see no silver lining." This chapter and the book do not discuss these differences in detail, but it is important to keep in mind that many of the differences in findings on inequality are the result of different technical and normative assumptions. We first turn to a description of the varied processes that globalization entails, and how each of these impinge on social policies.

The Many Faces of Globalization

There are at least three spheres of globalization that are important here, each with implications for descriptions of poverty and inequality trends, as well as the analysis of public policies: economic, political, and socio-cultural. While the current phase of globalization is different from earlier ones, it is important to keep in mind that economic, political, and socio-cultural

[3] Wolf (2004). In his 2008 book, *Fixing Global Finance*, Wolf does concede that the globalization of the 1990s and 2000s has led to unsustainable imbalances.

developments interacted on a world scale throughout the colonial period (Wolf, 1982), and history has also taught that processes of globalization are not irreversible, and continue to be plagued by crises (Krugman, 2009). Technological change and the declining cost of communication, however, have given the current phase of globalization a unique dimension. According to Reich (2008), the key driver of "supercapitalism" has been marked by enormous increases in inequality and loss of institutions that tempered social problems till the 1970s. With the rise of new economic powers like China and India, globalization has obtained a new dimension, of increasing South–South and South–North economic linkages, but also with global implications as both the most recent financial crisis and the debates on climate change show.

In the economic sphere, four sets of processes have been important (Brawley, 2003; Yeates, 2001). First, international financial flows have skyrocketed, from almost negligible in the 1950s to a trillion dollar a day in the early 1990s. This was accompanied by deregulation of financial markets, and the rise of mergers and international acquisitions, thus increasingly challenging the welfare states that had been built on models of national economies, taxation, and social contracts. Nevertheless, a strong "home bias" continues to exist in investment, and equity capital held by individuals is still concentrated in domestic firms, a tendency that may be reinforced through the current crisis. Emerging markets' finance has come to play an important role, including through the global financial crisis in 2008, with China and others continuing to finance, particularly, US debt.

Increased capital mobility has been associated with international financial crises, which have caused new forms of vulnerability, and this has led to renewed calls for capital control (for example, in Malaysia and Chile after the crises of the late 1990s). Financial liberalization has been associated with increasing volatility, which is a particular concern for small and poor countries. The 1980s and 1990s already saw about 70 financial crises, many with an international dimension.[4] Many of these, like the East Asia crisis, started with increases in current account deficit and fiscal deficits, followed by drops in capital inflows that financed the deficits, and reduction in countries expenditure, leading to recession. These were often short run, but nevertheless, often had important implications for its social policies.

---

[4] Adelman (2000: 1053). Krugman (2009) discusses the failure of economists to recognize that "depression economics" continued to exist, thus failing to recognize warning signs for the 2008 crisis.

The 2008 financial crises started in the US but very rapidly impacted the rest of world, including emerging market economies which suffered from declining exports and declining net capital import. "Global financial intermediation is broken," wrote Alan Greenspan in late 2008, describing how cracks in the system appeared in August 2007 with the subprime mortgage problems, turning into a full-blown financial crisis with the default of Lehman Brothers in September 2008. This was followed by large-scale government interventions across the world to restore global financial stability, and as this book is finalized, the fiscal stimulus packages are unfolding, with the question how the public debts incurred through the immediate response will be balanced.

Crises tend to depress living standards of the poor and others, which is one reason why social policy tends to receive increased attention during economic downturns. For the poor, the long-term impacts of the crises of the late 1990s, for example, have been serious, though policy interventions, as discussed later in the description of the new social protection agenda, managed to mitigate these impacts. The impacts of the 2008 financial crisis and potential for changes in regulation are unclear at the time of writing of the book, but the crisis did highlight the extent of deep global financial integration, including that of emerging economies. The impact was felt in India, including in the relatively skilled export-oriented software and services sectors, as well as, for example, the diamond industry. Notably, large numbers of export factories in China closed immediately during the economic downturn and throughout 2008, and large numbers of migrants returned to their home villages, with estimates that 20 million workers may have lost their jobs; at the same time, the international community was hoping that a fiscal stimulus of China's domestic economy could accompany an adjustment of global imbalances (de Haan, 2010a, 2010b).

Second, globalization means growing foreign direct investment (FDI), a growing number of multinational companies, and integration of markets and business strategies. However, investments have remained concentrated between economically advanced countries and the newly emerging markets, and poorest countries may have been ignored rather than swamped by international investors, even though the foreign investment tends to be a large part of poor countries' GDP.[5] Countries in the North tend to be much

[5] Sachs (2005: 354) shows that richer countries tend to have more total FDI. UN Statistics (Brawley, 2003: 88) indicated that FDI in lower income countries constituted about 15 percent of GDP and 9 percent in richer countries. The FDI flows to Africa in 2008 reached a record level of US$ 88 billion, following eight years of consecutive growth, but was expected to fall by 67 percent in the first half of 2009 (UNCTAD, 2009).

more open than countries like China, Indonesia, and India,[6] but the trend unmistakably has been toward further integration, thereby challenging the social policies that were created during periods of dominance of closed economies.

Capital flows to emerging economies expanded rapidly from the early 1990s till the 1997–98 financial crisis, and then again from 2002 onward, increasingly constituting two-way flows (D'Souza, 2008). International (net) private capital flows to emerging markets alone reached US$ 929 billion in 2007, but were expected to fall to US$ 165 billion (*Economist*, 2009). An increasing number of multinational companies are from emerging market economies,[7] which because of India's and China's size, are expected to have a much bigger global impact than the earlier Asian success stories, and with at least as much movement across borders (for example, Chinese companies' production in Cambodia to benefit from trade preferences). Sovereign wealth funds have existed since the 1950s (in Kuwait), but have recently experienced enormous growth with overseas investments from China, India, Russia, etc., implying not only increased investment flows, but also an increasing role of the state—with some expecting that this will also contribute to challenging the dominance of the Washington Consensus (see also Chapter 3).

The third element of economic globalization refers to trade flows, including for services, which directly impacts on states' ability and strategies for taxation and redistribution. International trade has increased fast and constantly since the Second World War. From 1980 till 2003, while world output doubled, world trade trebled (D'Souza, 2008: 34). Much of the increased trade has been between developed countries, partly due to liberalization under General Agreement on Tariffs and Trade (GATT). Trade dependency is much higher in Africa than in OECD countries: exports form 30 percent of GDP for sub-Saharan Africa and 19 percent in the OECD (UNDP, 1999: 2)—but the large size of the informal economy in poorer countries make such comparisons difficult. Again, particularly

[6] A globalization index was presented in *Foreign Policy* by A. T. Kearny and Foreign Policy (2004), ranking countries on 14 variables related to globalization, on economic integration, personal contact, technology and political engagement.

[7] In 2003, 31 companies from the emerging market economies appeared in Fortune 500; in 2008, this had risen to 62, and in ten years, this may go up to one-third of the total (*Economist*, 2008b). Van Agtmael (2007) provides a detailed description of the emergence of emerging markets companies, suggesting increasingly rapid changes in economic structures, and Khanna (2008) describes how Washington's global position has been challenged by Beijing and Brussels.

during the 1990s, the emerging markets have been changing the global scenario: after 1989, China's exports have expanded phenomenally, while the 1997–98 financial crises strengthened resolve in many emerging economies to enhance exports and their trade surplus. The search for energy resources to fuel China's and India's economic model may be reinforcing the trade dependency—and vulnerability to shocks of prices of natural resources—in Africa (Weeks, 2009). In 2009, global trade is expected to fall for the first time since 1982.

Structural adjustment has usually implied a reduction, often externally imposed, of barriers for international economic trade and financial flows, alongside fiscal and monetary restraints, and realignment of exchange rates. Of course, the composition and timing of these reforms vary enormously, and small, poor countries tend to have less space to negotiate with international agencies. For example, India—unlike Argentina and South Korea, for example—kept strong restrictions on currency convertibility (protecting it from effects of the financial crisis in 1997), but liberalized current accounts and controls on technology imports, and started to dismantle industrial licensing. China also has kept control over international capital flows, and carefully intervenes to keep its exchange rate at a level that suits its diverse economic interests. While India's social policies appear mostly driven by histories and democratic politics, and Africa's by an inability to maintain the policy traditions of the 1950/1960s, East Asian countries carefully calibrated its social policies to support economic reforms.

Fourth, globalization entails increased international migration, even though the increase is not as large as often assumed: the streams in migration in the late 19th century were probably larger. Much attention is paid to migration to the North, for clear political reasons, because of the impact on, for example, welfare state provisions and national cohesion. However, most of the globe's human mobility remains regional, and by far the largest part remains within borders (with migrants often excluded from many social policy provisions), although in many cases—notably China—this is also directly linked to globalization. International remittances have grown substantially, now over US$ 200 billion, far ahead of official aid flows, and estimated to form about 12 percent of Nepal's GDP in 2004, for example (CBS Nepal, 2006). But remittances, too, are subject to volatile movements, including the current financial crisis, with deep impacts on countries like Pakistan, Indonesia, or the Philippines.

The nature of international migration has changed, as demand for labor in the North is changing, with skilled migrants forming an increasing proportion of total migration flows. The most recent growth phase of multinational companies in and from emerging market economies includes an active search for highly skilled workers from these countries as well as reaching out to its rapidly growing middle classes (*Economist*, 2008b). These changing patterns reduce the probability of international migration, thereby reducing inequalities, as these migrants tend to be the better off. But the structure of migration also has potential implications for national welfare provisions, if the internationally mobile opt out of national schemes (Deacon, 2004), and the potential for political pressure to enhance or create universal schemes may be reduced.

In the development debate, the economic aspects of globalization receive most attention. But these economic processes rely on political ones. Globalization has been associated with a degree of political unification or at least convergence, under the control of US dominance, including over international institutions—which, according to Amsden (2007), left much more space for developing countries to choose their own development path during 1950–80 than after. The roles and powers of national governments are thought to have diminished, and regulatory capabilities and governance have become increasingly subject to global norms.

This book will try to document, however, that national political agency has not vanished. As privatization, liberalization too is not a passive process, but involves institutional transitions (Rodrik and Subramanian, 2004). Success in liberalization involves adaptation to specific conditions, for example, in India, building on already strong institutions; innovative forms of ownership like China's town–village enterprises; changes in labor market institutions; and most recently, state-supported overseas investment, including to enhance energy and food security. And as many of the countries in Asia show, economic opening up requires careful public policy to ensure rising disparities do not fuel too large an opposition to reforms. The public policies of those emerging economies, including its social policies, are evolving at remarkable speed, as Chapter 7, and to some extent Chapter 8, will demonstrate. On the other hand, particularly in the poorest countries, the capacities to deal with let alone negotiate these global rules are limited.

Various aspects in the cultural sphere are equally important, even though this book focuses on economic ones. Religion has and continues to be a "globalizing force" (Payne and Nassar, 2006: 27), with perceived challenges to national state authority—as events in both the Netherlands with the rise of right-wing parties and the response of the Chinese state to religious movements show—and often, inextricably linked with global economic forces, notably around access to oil. Consumption patterns and life styles have become much more globalized as well, with communication technology playing an important role, alongside international companies promoting global brands, music, and fashion trends and events (with China and the 2008 Olympics bringing interconnectedness to yet another level). Awareness of events elsewhere around the world has increased through trendsetters like CNN and Al-Jazeera, and, of course, the Internet. Protests against globalization, for example, against WTO or G8 meetings, are now an integral part of globalization itself.[8]

Finally, globalization thus also involves transfer of ideas. This also is not a new phenomenon.[9] For many observers, globalization has involved the spread and justification of neo-liberal economic policies and ideology, claiming

> that the world has moved permanently into a new and promising era; that the growing density of market relations allows more stable as well as faster growth (and) that a single set of policies—liberalization of markets for goods and finance, small government and fiscal discipline—is best for capturing the benefits of globalization. (Wade, 2000, quoted in Harriss, 2001)

But this ideology is not passively absorbed. Reference to global institutions, adjustment, and globalization has become an integral part of the politics in many poor countries, for example, in attempts to build regional economic and political blocks such as the African Union and New Partnership for Africa's Development (NEPAD), that are seen as a shield against forces of globalization (as is the European Union [EU]) and an international epistemic community of policy analysts (Deacon, 2005) which has continued to argue against the dominance of a neo-liberal ideology of residual welfare promoting, with some success, for more inclusive approaches.

Thus, for an analysis of how social policies evolve, it is critical to understand globalization in its various dimensions. National economics have changed fundamentally, with increased mobility of capital and labor, and this directly impinges on possibilities to formulate economic and social policies. At the same time, policy processes are increasingly influenced also by

---

[8] According to Ferguson (in Dow, 2003), amongst the social disruptions caused by globalization is the perception that people are not in control and have no role in defining their reality. It is thought that the majority makes large sacrifices because of external forces, which reward only a few. This leads to growing social alienation.

[9] Jonathan Spence (2002) describes how China has drawn on international technical advice from the early 16th century onwards, and misplaced hopes of western advisers "to change China."

global norms and institutions: this shapes new opportunities, but also new challenges, particularly as both global and national inequalities have tended to rise in the most recent era of globalization, as described next.

Inequality during Globalization

The period since the 1950s has brought about historically unprecedented increases in economic welfare. In terms of economic growth and poverty reduction, during the last 50 years, more progress may have been made than in the thousand years preceding this (Sachs, 2005: 27 ff.), even though good global data, for example, on poverty have been available only since the 1980s.[10] Progress in many human development indicators, too, has been very substantial, partly because of improved economic resources, partly because of progress in technology, and partly also because of national governments assuming responsibility for the well-being of all its citizens (countries achieved very different levels of well-being at similar levels of GDP).

Very few people, including the strongest supporters of globalization, would argue that the benefits of this increased prosperity have been equally distributed. But any slightly more precise analysis of how unequal this has been depends greatly on the unit of measurement and type of inequality under consideration. If one was to take the extreme case of the world's richest and the world's poorest people, there is no doubt that over whichever period chosen, differences have increased—even though inequality figures are likely to understate this to a great extent as surveys seldom include the countries' richest (Bardhan, 2007). Milanovic (2005) calculates that at the beginning of the 21st century, the richest 5 percent received one-third of total global income, the same amount as the poorest 80 percent, and believes that globally, differences between the richest and poorest individuals are increasing (also, Sutcliffe, 2007).

The incomes of the richest and poorest countries have diverged at least since the last century-and-a-half. Bourguignon and Morrisson (2002) show steadily increasing global inequality between 1820 and 1992. Pritchett (1995) concludes there has been massive absolute divergence in the distribution of incomes across countries, not less than six-fold between 1870 and 1985. In terms of inter-country inequality, the long-term trend,

[10] The 2008 revisions of global poverty data following new price data show that, even now, much uncertainty remains regarding estimates, with, for example, the number of poor people in China doubling as a result of new estimates (Chen and Ravallion, 2008).

according to Pritchett, was "divergence, big time"—thus, at least partly contradicting economists' expectation of "conditional convergence" that economies with lower income levels would grow faster. According to the World Bank, inter-country inequality has been "increasing especially" since 1980 (World Bank, 2005a: 62 ff.).

A global Gini coefficient—one of the most popular measures of inequality in distribution of income or wealth—does not show such a straightforward picture. According to some analysis, the world's distribution of income has become "less unequal" over the last two or three decades.[11] The explanation for this is simple: the income growth in China and India, two large and previously very poor countries, has been far above global growth rates, thus bringing inequality down. Of course, this gives rise to new form of inequality, within the so-called Global South (even though China and India still have a long way to go to catch up with the North) and within countries, as we discuss later. But again, the indicators chosen matter a great deal. The Gini coefficient used for these calculations is a relative measure; if an absolute measure of inequality is chosen, inequality has been steadily rising since 1970 (van der Hoeven, 2000; World Bank, 2005: 63). Differences in wages between the best and worst paid, and the differences in returns to labor as compared to returns to capital, also show clearly rising trends.

There is also increasingly reliable data on global inequalities in non-income dimensions of poverty (UNDP, 2005; World Bank, 2005). Human development indicators have seen tremendous progress. Since the 1960s, the global distribution of education in terms of years of schooling has become less unequal. Many of the poorest countries saw large increases in enrollments, leading to some reduction in non-income dimensions of inequality. Of course, large variations continue to exist, within countries, between men and women, and, for example, in indicators related to quality of education even when access to education is becoming less unequal (UNDP, 2005; World Bank, 2005a: 61–62).

Life expectancy is estimated to have doubled over the last two centuries, and during the last half century, there has been global convergence in this respect as well. But the convergence was halted in the 1990s. During the 1990s, life expectancies in many places in sub-Saharan Africa and some other countries were lowered, mainly because of HIV/AIDS, leading to

---

[11] Sala-I-Martin (2002); Sutcliffe (2007); World Bank (2005); According to Ravallion (2003a) there was no convincing sign of a significant change in "overall" inequality over the last 20 years.

a gap with OECD countries that is larger than it was in 1950.[12] Health improvements slowed down during the 1990s and global progress became more uneven, and the negative trend was not restricted to sub-Saharan Africa and Eastern Europe (Cornia and Menchini, 2005, using global Demographic and Health Surveys [DHS] data). Within-country progress also was frequently uneven, and factors other than the spread of HIV/AIDS contributed to this divergence, such as extension of primary health care or lack thereof, as well as local conflicts and disasters, the erosion of family support, and slower and more variable economic growth and rising income inequalities.

The overall picture over the last half century is thus mixed. The gap between the world's poorest and richest has been growing very rapidly, but at the same time, large numbers of poor people, particularly in China and to a lesser extent in India, have seen incomes and other indicators of well-being rising. Human development indicators have shown some convergence, but some of the trends were reversed, at least in some areas, and in other indicators, sign of convergence are still not visible. A part of these rising and continuing global inequalities are due to increasing inequalities within countries, and we next turn to some examples, to better understand what policies have managed to reduce differentials, and under which conditions this failed.

Inequality within Countries: Regional Patterns

While research has shown that countries' economic growth, on an average, reduces poverty and does not systematically increases inequality, an overview of country trends shows fairly convincingly that during the last three decades, there have been more cases of rising than decreasing inequality. In Cornia's (2004) study, 53 of 73 countries showed rising inequality, which may have been a reversal of the trend of declining inequality until the 1970s (Cornia, 1999). Meschi and Vivarelli (2009) show rising inequality using a composite indicator for both middle-income and low-income countries during the 1980s and 1990s.

Across OECD countries, levels of inequality vary as well, though not nearly as much as across the Global South. The US is among the more unequal countries, with a Gini of 0.41, and the bottom 20 percent of the population earning 5.4 percent of total income. In egalitarian Sweden,

---

[12] World Bank (2005: 58–59); the differences in income only partly explain the differences in health indicators.

the Gini is 0.25, and the bottom 20 percent earns 9.1 percent of total income. In many of the OECD countries, like the US, the UK, and New Zealand, earning inequalities have increased during the period of globalization. Kevin Murphy calculated that in the US, in 1976, CEOs earned on average 36 times as much as an average production worker; in 2005, this was about 369 times.[13] The extremes have diverged in particular, with the share of income of the richest 1 percent going from 8 percent to 16 percent over the last two or three decades.[14] The failure of public policies to address inequalities in opportunities became a central part of the Democrats' 2008 election campaign in the US, but subsequent debates on health care reform indicate how deeply rooted the opposition to a redistributive state is. Apart from the US, Gini coefficients have been rising in the UK, the Netherlands, Belgium, and Norway (still very equal), but not, for example, in Canada, Italy, and France (Smeeding, 2005). Returns to skills, returns to capital rather than labor, technological change, and absence of adequate safety nets and changing public/private mix in spending for social protection are often quoted as main contributing factors to rising inequalities.

Former communist countries, in Eastern Europe and the former Soviet Union, used to have very low levels of income inequality. But income inequalities have risen with the collapse of communism and reforms, most notably in Russia where the Gini index is now around 0.40, and forms of extreme wealth have become visibly inside and outside the country. But in other countries in the region, inequality remains moderate (Poland, 0.35) or very low (Hungary, 0.27) (data early 2000s: World Bank, 2007).

In Latin America, inequality has traditionally been very large, as we discuss in detail in Chapter 5. This has been a direct result of the colonial history, and limited transformation since, despite a history of state intervention, for example, in industrialization. Income inequality measured by the Gini coefficient is around 0.50 across the continent, and the income inequality appears directly related to inequalities in access to land and education, and to social inequalities in the form of ethnic and racial divides. Inequalities have been high on the agenda in many countries in the region, with some positive results.

While Latin America has for long had the dubious reputation of being the most unequal region, Africa is not generally associated with such

[13] Vermeend (2008: 41); he criticizes the idea that high bonuses are beneficial for companies, as it appears that it has led to excessive risk taking (as the 2008 financial crisis highlighted).

[14] Various issues of the *Economist* (2003, 2006b, 2007). The Gini coefficients quoted are from World Bank (2007).

inequalities—even though ethnic diversity and conflict have been considered crucial. However, with the household survey data that have become available fairly recently, and the growing international concern for inequality alongside poverty, it has become increasingly clear that income inequality is as high in Africa as in Latin America. But unlike Latin America, there is much variation in African countries' inequality, in terms of income as well as assets, as we document further in Chapter 6. Apart from South Africa, highly unequal countries in terms of income include Namibia, Central African Republic (CAR), and Zimbabwe, while income inequality is low in Tanzania and Benin, for example. Little information exists about changes in inequality but, as elsewhere, increases in income inequality (for example, in Ghana, Ethiopia, and Uganda) appear more common than decreases. As in Latin America, but less well documented in the development literature on Africa, income and asset inequalities are often compounded by social disparities, which also find their reflection in state institutions.

The picture of levels and trends thus is complex. Nevertheless, levels of inequality have been going up—there are more cases of rising than declining income inequality, even though a number of countries have actively managed to keep inequality low, including in western and eastern Europe. With data that have fairly recently become available, we now know that the world's poorest continent is also very unequal. And the averages as documented by Gini coefficients should not let us forget the often deep-rooted regional and social inequalities—not only because they matter in themselves but also because they are constitutive forces of public policies and administrative arrangements. In Asia, as we describe next, levels of income inequality have been relatively low, probably, to a great extent due to much more equal distribution of land. But in many countries there too, inequalities have been rising, notably in China, Bangladesh, and Thailand, and arguably in India as well, despite a fairly steady Gini coefficient.

Is Asia still the Low-inequality Region?

By comparison with Latin America and Africa, inequalities in Asian countries appear low, as Table 2.2 demonstrates. Countries with the lowest levels of income inequality in Asia are as diverse as much richer South Korea, where inequality decreased during the 1980s (You and Lee, 2001: 298), predominantly rural Pakistan, India, and Bangladesh, and countries of economic success like Indonesia and Vietnam.

Data on Bangladesh have been disputed, and overall, its income Gini has remained relatively low. Over the last two decades, human development

Table 2.2 Well-being and Inequality in Asia

	Human development			*Poverty headcount (%)*			*Inequality*					
	HDI 1975	*HDI 2005*	*Change*	*US$ 1/day*	*US$ 1.25/day*	*Year latest survey*	*Gini coefficient*	*Share poorest 20%*	*Year*	*Trend*		*Years*
Bangladesh	0.35	0.55	0.20	41.3	49.6	2005	0.33	8.6	2000	38	42	1989–2000
Cambodia	0.54 (1995)	0.60	–	34.1	40.2	2004	0.42	6.8	2004	–	–	–
China	0.53	0.78	0.25	9.9	15.9	2005	0.47	4.3	2004	29	46	1981–200
India	0.42	0.62	0.20	34.3	41.6	2004–05	0.37	8.1	2004–05	32	33	1984–2000
Indonesia	0.47	0.73	0.26	7.5	21.4	2005	0.34	8.4	2002	37	40	1970–2002
Korea, Rep.	0.71	0.92	0.21	<2	–	–	0.32	7.9	1998	–	–	–
Malaysia	0.62	0.81	0.19	<2	<2	2004	0.49	4.4	1997	–	–	–
Nepal	0.31	0.53	0.22		55.1	2003–04	–	–	–	34	41	1995–2003
Pakistan	0.37	0.55	0.18	17	22.6	2004–05	0.31	9.3	2002	37	40	1979–200
Sri Lanka	0.62	0.74	0.12	5.6	14.0	2002	0.40	7	2002	–	–	–
Thailand	0.615	0.78	0.17	<2	<2	2004	0.43	6.3	2002	–	–	–
Vietnam	0.59 (1985)	0.73		8.4	21.5	2006	0.34	9	2004	–	–	–

Sources: UNDP (2009b); World Bank (2007: Table 2.7) and 2008 Supplement (World Bank, 2008); inequality trends of various country studies.

Notes: Poverty data are presented for both the old PPP data, and the revised US$ 1.25 poverty line following the revision of the PPP data; the old data are shown here for sake of comparison, as most information presented in this book is based on the old PPP data. See the World Bank website for explanation of the new data.

indicators have improved greatly, partly under the influence of its large NGOs like BRAC and Grameen. But income inequality seems to have increased since the 1990s, and the bottom 20 percent may have profited very little during the period of liberalization and economic growth.[15] Infant mortality and female literacy indicators remain very poor, similar to Pakistan, and much worse than in Sri Lanka (Chatterjee et al., n.d.: 21), suggesting both significant gaps in public policies and underlying strong gender inequalities.

A second country with a low Gini coefficient is Indonesia, though most recent data do show an increase in the Gini (World Development Indicator [WDI] data). Poverty has been reduced rapidly in Indonesia since the late 1960s, under an autocratic regime. According to Timmer (2004), Indonesia's long-term growth path has been very "pro-poor": the poor benefited from economic growth and suffered during declines.[16] The income Gini remained low, and access to health and education became relatively equal. Indonesia's provinces have experienced convergence of income over time (World Bank, 2005: 204). The Asia crisis of the late 1990s led to significant economic setbacks, political upheaval, and a process of democratization.

Vietnam's inequality trends have been somewhat disputed, but most recent evidence suggests that the country has managed to avoid the rising inequalities of China. Both the pro-poor economic and social policies of the current government and the preconditions of the pre-reform period have been key to keeping inequalities low alongside Vietnam's impressive growth performance.

The long series of comparable surveys in India dating back to about 1960 highlight that India has experienced substantial rates of economic growth and poverty reduction,[17] while the share of agricultural employment has declined. Little change in income inequality has been observed, with a

[15] However, Durevall and Munshi (2006) found no evidence that liberalization increased wage inequality between skilled and unskilled workers.

[16] There are various definitions of "pro-poor," and the differences mirror the debates over definition of inequality; in the definition applied in the joint donor research program which Timmer contributed to, pro-poor simply meant growth that benefits the poor, independent of changes in inequality. In China too, growth has been "pro-poor" even though inequality increased rapidly. Grosse, Harttgen, and Klasen (2008) apply a measure of pro-poor growth for non-income dimensions, and apply this to Bolivia during the 1990s, highlighting that improvements among the poor does not necessarily imply they catch up with the better-off.

[17] Measured by National sample Survey (NSS) data, poverty reduction has remained rather modest (42 percent in terms of the new US$ 1.25 norm), but this figure changes substantially (and decline is much faster) if data from the national accounts which show a much more rapid increases of consumption are taken into account (Ravallion, 2009: Appendix).

Gini staying around 0.35. Nevertheless, variation in both the rate of economic growth and the rate in which the poor benefit from economic growth vary considerably across the country. The relatively low and constant Gini coefficient hides diverging trends in income and human development indicators, across and within states,[18] and disparities in nutrition despite decades of national food self-sufficiency and food distribution programs. India's social disparities are very large, and overlap to some extent with regional disparities, which appear to be increasing.[19] Finally, inequalities in land and education are extremely large in India, and educational inequality measured by distribution of years of adult schooling is higher than in most Latin American countries.

Rising and High Inequalities: China, Thailand, Malaysia

Malaysia, China, and Thailand are the regions' most unequal countries, with levels of inequality that preoccupy public debate as well as official government responses.[20] The rising inequalities mean Asia is no longer the equal region it has long been associated with (Bardhan, 2007). Malaysia's levels of inequality have been much higher for a long time, but declining slightly since the introduction of the New Economic Policy in 1970. Income inequality in Thailand has been rising steadily alongside economic growth. The sectoral shift from agricultural to non-agricultural activities (Motonishi, 2003) and disparities in regional growth, particularly the concentration of economic activity in Bangkok and the Center (Richter, 2006), have contributed to this rise.

[18] Datt and Ravallion (2002). In 1999–2000 the state-wise variation was from 6 percent in Punjab to 47 percent in Orissa. The variation across "NSS regions" is even larger, and increasing (de Haan and Dubey, 2003; de Haan, Dubey, and Sabharwal, 2009).

[19] State level analysis for Orissa show that these social disparities are at least as severe within India's poorest regions, and the various forms of disparities overlap and mutually reinforce each other (de Haan, 2008).

[20] Ahuja et al. (1997) and Watkins (1998) were among the early studies focusing on inequalities during East Asia's miracle. Nepal's Gini coefficient jumped from 0.34 to 0.41, while the poverty headcount fell from 42 to 31 percent between 1995–96 and 2003–04, a period of conflict. Remittances became an increasingly important component of growth but also possibly a source of rising income inequality (CBS Nepal, 2006; World Bank and DFID, 2006).

China's rising inequalities have attracted a great deal of attention internationally and nationally, and are considered as among the key challenges for its sustainable development.[21] Since 1949, though with setbacks particularly during the Great Leap Forward,[22] China created income equality and egalitarian access to health and education facilities—though always with a strong rural–urban divide. The enormous increase in inequalities since the reforms of the late 1970s, accompanying 9–10 percent economic growth rates, and while lifting hundreds of millions of people out of extreme poverty, has been well documented. The Gini coefficient has skyrocketed to over 0.45, with little sign of levelling off. This consists mainly of rural–urban and inland–coastal disparities, but also growing interpersonal and social group inequalities. Disparities in health and education too have increased since the reforms began (Zhang and Kanbur, 2003). Different factors, policies, and policy phases impinge on these (Kanbur and Zhang, 2004). Pre-reform, rural–urban disparities were large, related to government promotion of heavy industry, restrictions on labor mobility, and social security for urban inhabitants. Reforms diminished the importance of policy-induced inequalities. But increased openness alongside fiscal decentralization contributed to increases in disparities between coastal and inland areas over the last two decades.[23] After a period where increases in inequality were publicly accepted, public policy since the early 2000 has become keenly interested in this rise, partly because of the threats posed to public health and threats of social unrest. Government policies now promote the idea of a "Harmonious Society" and balanced development (regional, social), alongside policies to promote continued economic growth, a trend which has been reinforced by the 2008–09 crisis.

There is little doubt and indeed open recognition that China's opening up have contributed to these rising inequalities (though different opinions exists about how much of a concern rising inequalities are with such large poverty reduction), which in turn, and with some delay, challenges its model of economic growth and political control. Other countries like Vietnam appear to have escaped such a dramatic rise in disparities, thus suggesting that increasing inter-country inequality is not an inevitable by-product

[21] An early international publication emphasizing the growing disparities was World Bank (1997); recent publications included the edited WIDER volume (Wan, 2008) and Gustafsson, Shi, and Sicular (2008).

[22] Kanbur and Zhang (2004) show that inequalities peaked during the Great Famine and at the end of The Cultural Revolution as well as in the current period of global integration.

[23] Wei and Wu (2001) argue that globalization led to reduced rather than increased rural–urban disparities.

of globalization. The link between globalization and inequalities is the subject of the next section.

Globalization and Inequality: Context and Policies Matter

As already mentioned, views on the impact of globalization have differed radically, and it is unlikely that a consensus will be reached, even as the global economic crisis has caused many to reconsider their views, but will also further complicate assessments of the impact of globalization. When globalization is shown to be increasing inequalities, this can be because markets work, because markets fail particularly for the poor, and/or because existing rules benefit the better off (Birdsall, 2005: 22 ff.). Given the complexity and multidimensionality of globalization, it is unlikely simple conclusions about impacts will emerge, and it is critical that social policy analysis recognizes this complexity. Initial conditions strongly affect outcomes in terms of economic growth and well-being, as do fiscal possibilities, political commitment, and public pressure to introduce social policies, as the case of Vietnam that seems to have averted extreme rises in inequalities indicates.

Economic studies and cross-country regressions have been very influential in the debate on the impact of globalization, and the authority ascribed to results of such studies seems undiminished despite strong technical reservations.[24] First, this literature has emphasized a positive relationship between openness and economic growth. But the record on economic growth has not been as uniformly positive during the period of globalization as is commonly assumed (Milanovic, 2003). More specific to the South, the impact of stabilization and structural adjustment on growth has generally been disappointing, leading to a conclusion that adjustment may have been necessary but not enough to promote growth and hence, poverty reduction (Killick, 1999), highlighting inter alia the need for careful assessment of the broad spectrum of public policies.

In both India and China, economic growth preceded opening up. Most of China's poverty reduction had happened by the time the economy started

[24] There are major questions about the robustness of the type of analysis, regarding the appropriate indicators, about the relevance of cross-country regression for the experience of individual countries, and the problem of comparing countries with very different starting positions. See, for example, Banerjee et al. (2006) for a critique of use of this type of research within the World Bank.

opening up. China's entry to global markets was preceded by communist (social) policies that had created a relatively healthy and educated workforce, land reforms that created both food security and an increasingly mobile labor force (as in many other parts of East Asia, and Vietnam), and state-supported rural industrialization. Moreover, integration into the global economy was supported by the (ethnic) Chinese emigrants who had built up substantial economic potential outside communist China, and in turn, government policies have actively encouraged the role of returnees.

Even now, countries like China and India are far from completely open and foreign investment is limited. Technical economic arguments and political economy considerations have driven a careful and gradual approach. The link between openness and growth may well be a virtuous cycle rather than direct causality: openness may lead to faster growth (but does not always do so), which in turn generates larger trade; "the positive openness-growth link is neither automatically guaranteed nor universally observable" (Nissanke and Thorbecke, 2005: 7). Moreover, the volatility that accompanies financial liberalization may hamper economic growth, because of declines in investment in human capital, falling investor's confidence, and uncertainty undermining the political or societal support required to implement structural reforms. In the context of crises as well as during "normal" times, public policies thus are critical for growth patterns.

Second, cross-country analysis have emphasized the almost tautological fact that economic growth is necessary for sustained poverty reduction (Dollar and Kraay, 2002). A more difficult question, which received very little attention during the 1980s and 1990s, is whether economic growth leads to increased inequality, which, as mentioned earlier, is as critical for our social policy analysis as the question about reductions in poverty. For long, it was assumed that early economic growth would lead to rising inequality, as summarized in the so-called Kuznets curve (which was established more through intuition than through good analysis of data, which was not available at the time). Recent evidence from research based on new poverty data showed that there was little evidence of this curve (China notwithstanding), and that inequality indicators such as Gini coefficients change only very little or slowly. Moreover, research in Africa, as highlighted earlier, found that many poor countries also are highly unequal.

But these findings that economic growth is good for the poor and not systematically associated with rising inequalities refers to an average relationship, and one might expect that most nations' policy makers care less about a global average than about how their country is doing in terms of specific potential threats of rising inequalities. Importantly, the finding that, on an average, inequality does not change is consistent with another finding that income inequality did rise in about 50 percent of the cases of growth that Ravallion (2001) analyzed. This again is in line with the important but less oft-quoted finding that the extent to which growth contributes to poverty reduction (measured by so-called growth–poverty elasticities, or by measures of pro-poor growth) varies enormously: in some countries, one percentage point growth contributes to a 3.5 percentage point decline in poverty, but at the other end, there are countries where a one percentage point growth is related with only 0.6 percentage point poverty reduction (Nissanke and Thorbecke, 2005: 10). In Africa, the poverty reducing effect of growth is much larger in Ghana than in Namibia (Fosu, 2009). And in India, a similar large variation in poverty elasticties and pro-poor growth across states has been found, which was linked to both initial conditions and public policies.[25] Context thus matters, greatly, including the public policies that were at the basis of growth as well as its pattern of distribution.

Attributing changes in income inequality or poverty reduction to specific policies is very complex, as inequality outcomes result from a wide range of factors. Changes in income distribution, of course, cannot be attributed to globalization alone. For example, inflation usually changes the distribution of income, and technological change can lead to wage dispersion. Impacts on income inequality from liberalization and privatization were found to be relatively small in Argentina (Berg and Taylor, 2001: 39; Gasparini, 2004), but financial sector liberalization that took place in Latin America during the 1990s increased income inequality (Lopez, 2004). Trade openness increases income inequality according to some studies. Lundberg and Squire (1999) in a then controversial paper suggested that openness to trade did not enhance income growth of the bottom 40 percent of the population. But others have come to opposite conclusions, and yet others find there is no impact and/or they are different for types of country,[26] and emphasize the problems of attributing these changes to economic or policy variables.[27] While Berry—who does not find evidence that capital

[25] Besley, Burgess, and Esteve-Volart (2004); Datt and Ravallion (2002).

[26] Meschi and Vivarelli (2009) showed that the types of trade and trading partners mattered for inequality effects: for example, trade by middle-income countries with high-income countries worsened income distribution.

[27] The complexities of the impact of trade liberalization on inequalities are described in Lopez (2004) and Ravallion (2003a).

account liberalization has contributed to rising inequality—makes a "reasonable guess...that increased openness has been at least partly to blame for increased inequality," partly because of labor-displacing technologies (Berry, 2006: 61).

At the same time, the outcomes of increased openness on poverty or inequality will be different in each individual country (Winters, McCulloch, and Cirera, 2001). In Bangladesh, opening up to trade did not lead to narrowing of wage gaps between skilled and unskilled labor. Liberalization is less likely to reduce wage differentials if unskilled labor was protected before the reforms (Hoekman and Winters, 2005; Jenkins, 2003). Economic restructuring as a result of globalization creates new employment, but also leads to job loss in previously protected industries, and the impact of these changes, of course, depends greatly on public policies, including existing safety nets. The jobs in the new industries tend to be vulnerable, as technology, global sourcing, and economic fluctuations make companies move easily, while safety nets tend to be weakly developed, including in China. Economic integration can reduce wage or income inequality, for example, if foreign firms provide jobs to mainly unskilled women, who use remittances to support their families—but this is typically at the cost of long working hours, poor working conditions, and separation from children.[28]

Does increased competition or trade lead to a race to the bottom, in terms of labor conditions? Burgoon (2001) indicates that a race to the bottom is by no means inevitable or automatic: in countries where people are compensated if they lost out because of trade, competitiveness appears to be improving in the long run. Cigno, Rosati, and Guarcello (2002) suggest that globalization may not have raised the incidences of child labor (though data are unreliable, and it is important to note that not all child labor is objectionable or damaging for children's prospects). While economic pressures no doubt increase under globalization, openness can be accompanied by global convergence around labor and other norms, even if with a lag, as experience in China before the crisis seems to suggest. Pressure for competitiveness may even lead to creation of political institutions that help reduce corruption. But none of these developments are automatic, and call for proactive social policies accompanying economic reforms.

Impacts of international labor mobility on inequality, similarly, are heavily disputed (de Haan, 2006). At a global scale, labor mobility is likely to lead to reduced global inequality, as economic migrants usually improve their income by moving from poorer to richer areas, and migrants

[28] Borraz and López-Córdova (2004); Kabeer, Mahmud, and Van Anh (2003); Kerr and Sweetman (2003); Jingzhong, Murray, and Yihuan (2005) for China.

very seldom are unemployed, partly because they lack a social safety net. However, international migration is increasingly dominated by the better skilled following changing production patterns and immigration policies. This does not diminish the global inequality reducing effects, but does reduce the potential for reduction of inequality within countries of origin. The higher skill levels required also imply greater investments in education in home countries, the costs of which need to be offset against the positive benefits of migration and remittances.

Finally, macroeconomic instability following liberalization often was associated with increased inequality (Medrano, Sanhueza, and Contreras, 2006). Crises affect the poor and impact inequality in many ways, and the share of labor in national income often declines during crises (van der Hoeven and Lübker, forthcoming). Price changes nationally and internationally, and exchange rate depreciations, subsidy or tax changes, closure of public or private companies, etc., all can change inequalities, affecting poor and rich, men and women differently. In absolute terms, poor people may lose less than the better off, but the impact of such losses on the poor is usually bigger as they have fewer resources to protect themselves. Moreover, economic hardship while often making people fall back on traditional support networks, may also lead to a weakening of such networks. Continuing volatility and the recognition of the damaging impact has over the last decade led to increased attention to social protection policies, and a reconsideration of a potential trade-off between social protection spending and growth, to which we come back later.

Globalization and the Need for Proactive Social Policies

It is unlikely that there will soon or ever be consensus about the benefits and losses from globalization. The overview of trends here has stressed how much conclusions depend on definitions and units of analyses. One can substantiate the point that recent decades have been beneficial for the South, notably China and to a lesser extent, India, but equally convincing is that inequality between the poorest and the richest countries and people has increased enormously. While on an average growth may not lead to rising inequalities, there are more cases of rising than decreasing inequality, and many of these are in Asia. Inequality measures are complex, and countries with relatively low income inequalities may suffer from huge disparities in other forms of wealth. A range of factors determines what type of economic growth is generated by globalization, and which sections of the population benefit from different types of economic growth.

The impact of globalization on any indicator of well-being, and even on economic growth, is due to a large number of factors, and generalizations do not appear meaningful: "it is often statistically difficult to disentangle the effects of globalization from those of the ongoing forces of skill-biased technical progress, as with computers; structural and demographic changes; and macroeconomic policies" (Bardhan, 2007). Globalization was responsible for China's rising inequalities, as with new opportunities the better-endowed are in a better position to utilize them. But the expansion of labor-intensive industrialization has also helped large numbers of workers, and the restructuring of the economy moved many people out of agriculture and poverty. In India, the decline in poverty slowed down since the early 1990s, the period of intensive opening of the economy. Agricultural growth slowed, but this was probably due to a decline of public investment in, for example, irrigation, rather than due to globalization.

Specific groups suffer from globalization and the structural reforms that accompany this, and impact assessments, as discussed in Chapter 4, are critical for international development approaches. In assessing the impact of globalization, we need, of course, to take into account how pre-reform public policies caused inequalities and hurt poorer groups, such as regressive public spending or administrative barriers to migration (such as the *hukou* system in China). Globalization can both reinforce these and alter them. Apart from redressing these biases, according to Ravallion (2003a: 20–21), there are many things governments can do to enhance positive impacts, "combining growth-promoting economic reforms with the right policies to help assure that the poor can participate fully in the opportunities unleashed by growth." In terms of the impact of trade liberalization and other reforms, a wide range of "initial conditions" are crucial, including macro stability and fiscal discipline, private property rights, primary education, the poor's access to land and credit, local knowledge and participatory political systems, and administrative capacity to steer reforms.

But this in turn highlights the importance of public policy commitment and capacity, and this book will help enhance understanding of what kinds of policies and institutions help reduce inequalities in the context of globalization. These questions were equally important in the period of more closed economies and developmental states. However, globalization has radically changed the way we should ask the questions, as international economic connections make demands on state policies to ensure a competitive labor force and social protection to be able to react to the increased number of international economic crises far more urgent. At the same time, the traditional mechanisms of taxation, regulation, and redistribution have come under pressure. In the second part of this book, we will describe ways in which countries have responded to the forces of globalization, and discuss the necessary capacity to undertake reforms—which is very different in the strong states of China and India from that in many of the poorest countries in Africa, where a growing proportion of the world's poor live. Before we turn to country cases, we first review the debate on state intervention, particularly whether globalization has led to a demise of the state.

3

Demise of the State?

The previous chapter concluded that the impacts of globalization on well-being and inequalities are diverse, and that much depends on state intervention, in cushioning the negative effects of, for example, liberalization on the labor market, but also in creating the preconditions for successful integration in the world economy. This highlights the question about states' capacities, and whether globalization has caused a "demise of the state," specifically a decline in capacity to design and implement social policies as some authors have argued, and the impact that this would have on inequalities, for example, the increasingly dual structures of social services.

Like other public policies, social policies have been challenged by globalization. Increased investment and trade across borders challenges states' traditional possibilities for taxation and hence, provision of services and redistribution, and enhanced capital mobility has reduced the margins for fiscal policies. Regulation of production and labor conditions, and redistribution of income have become increasingly unpopular—at least before the financial crisis broke out in 2008—and are perceived to be more difficult to implement with increased capital mobility. Increased international labor mobility and emerging global markets in health, education, and social insurance, all potentially contribute to undermining welfare provisions within countries.

To prepare for the discussion on countries' social policies, this chapter reviews the debate on the "demise of the state" (see also de Hann, 2007b), highlighting the diverging views on this in the literature, and the many questions that remain. This chapter will argue that processes of opening up are generally not associated with less state intervention. The chapter presents evidence that countries with more integrated markets do not spend less and often spend more on social sectors, and discusses why this should be the case. The chapter then moves on to a normative argument about why and when public spending is necessary, not only for human development and redistribution but also for economic growth, and why the quality of such spending needs improvement.

A Minimalist State? The Debate

Does globalization undermine nation-states? Has the age of globalization led to a minimalist state, as many politicians on the right have argued it should, and many advocates on the left have feared? Political scientists have claimed that globalization has not only led to astonishing growth of inequalities but also destroyed the stability of post-welfare capitalism, and undermined social cohesion. According to Deacon (2000) and the World Commission on the Social Dimension of Globalization (2004), globalization is unraveling the social bond as well as weakening national institutions. Hirst and Thompson emphasize that globalization has undermined state capacity for economic management and provision of basic services and public goods, thus realizing 'the ideals of the mid-nineteenth century free trade liberals' (Brawley, 2003: 36). The instability created by the new global markets, and the size and importance of multinational companies whose turnover is larger than the gross national product (GNP) of many smaller poor countries have been considered to constrain national governments' policies, their taxation, regulation, monetary policies, and ability or willingness to subsidize social sectors. An increasing number of commentators have taken similar positions when commenting on the 2008–09 crisis, which indicated countries' inability to shelter itself from international economic volatility.

But the academic literature is divided over the question, and many instead argue that globalization restructures and transforms the state. Moreover, conclusions are strongly informed by frameworks adopted to analyze the impact of globalization on national policies (Yeates, 2001).[1] A "strong" globalization hypothesis, which the authors quoted above by and large follow, focuses on globalization as an external phenomenon that states and populations perceive passively, and which directly erodes state sovereignty

[1] A parallel strand can be found in the literature on policy transfers, which can happen through coercion, convergence, diffusion, and learning (Governance and Social Development Research Center [GSDRC], 2008). Policy learning and transfers are, of course, not unique to North–South relations, but, for example, lessons from England and France were an important "part of a comprehensive process of learning within the framework of the specific development of Prussian Germany on the way to the modern industrial state" (Reulecke, 1981: 45).

and capacities. Abedian and Biggs (1998) indicate that economic globalization undermines South Africa's spaces for economic policy making, increases pressures to reduce budget deficits, and restricts fiscal powers. Tanzi (2000) agrees when he concludes that globalization will impact governments' ability to provide social protection. He expects a fall in tax revenue and scope for regulation because of tax competition, rapidly increased electronic commerce, and mobility of production factors. Timing and sequencing of policies are also crucial: for example, reduction of import tariffs and quotas may undermine country's industrial capacity faster than it creates incentives. The global economic pressure is intensified through a global convergence of policies and norms, particularly around budgeting systems and privatization and public–private partnerships. Many social policy analysts similarly have stressed the force of globalization, including those of global institutions, which has contributed inter alia to the "residual" notion of social policy as highlighted earlier.

The second approach identified by Yeates (2001) sees globalization as partly under control of nation-states, and, thus, sees states as contributing to creating globalization (for example, Walby, 2003). This approach emphasizes capacities of states to adapt and be proactive, and even to choose to limit their sovereign powers, even if not "voluntarily." In this analysis, national politics and political economy—and, for example, the strength of organized labor (Rudra, 2002)—play an important role in determining the course of access to global markets, as the East Asia success stories clearly indicate. Even if globalization is portrayed as inevitable, the timing and pace of globalization still depend on political responses and pressures—India's gradual path of globalization is a case in point. Globalization may engender particular political models, but this too is not automatic, and national histories, politics, and preferences continue to play an important role, China of course demonstrates.

Third, a strand of analysis focuses on political agency at international or transnational level, and the institutions that have exerted increasing influence on policy formulation and implementation, including of social policy. Social policy has been globalized through the emergence of poverty and social policy approaches within international financial institutions (IFIs), OECD, WTO, but also responses by regional organizations such as the African Union (2006), UN organizations like in West Asia (UN Economic and Social Commission for Western Asia [UN–ESCWA], 2008), the international epistemic community of policy analysts that we referred to earlier,[2]

[2] Bob Deacon's work is an example of this. He highlights the risks or changes in social standards under globalization—for example, the emergence of a global health market alongside privatization of social services—but also the possibility to influence this change.

and international civil society whose critique of globalization has become part of globalization itself and, for example, exerted great influence on approaches and funding for social services.

The study of government's capacity to formulate and implement social policy needs to adopt elements of all three approaches. A concept of evolving social policy needs to understand the different and changing ways in which states are positioned in the global system, as well as the different ways in which these positions are perceived, and how internationals organizations are contributing to these dynamics. Globalization has been perceived as undermining OECD's Keynesian fiscal, monetary, and employment policies. Globalization since the 1960s indeed has had a unique impact on the post-war welfare state (Mishra, 1999). Economic policies are increasingly intertwined with global policies and competition for investors, and even with immigration dynamics which have resulted in the rise of anti-immigrant sentiments and concerns about national identity. Those dynamics can lead to surprising changes and need to transform social policies, as the case of the Netherlands, described in Box 3.1, shows.

In Africa in particular, globalization has been inextricably associated with imposed adjustment (Manji, 2000: 18), declining capacity for national policy making after the optimism during early independence, and "a growing process of transnationalization of social policy" (Aina, 1999: 85). International development assistance remains crucially important in many countries—for example, as the following table (Table 3.1) illustrates, in Ghana, Kenya, Malawi, Tanzania, Uganda, and Zambia—and often aid is more important than remittances from migrants. Sustained large aid volumes have reduced incentives for improving revenue generation and systems

Table 3.1 Aid Dependency in Africa

	GDP per capita (US$) 2005 PPP	*Official development assistance (ODA) per capita (US$) 2007*	*Inflow of remittances per capita (US$) 2007*
Botswana	12,387	56	75
Ghana	2,480	49	5
Kenya	1,240	34	42
Malawi	667	53	0
Nigeria	1,128	14	62
South Africa	11,110	16	17
Tanzania	744	49	5
Uganda	1,454	56	27
Zambia	1,023	88	5
Zimbabwe	2,038	35	–

Source: UNDP (2009b).

of taxation. It is felt that countries have lost control over public policies to global institutions, and are subject to externally imposed constraints on social policies. It is felt they have been pushed into liberalization and privatization, under influence of neo-liberal ideologies and strategies for restructuring of world economy. Initiatives like NEPAD and strengthening of the African Union are an attempt at regional integration to harness the continent against global forces.

Big countries like China and India that are less dependent on global institutions are positioned in a very different way—even before they became a major force in global finance. They have been able to manage the processes of integration into global markets, maintaining national public policy approaches, modifying these to new requirements of global systems, as described later in this book. China, after 30 years of reform, further demonstrates that the global economy for the foreseeable future will contain very different national political regimes; and the growing importance of China in Africa may lead to more divergence in this respect, with China's stated international development policy of non-intervention but different models of economic policy.

The social policy analysis in this book emphasizes the importance of interaction between national action and global forces, stressing the need for proactive analytical and normative perspectives. Assertions about the impact of globalization have been subjected to empirical quantitative analysis: ways of taxation are changing and becoming more difficult; and capital liberalization has created a downward pressure on government spending, but higher levels of trade have not, though trade liberalization posed more challenges for revenue generation in poor developing countries.[3] But overall, states have not been shrinking, as we discuss next, and national policy remains crucial. Similarly, increased competition does not necessarily lead to a fall in labor standards. The regulatory roles of states are redefined, under the influence of both civil society, including northern trade unions, and global institutions like ILO and WTO,[4] but evidence across the world does indicate that states continue to play important roles.

---

[3] Aizenman and Jinjarak (2006); Brawley (2003: 113); Clements, Gupta, and Inchauste (2004: 13).

[4] For example, in June 2007 Chinese government representatives for the first time had to report on China's record on preventing worst forms of child labor. The evidence consisted of new legal and other national measures, but it is not inconceivable that global fora like these do influence progressive national policy making and implementation, and the evidence does indeed quote international collaboration particularly with US and ILO (International Labour Conference, 96th Session, May 30–June 15, 2007, Geneva).

It has been observed that globalization has been accompanied by reduced concern about the welfare of the population. However, this in itself has also created new terrains for debate, both internationally, with the focus on poverty reduction and governance following a period of unmitigated adjustment, and nationally, as a result of direct pressures of old and new interest groups and protests that follow reforms. While globalization in the form of increased movement of investment and capital across borders makes it harder for states to regulate economic activity, it also may lead to a decline in acceptance of politically sanctioned rents (Brawley, 2003: 66). While forced policy convergence, particularly in aid-dependent countries, may reduce space for public policy formulation, according to some, globalization "may" have beneficial—and no doubt deeply contested—impacts such as transforming the patrimonial character of states (Budd, 2004). For example, international research and advocacy has made the existence of corruption—which often hurts the poor more than the better off—more visible. Globalization has been associated with enhanced role of the private sector at the cost of public intervention, but is simultaneously "about more accessible and transparent national policy domains, public policy convergence, and greater interdependence as people experience the effects of others' management of cross-border spillovers" (Kaul and Conceição, 2006: 9).

Even if space of public policy making has been restricted, policy makers and national elites (both increasingly connected globally) and their political views continue to matter. With respect to India, a former senior civil servant, Mander (2004), observed that during the 1990s, the country's political elite seemed to have lost the concern for the deprived that had prevailed in the earlier period after independence. Liberalization itself was introduced by stealth during a period of political–religious turmoil of the early 1990s, and its social consequences became more central again with the change in government in 2004. China's social policies since the 1970s were marked by an often open recognition—with little public debate, reflected in the way social services collapsed—that inequality could, if not should, increase. This assessment was always contested, but started to change with a different political leadership and when the costs of rising inequalities and corruption in terms of the Party's legitimacy were becoming clearer. Finally, rising wage inequality in OECD countries was, according to Atkinson (1999), not only due to globalization and competition from low wage countries but also linked to an ideological shift that implied less popularity for redistribution and more individualism (one of the components of the dramatic changes in the Netherlands).

Thus, the debate on globalization and capacity and space for public policy making remains unresolved, and different perspectives continue to prevail. With the crisis of 2008, the voices for enhanced state intervention again got the overhand, and it remains to be seen whether the growing intervention to restore financial stability will be temporary—as economists like Greenspan argue it should be while acknowledging that the politics of withdrawing government intervention are complicated. In any case, as the analysis in this book will substantiate, links between globalization and government intervention are multifaceted, and different in each country. Within this complexity, for social policy analysis, the question of public spending is critically important—and much debated—and we turn to this next.

Social Sector Spending: Trends

Social spending in low-income countries has received surprisingly little attention in academic literature.[5] The reasons for this are varied. Comparable data are hardly available, with major international agencies having paid little attention to data collection. Classifications vary across countries, and can, by themselves, be problematic. Spending data can refer to central government spending only, excluding state/province and local government spending, which, for example, affects conclusions about health policies significantly. While for OECD countries it is possible to provide acceptable comparisons of levels and patterns of spending, for countries in the South, this poses many more problems, and has generally been available only since the (late) 1970s. And of course, there have been serious disagreements on the issue, notably in the heated debates on and policy advice regarding structural adjustment, which on the whole has not stimulated in-depth scholarly debate.

Global data showed no downward (or upward, for that matter) trend in the share of the state in national GDP since 1990 (see Table 3.2). High-income countries have, on an average, larger states: government revenue

[5] None of the major research programs on social policies quoted earlier included substantial study on spending (but see Hujo, 2008), and the subject was absent during the Arusha social policy conference. An International Food Policy Research Institute (IFPRI) overview of studies on governance found only two studies that focus on social expenditures and poverty, with differing results (Resnick and Birner, 2006: 27). Baldacci et al. (2008) used panel data from 118 developing countries during 1971–2000. W. Arthur Lewis suggested that the public sector in the South should be spending 20 percent of GDP on services, excluding defense and debt repayment (in Herbst, 2000: 118).

in high-income countries was about 25 percent of their GDP, while it was about 15 percent in low-income countries. While there has been a general rise in tax revenue as share of GDP across the OECD, the variation among OECD countries is large. Levels of government spending in OECD countries have not been converging, while taxes on capital remain varied,[6] and spending has been shifting from public toward private arrangements.[7] And one study that shows some convergence indicates an upward trend in spending through a catching up by low spending countries (Rothgang, Obinger, and Leibfried, 2006).

The differences reflect ideologies regarding limiting state interventions in many English-speaking countries on the one hand, and those regarding the need for state intervention and redistribution in continental Europe on the other. As we illustrated in Box 1.2, "reasons why Americans and Europeans differ on their choices of welfare state and redistribution run very deep into their different history and culture" (Alesina and Glaeser, 2004: 13). Other factors that explain the substantial and continued cross-Atlantic social policy differences include political institutions, such as proportional representation, the role of the constitution in allowing changes in government policies, and federalism. Further, racial divisions and preferences in a more heterogeneous country like the US—where poverty is concentrated in minority groups—can deter redistribution.[8]

As a proportion of GDP, poorer countries' governments, on an average, tend to tax and spend less than richer countries. But spending is still substantial, probably well above OECD countries' historical records

Table 3.2 Government Revenue and Spending as Percentage of GDP

	Current revenue			*Total expenditure*		
	1990	*2000*	*2008*	*1990*	*2000*	*2008*
World average	22.7	24.7	27.4	25.8	25.8	28.1
Low-income	15.5	15	n.a.	18.4	18.3	n.a.
Middle-income	17.3	17.7	20.2	22.1	21.3	19.7
High-income	23.8	n.a.	27.9	26.6	n.a.	28.9

Source: World Bank (2003b).
Note: 2008 figures are from World Bank (2010) and may not be entirely comparable.

[6] Brawley (2003: 63). According to Dreher (2006: 197) "few economic variables robustly influence tax rates—probably because decisions to change taxes are dominated by political considerations."

[7] Goudswaard and Caminda (2010), who show a positive impact of public spending on income redistribution in OECD countries, and a negative impact of private spending.

[8] The emphasis on political institutions is re-affirmed by Taylor-Gooby's (2005) critique of Alesina and Glaeser, which highlights the importance of left wing politics in Europe.

(Siebrits, 1998: 309), and has not been decreasing recently, including in social sectors.[9] Moreover, there is enormous diversity across the South. For example, while the average for low-income countries is 15 percent, total government revenue as percentage of GDP is around 10 percent in Bangladesh, while it is about 25 percent in equally poor Kenya. Neither can one observe a universal trend of a shrinking public sector, though with important exceptions like Ghana. The variation for 29 of the countries referred to in this book for which data are available (excluding Korea) is plotted in the following graph (Graph 3.1).

Similar large variations exist in the proportion of government spending to the various sectors, including within the social sector, and there is very little serious analysis of what causes these differences. For example, poorer countries tend to invest more public resources in education, as compared to health, as data from Argentina, Thailand, India (particularly recently), and Bangladesh, for example, illustrate. Moreover, there are large differences in the proportion of this spending to primary education: Zimbabwe and China spent 15 times

Graph 3.1 National Income and Government Spending

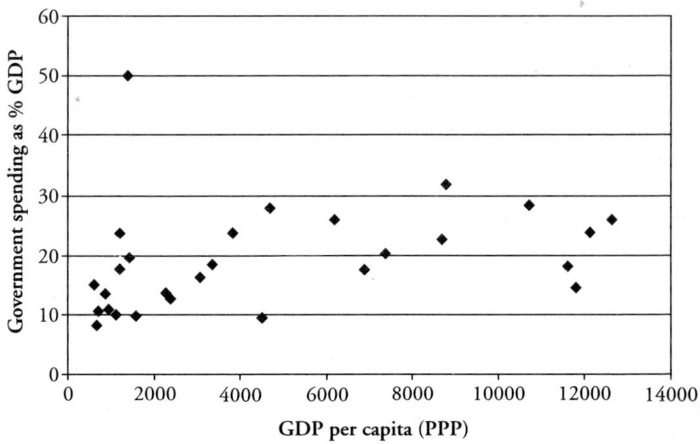

Source: Data WDI online, available at http://data.worldbank.org/data-catalog/world-development-indicators (accessed in December 2009). See Annexure for country data.

[9] Abu Sharkh and Gough (2008); but see Rudra (2002), who does note a decline in welfare spending (excluding health and education), for which data is even less reliable. In an earlier paper, I suggested there may be a link between levels of income inequality and government revenue/spending, but WDI data for 29 countries referred to in this book do not confirm such a trend, nor does there appear to be a link between GDP per capita and government revenue (see Annexure for presentation of data).

more public money on tertiary education than on primary education. South Korea was one of the few countries where more public money was spent on primary than on tertiary education, but private contributions to education were high too. The relative high spending on education, relative to health, not to needs, may be motivated by the synergies that may derive from a well-educated population, and/or by public pressure (as in India during the 1990s), but it remains a subject of investigation why countries spend in social sectors as they do, and whether these are the right choices.

Globally, health funding may be least prioritized (Musgrove, Zeramdini, and Carrin, 2002). Recent "vertical" donor initiatives in the poorest countries, including by new private international organizations like the Gates Foundation, may be changing this, though there are concerns that these do not contribute to a strengthening of the health sector as a whole (see next chapter). As the data presented later show, there is much variation across countries in public health expenditure: it is relatively high in Mexico, for example, but very low in Uganda, Vietnam, Indonesia, and India—where typically private, "out-of-pocket" spending is high.

Least information is available on social security or safety net expenditures in the South, even though such expenditures are substantial. Besley, Bergess, and Rasul (2003) brought together the international data on safety net expenditures between 1972 and 1997, highlighting "wide variation in the levels of expenditures on safety nets across countries," which cannot be explained on the basis of governments' information about "optimal" levels of expenditures. Donors have been important in determining patterns in low-income countries, perhaps increasingly so. The recent crisis may drive spending on social security up, as it typically forms a large proportion of the fiscal stimulus in better-off countries, and donors are prioritizing protecting the poor and vulnerable against the impact of the crises.

Knowledge about trends in social spending is naturally even sparser. Discussions about the impact of structural adjustment have generated much controversy, with common claims that such programs have restricted social spending.[10] However, Killick (1999) noted that "SAPs have not made a decisive difference to social service provision, which has generally been among the more protected categories of government spending" (also, Killick, 2005). The IMF and World Bank research has challenged continuous claims—by NGOs and others—of a decline in social spending. Presence of IMF-supported programs did not reduce spending in health or education, according to a report by the IMF's evaluation office. Recent increases in

[10] Often, processes of adjustment and liberalization have been associated with economic crises, which makes trends in social expenditure even more difficult to interpret.

donor funding through debt relief have led to a substantial relative increase in social spending. Nevertheless, civil society continues to criticize the IMF regarding fiscal space for social service provision.[11]

Taylor's (2001) overview of case studies on social spending during liberalization also shows diversity in trends. South Korea, Colombia, and Cuba increased its social spending after the 1997–98 crisis, but South Korea did so from low levels and a neglect of most forms of social policy (Kwon, 2005a). On the other hand, Zimbabwe, like Russia and Turkey, was forced to cut back social spending following the fiscal constraints during external liberalization. Neither Argentina nor India cut back in social spending during periods of liberalization. While in Ghana, which has adjusted relatively diligently for an extended period of time, state expenditure has declined significantly and social sector spending declined in the first decade of reform, overall state spending does not seem to have declined during the 1990s, and the share of spending going to social sectors has not been declining either. A further, and also under-researched, aspect of social spending in the South is its "volatility," particularly in aid-dependent countries, which we illustrate later with respect to Ghana.

These findings and studies thus confirm the conclusion that there has been no generalized downward trend in social spending as proportion of government spending or of GDP (Mishra, 1999: 50). The research on OECD trends point to one of the possible reasons why social spending may not be declining. In 1978, it was found that social expenditure and openness to trade were positively correlated.[12] The welfare state formed a precondition for economic liberalization: social protection provisions are the alternative for the protection previously provided through economic policies of tariffs and quotas. Similarly, in Spain, universalistic social policies were preconditions and created popular support for the modernization of the post-Franco economy (Boix, 2008). Not that all OECD countries have taken the same trajectories under globalization, far from it. The point is that globalization seems to have made state intervention different, but not less important, and that national ideologies and institutions like trade unions and parliamentary systems continue to drive differential responses.[13]

[11] IMF (2003) and Martin and Seguro-Ubiergo (2004) on adjustment; Paternostro, Tiongson, and Rajaram (2005) on trends under debt relief; an Afrodad view is posted at http://www.bretton woodsproject.org/art-562469

[12] Gough (2008); also Rodrik (1998). De Grauwe and Polan (2003) conclude that there is no necessary trade-off between social spending and international competitiveness, but with an important role of efficient governments. But see Rudra (2002) for evidence to the contrary.

[13] According to Bowles (2000: 20) states and trade unions as "traditional vehicles of egalitarian aspirations ... have a different but no less important role to play in a highly competitive world than in closed economies."

As highlighted by Tanzi (2000) for developing countries as well, globalization leads to contradictory pressures: the ability of the state to raise taxes may be reduced with globalization, but pressure for state involvement is increasing as certain groups are perceived to be suffering from globalization, or as national identities are thought to be under threat, as the case of the Netherlands in the Box 3.1 demonstrates.

In small and weak states, it is unlikely that similar patterns will be found (Deacon, 2000), but there too, responses are not likely to be independent of national institutions and histories. In any case, the argument highlights the importance of strengthening of national policy making, and

Box 3.1 Globalization and Backlash in the Netherlands

The Netherlands has had a reputation as an open and liberal country, with an impressive welfare state. It also was the country that gave rise to the expression "Dutch disease," where a rise of income from natural resources led to serious economic crisis, and where the unsustainable impacts of the welfare state have been very manifest. The Netherlands managed the crises through the social contract of consultative mechanisms known as the "polder model," and has for a long time had relatively good economic growth and low unemployment, while the state has maintained a strong redistributive function.

The 2000s witnessed a very different type of transformation, which was directly the result of the Netherlands' position in the global economy. While the rise of emerging economies is seen as an increasing threat, and the financial crisis of 2008–09 had a relatively large impact on the relatively open economic (financial) sector, most of the public debate revolved around three issues. In the first place, the citizens lost confidence in the established political system, which helped to open space for "plain-speaking" right-wing politicians, and was accompanied by increased individualism. Second, very surprisingly, Dutch sentiments turned radically against the European community, and diplomacy became increasingly bilateral. Finally, public debate became extraordinarily preoccupied with the problem of "integration" of immigrants (particularly the category of unskilled migrants recruited in the 1950s and 1960s) and a definition of what it means to be Dutch, with the possibility that its immigration policies will end up running counter to the policies to attract knowledge migrants.

These changes are complex, and perhaps unique and temporary, but the key point here is to indicate how the Dutch state has been forced to redefine itself. The Netherlands clearly experienced a backlash against globalizing forces, and social policies are both challenged and become the instrument for realigning the country's position in a globalizing economy.

Source: de Haan (forthcoming 2010).

for international approaches to become better attuned to the politics of aid (de Haan and Everest-Phillips, 2010). State intervention, including regulation and taxation when service provisions are privatized and opened up to international markets, is increasingly challenging. But politics and social processes remain crucial for the ways in which social policies evolve at the beginning of the 21st century, including as the effect of the financial and food crises makes itself felt to all corners of the Global South. We will return to country-specific politics and social policies in Part II of this book, but in the next section, we first turn to the normative question—supported by empirical evidence—why social spending matters, for well-being directly but also for economic growth.

Why Social Sector Spending is Important

> [That public policies] need to combine human resource development with economy-wide policies favourable to growth has been well recognized in discussions of policies for fighting poverty…The key message emerging from recent research is that achieving a policy environment conducive to growth interacts multiplicatively with human resource development. By doing just economic reform or just human resource development, one may achieve very little in terms of poverty reduction, but doing both can take a nation a long way. (Datt and Ravallion, 2002)

Alongside the debates on the role of the state, the role of social spending in broader public policies has been heavily debated in the advocacy-oriented development literature. As Peter Lindert has noted with respect to much-better documented OECD literature, the differences in views are likely to remain; in the case of the South, we simply know much less about social spending but the debate is equally polarized. The following lists a range of reasons—discussed in more detail in de Haan (2007b)—why social spending and better knowledge about it are important.

Education and health indicators depend of levels of economic development, but different social policies can cause large differences in outcomes at similar levels of GDP. For example, South Asia has unusually highs levels of undernutrition, whereas on the other hand, Vietnam showed rapid improvements in nutritional status (Glewwe, Koch, and Nguyen, 2002). Earlier, both Sri Lanka and Kerala showed that high levels of health and education indicators can be achieved at relatively low levels of GDP, and public policies clearly played a role in the form of "support-led security" in the terminology of Drèze and Sen (1989). The literature—on the histories of OECD countries as well as the Global South—has shown how important public investments are for enhancing well-being, and that sustained levels of social investment have contributed to high health and education achievements.

A substantial body of cross-country analysis exists on the links between government intervention and economic growth. There is evidence that increased public investment may reduce growth because it is less efficient, may compete with private capital, or crowd out private investment, and that fiscal "deficits" can constrain growth. But the potential negative impact of larger states on growth does not necessarily apply to all forms of investment, and quality may be more important than quantity. Analyses like Lofgren and Robinson's (2004) and Fan and Rao's (2003) emphasize that reallocation of government sources to, for example, agriculture or infrastructure, can enhance growth and poverty reduction. In most cases, positive relationships between spending and outcomes depend on governance indicators and "sound" policies, as Peter Lindert, for example, has shown for OECD histories of social policies. Graph 3.2, which plots the Human Development Index (HDI) against total amounts of spending in health and education for a large number of developing and middle-income countries, suggests an overall positive relationship but with large variations.

While economic growth provides the basis for sustained government policies as well as income poverty reduction, a range of positive links from social policies to economic growth are suggested in the literature (de Mello, 2002), suggesting that social spending is not only "consumptive," as neo-liberal development models and even Chinese practices suggest, but are investments in productive capacities. According to Birdsall, Ross, and Sabot (1995), East Asia showed that rapid growth in growth was associated with "prior" spread of access to education (as well as land), even though a relatively large part of the investments were private: widespread education

Graph 3.2 Human Development Index and Public Spending

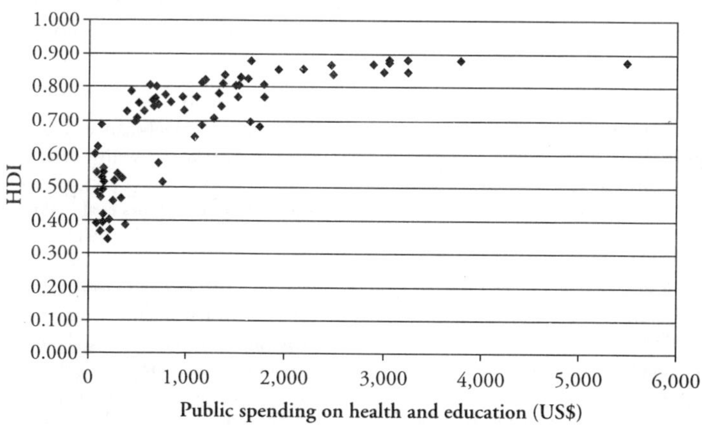

Source: UNDP (2009b).

played a central role in the success cases of East Asia, where government and elites shaped the conditions for global competition. IMF research shows that education and health spending have a direct impact on the accumulation of education and health capital, and an impact on growth, though often with a lag.[14] Improved educational attainment means more skilled and productive workers, higher output of goods and services, and easier absorption of new technology.[15] But—as with the links between economic and social policies more generally—an education–growth link is not automatic. It depends on good governance and sound macroeconomic policies, and returns to education are dependent on the existence of employment opportunities (Hillman and Jenker, 2004: 258).

Similarly, health and nutrition contribute to long-term economic development, by improving productivity, lowering fertility, and better educational outcomes, for example. Malnutrition contributes to infectious disease mortality, childhood diarrhea, acute respiratory illnesses, affects pregnancy, and limits cognitive development (WHO, 2001). Studies have shown significant costs of, for example, malnutrition or HIV/AID on GDP.[16] Again, the history of OECD countries suggest that few countries developed without significant public intervention in health, which often arose as much out of self-interest of elites as of charitable concern for the poor alone. The way the Severe Acute Respiratory Syndrome (SARS) crisis evolved in China suggests that globalization added a significant argument for rather than against public investment in health.

Social security provisions and spending can have negative effects on public finance (notably, pensions), constrain investment, reduce labor mobility, and "crowd out" private support (Besley, Burgess, and Rasul, 2003). But it can have positive impacts on economic growth too, in a variety of ways. The idea of an overall trade-off between insurance and growth has been questioned increasingly,[17] and the benefits of social security spending in

---

[14] Baldacci et al. (2004, 2008); Pattillo, Gupta, and Carey (2005).

[15] Econometric studies have shown that returns to education can be substantial, in particular for education of girls. Female education is associated with a range of positive development outcomes, including nutritional (Schultz, 2002).

[16] The costs of malnutrition may exceed 2 or 3 percent of GDP (Chopra et al., 2002), and GDP may fall 25 percent over 20 years in countries heavily affected by HIV/AIDS (USAID, 2005: 41–42).

[17] "It is known that a market economy can generate too much risk and inequality, judged solely from the viewpoint of aggregate output ... This theoretical possibility has given a new lease of life to targeted transfers as the main instruments for publicly-provided 'social protection' in poor countries, which is seen as being good for pro-poor growth ... by providing insurance or helping credit-constrained poor people be productive workers or take up productive opportunities for self-employment" (Ravallion, 2003a: 3).

terms of addressing market failures can offset the costs to the economy of taxation (Barrientos, 2004b). Designed in the right way, financial markets can benefit from social security policies. Pension schemes can be a means to enhance savings and financial market development. The Central Provident Fund in Singapore was used for capital mobilization (Kwon, 2005b: 9). Social provisions can also have a beneficial impact on governance, as regular transfers, for example, to elderly, can enhance the accountability of government and the social contract (HelpAge International, 2003)—again, this beneficial impact depends on design, as the same benefits can be administered corruptly and under patronage and thus, reinforce socio-economic and political inequalities.

Beneficial impacts cut across sectors. As insecurity and crises can have long-term negative consequences for education and early childhood, social transfers can help enhance demand for and access to education and health services. Maternity benefits can improve health status; unemployment benefits can facilitate job searches and training; and injury benefits can enhance employers' incentive to reduce work hazards and make their workplaces safer. Benefits for older people have the potential to enhance their social standing and their health; moreover, elderly sometimes use their pensions to fund education of grandchildren, support orphans, or invest in economic activity (HelpAge International, 2003, 2004, 2007).

Finally, social sector spending has clear political objectives. Historically, social security provisions have been used to "buy social peace," or "regulate the poor."[18] This is one of the reasons why more open economies tend to have larger welfare states (or develop these over time, including during crises). Unemployment benefits can mitigate political opposition to enterprise restructuring, and social protection provisions can help in economic adjustments, and to reduce wage demands. As the second part of this book describes, this objective has been of importance, notably, in the "productivist" welfare states of East Asia, including most recently China.

Redistribution and Growth are Compatible...

The previous chapter described that there is no straightforward link between economic growth and inequality, even though we have seen more cases of inequality rising than declining. One of the reasons, of course, is that governments redistribute income or opportunities. While inequality and

[18] Piven and Cloward (1972). Social policy also has a broader role of social disciplining, illustrated, for example, in the successful Singaporean approach to public housing (Chua Beng Huat, 2005: 106).

redistribution did not receive much attention since the 1970s, it has been "back on the agenda" since the late 1990s. This has been fueled by research focusing on the instrumental case for addressing inequality, and the emphasis that there need not be a trade-off between redistribution and growth, and this strand of literature is, of course, of critical importance for a social policy framework that emphasizes both the public policy responses to inequality, and how these responses in turn shape market processes.

There are a number of arguments about inequality and growth, relating to different types of markets.[19] Less unequal income distribution and lower poverty can mean a larger internal market and higher savings, and therefore, higher growth and more innovation. High-income inequality also means fewer people have access to credit, thereby possibly lowering growth. Spatial inequalities can mean poor people have less opportunity to contribute to productive activity. Further, distribution of assets can have an impact on economic growth. Inequality in access to land has shown to have an impact on economic growth, particularly if it is combined with other forms of inequality. As noted by Myrdal (1973) already, redistribution of opportunities in health, education, and labor markets can be a productive investment in the quality of people and their productivity.

Similarly, gender inequalities, apart from having an impact on various forms of human development, also can affect economic growth, as World Bank authors like Tzannatos (1998) and Blackden and Bhanu (1999) argued already over a decade ago. Discrimination in access to productive resources can reduce overall productivity. Gender inequality in education lowers average human capital, and can impact both investment and population growth. Labor market discrimination, or absence of child care which makes it more difficult for women to enter or continue employment, can reduce potentials for economic growth and increasing productivity. However, not all forms of gender inequality negatively impacts economic growth, as export-led growth in many places has been accompanied by wage inequalities—though these may be challenged in the longer run.

Finally, and perhaps most controversial but crucially important in the debate on social policy, as we will see later in this book, there can be a link between inequality and various political and institutional factors, which in turn can affect growth. Inequality can undermine good public policy, and social divisions may make it more difficult to implement reforms or formulate crises responses (though new forms of consultations tend to emerge during crises, as in South Korea after the 1997–98 crisis).

---

[19] Birdsall (2005); Ravallion (2003a); Sabates-Wheeler (2008); Tzannatos (1998); World Bank (2005).

Discrimination is part of and can reinforce bad governance; vice versa women's empowerment can reduce corruption. Inequality may lead to pressure to redistribute income (and hence, costly transfers),[20] social unrest, and/or crime, hence having negative impacts on growth too. However, such links are by no means simple ones. For example, the large numbers of protest in China are not directly associated with inequality, but corruption and mismanagement by public authorities tend to be a more important cause. And inequality, particularly if it consists of a range of economic and institutional inequalities that reinforce each other, leads to pressure to redistribute only in particular circumstances, and even less often to effective pressure (Bebbington et al., 2008).

...but Positive Links are not Automatic

Thus, policies for social protection and redistribution can be consistent with policies for economic growth. Particularly in poor countries (or "low equilibrium economies"), while financing is most problematic, social security provisions can be particularly important, to enhance investment and basic security. But, as in the case of health and education policies, the question that is at least as important is how they are provided. And this points to a possible paradox: in many poor countries, much spending is not progressive, nor do the institutional or governance conditions exist to ensure that social spending is a free lunch, as Peter Lindert (2004) has argued, the welfare state "can" be.

Lindert's historical analysis of OECD states highlights the potential synergy of social and economic policies and objectives. The welfare state (and universal forms of provision) can be a free lunch, in the sense that the net costs of social transfers are zero. But this is the case only under specific conditions, notably of democracy and interest competition which enforce care in the design of transfers and taxes, including of universalistic approaches that can have a positive impact on growth, with uniform, less expensive, and less distorting rules. In many countries in the South where there is little doubt that social spending needs to increase for enhancing human development, many of these condition that ensure a positive economic impact of transfers are not met, and much of the cross-country literature quoted earlier stresses the impact of governance indicators (for example, Baldacci et al., 2008).

[20] The "median voter hypothesis" describes how voters' behavior can lead to pressure to redistribute income: if the income difference between median and mean voters is greater, the median voter would exert more pressure for redistribution (de Mello and Tiongson, 2003; Milanovic, 1999; Ravallion, 2003a).

Much evidence now exists, for example, in the form of "incidence benefit" studies that targeting of public spending in the South does not tend to be progressive.[21] Much social security expenditure such as pensions for civil servants is very regressive. An overview of existing benefit incidence of health and education spending (Davoodi, Tiongson, and Asawanuchit, 2003) concluded, for example, that the poor benefited less from public spending in education than the rich. Spending on primary education overall was less regressive, as one would expect, although not in sub-Saharan Africa (perhaps because at lower schooling levels, inequalities matter for primary education too). Even primary health care spending was not pro-poor. Overall, targeting seemed to have improved slightly during the 1990s, perhaps partly under the influence of renewed international attention. The new modality of cash transfers developed, particularly in Latin America, such as non-contributory pensions are distinctly more pro-poor. Yet overall, the Robin Hood paradox (Lindert, 2004: 15–16) still exists: redistribution from rich to poor, through social security, is least present when and where it is most needed.

The reasons for the Robin Hood paradox are deeply rooted. In the Global South, basic state functions—which formed a prerequisite for social policies in the North—often are absent. Moreover, "structural inequalities" and historically determined social divisions make social policies and particular universal approaches more important. However, at the same time, these very inequalities enhance the challenges to make these effective; as we describe later, the progressive policies for "Scheduled Castes" and "Scheduled Tribes" in India are an example of how deep-rooted inequalities can pervade the institutions that are designed to address these inequalities.

These challenges do not imply social policies cannot play a role in addressing these inequalities; what it does mean, in terms of this book, is a need to understand the politics of these social policies, and the conditions under which deprived groups or supportive elites are able to promote social policies that are both progressive and sustainable. Historically, public investment in social services have played crucial roles in enabling social transformations, but public funding can equally be monopolized and reinforce inequalities—only careful analysis can help to understand how progressive forces have emerged.

---

[21] CBS Nepal (2006: 36–37); Davoodi, Tiongson, and Asawanuchit (2003); Mehrotra and Delamonica (2007).

Globalization Needs better Social Policies

Thus, globalization has not led to a demise of the state. While the Washington Consensus implied optimism about a link between globalization and universal economic growth, the resurgence of nationalism and ideological divides, and most recently, the responses to the 2008 financial crisis show that the political motivations for social policy and spending will continue to predominate. Globalization and economic shocks exert contradictory pressures on state intervention, which in any case are mediated by national institutions and traditions. Quantitative evidence suggests that states often expand with economic growth, and that globalization has not (at least not uniformly) led to a minimalist state. While the pressure of international institution toward stabilization and structural adjustment has put states under pressure, this has not, in general, reduced social spending and programs in relative terms, nor the attention paid to these; however, as this chapter has documented, social policy analysis needs provide better understanding of levels of social spending, distribution across sectors, and the political motivations and outcomes in terms of well-being and distribution.

Countries that successfully integrated into global markets in general had proactive states managing integration and market processes. The rapid global rise of China and India in the last two decades, and their ability to respond to shocks to the system, should not blind us to the fact that they entered world markets in well designed and paced manners, in which they learnt from historical experience. East Asia's development path, varied as this may be across the region, indicates that public institutions played a key role, through both "economic" and "social" policies. Success stories in Africa, like Botswana, similarly show the importance of public institutions and stable social contracts. Reforms associated with globalization depend on the strength of governments and their public institutions, and public support for the planned reforms. Government intervention matters as much as it used to, and arguably, as international competition and accountability and the scale of economic crises are increasing, even more.

We return to countries' specific experiences of social policies in this context of globalization in the second part of this book. But we first turn to the international development debate, to explore how this has steered debates on the issues mentioned earlier, and whether it has incorporated the lessons of the history of globalization, and changing pressures on public policies.

4

International Development and Social Policy

While national policy traditions have continued to be crucial for social policy in the South, international development debate and practices have become increasingly important, through more invasive forms in aid-dependent countries and during economic crises, but also, for example, through the opening up of China and Vietnam, which made international development cooperation part of its reforms. Moreover, after a period of aid fatigue, there has been recent optimism about the role of international development. Well-organized civil society pressure and reform attempts within international organizations have led to significant initiatives around debt relief and commitments for increased aid, highlighted in the agreements at Gleneagles and the Monterrey Consensus, and reaffirmed by many at the time of the financial crisis. This chapter describes the most important trends in international development,[1] leaving aside the recent literature on conflict and post-conflict reconstruction, and assesses their potential to contribute to a cross-sectoral public policy view promoted in this book.

First, we discuss the theoretical approach of the post-Washington Consensus, and the progress this entails in terms of broad based and comprehensive approaches to development and poverty reduction. This includes

[1] See for more detail de Haan (2007b, 2009c), while de Haan (2009a) elaborates on the way donor politics and the way these are embedded in national politics and popular debates continue to inform aid modalities, reducing the chances aid can support capacity building for public policies and social transformation.

discussion of the implications of the "consensus" on scaling-up aid, and what this implies for public policy making. The second section describes sector-wide approaches and recent "vertical" initiatives, for example, in the case of HIV/AIDS, and whether these are compatible with a perspective that focuses on inter-sectoral public policy making. We then move on to the focus on poverty reduction and targeting: the poverty analysis that has dominated much of the international development debate, the social funds as an evolving donor response that started out as a direct response to the negative consequences of adjustment and reforms, and finally, the newer approaches to social protection and cash transfers. The chapter then describes the Poverty Reduction Strategies, which in the late 1990s were put forward as a major instrument under the process of debt relief for heavily indebted countries.

The Post-Washington Consensus

Attitudes toward state intervention and social policies changed with the economic crises of the 1970s. Restoring markets, structural adjustment, and reducing state intervention became core concerns, and goals of redistribution and the interventionist state lost popularity. But since the 1990s, following emphasis on the "human face of adjustment" and international civil society pressure, poverty has become accepted as central goal of international development efforts.

Writings on the "post-Washington Consensus" suggest new approaches to economic policies have emerged, with a wider role for public policies. The "Washington Consensus" emphasized the now-familiar policies of fiscal discipline, market-determined exchange and interest rates, protection of property rights, liberalization, privatization, and openness to trade, as well as (but less commonly debated) redirection of public expenditure toward education, health, and public infrastructure (Stern, 2002: 9).

Many observers have proclaimed the failure of the Washington Consensus. But in a large number of countries, fiscal and monetary stability was achieved during the 1990s, and East Asian states started to build up fiscal reserves after the 1997–98 crisis, which is one of the reasons they are now "weathering" the 2008–09 crisis. Recent growth and poverty reduction performance of countries that have adjusted also has been fairly positive. Many of the economic policies followed by China, for example, can be characterized as orthodox, even if the overall mix is not. On the other hand, globally the growth performance has not been uniformly favorable, and it has been acknowledged that the "supply response" to adjustment measures has been weak.[2] The financial crisis of 2008 has thrown up many questions around the lack of financial and banking regulation, after the 1997–98 crisis had discredited the IMF and its advice to stabilize the Thai and Indonesian economies.

Writings on the post-Washington Consensus take into account many of the critiques, even though much practice continues to be much more orthodox. According to Stern (2002), there was nothing wrong with the principles of the Washington Consensus, but it

> said nothing about governance and institutions, the role of empowerment and democratic representation, the importance of country ownership, or the social costs and the pace of transformation. The development community has learned the hard way, through the setbacks of the structural adjustment programs in developing countries of the 1980s, and the transition of the 1990s in eastern Europe and the former Soviet Union, that these elements are at the heart of the development challenge.

The post-Washington Consensus pays much more attention to the interaction between states and markets, and highlights recent processes of democratization that can support a vibrant market economy.[3]

However, the emphasis on the importance of governance for development outcomes and the provision of services quickly obtained a technocratic character (de Haan and Everest-Phillips, 2010). Governance was conceptualized primarily as a technocratic phenomenon—with apparently simple governance indicators—rather than a political process. The list of necessary governance reforms grew exponentially. The optimism of the early 1990s of implementing "good governance" gave way to more focused and realistic ideas around "good enough governance" (the term coined by Grindle, 2002) that tried to target fewer but more prioritized and feasible interventions, an understanding of the importance of local context for reforms. Political analysis was introduced in a number of international agencies.

The international development debate thus has been transformed from the Washington Consensus. The Monterrey Consensus put politics—domestic and international—at the heart of development, including for

[2] Killick (1999) concluded the evidence on the impact on poverty was not strong enough to conclude that adjustment either failed or succeeded, or even that these kinds of policy prescription would allow for reasonable expectations in terms of poverty reduction.

[3] Eyoh and Sandbrook (2003: 228) label the new approach a "pragmatic neo-liberal development model," and highlight the similarities with the "Third Way" promoted by Tony Blair and Bill Clinton. See also Owusu (2003).

programming on governance and for reforms. It stresses that governments in developed and developing countries alike must build public support, to translate development aspiration into action. It notes the need for political leadership: in the South for undertaking institutional and policy reform; and in the North to strengthen solidarity with poverty reduction efforts in the South.

But it is also clear that the new agenda has come with as many questions as answers. The commitments for increased aid are made while many observers have asked questions about the capacity for "aid absorption." There are well-documented concerns that additional aid may divert attention from enhacing quality and effectiveness of aid. As summarized by Manor (2005), views continue to differ around questions of absorptive capacity, possibilities for governance reform, likelihood that aid will be delivered in coordinated manner, donors' "unhelpful habits," and continued questions around aid dependency. The emphasis on governance appears to have difficulty conceptualizing the politics of public policy making, and how the international community relates to these politics. Moreover, governance analysis typically have neglected social policies, perhaps because these are seen as unimportant within the larger sphere of public policy; however, as the second part of this book will argue, social policies play a key role in establishing the social contract between governments and its citizens.

New Aid Modalities 1: Sector Approaches

Alongside the increased interest in governance, the 1990s saw the emergence (or return) of emphasis, within the donor community, on the importance of country ownership, leading to the development of sector programs, direct budget support, and partnership approach. Sector-wide approaches imply that "all significant [donor] funding for the sector supports a single sector policy and expenditure programme, under government leadership, adopting common approaches across the sector and progressing towards relying on Government procedures for all funds" (Foster, 2000: 9). This emerged as a response to various issues: donors had found that conditionality did not work, and sector approaches were a way of providing support against government commitment and track record in providing services for poverty reduction. They were an attempt to focus support on creating a sound policy environment rather than donors directly funding services in a project mode. Sector approaches were seen as solution to the fragmentation in budgeting processes, which had been related to large and project-oriented aid flows.

There have been successes with this new form of donor support (Cheru, 2006: 362). In 2000, around 80 sector programs existed, mostly in sub-Saharan Africa, and mostly in health and education (less so in agriculture, and apparently, few or no cases in social protection). It may have helped to enhance political commitment, efficiency in resource use, and capacity for sectoral policy formulation and implementation. But establishing joint donor support and monitoring has also been time consuming and costly, and a joint donor response, at times, has also been considered a disadvantage by recipient governments if this involved the risk of a complete halt to support.

At the same time, international development has been transformed by the emergence of "vertical initiatives," which focus on individual or groups of diseases, often initiated by private charities. Pharmaceutical companies have donated drugs to eliminate particular diseases, like the Mectizan Donation Programme, where Merck have donated Ivermectin to treat river blindness. The last decade has seen the rise of "new philanthropists," donating large sums of money for specific health-related projects: the Melinda and Bill Gates Foundation donations in particular are enormous, with resources outstripping the annual budget of WHO. There are now dozens of health funds and partnerships, with the Global Fund for Aids, Tuberculosis, and Malaria, the Global Alliance for Vaccines and Immunization, and the International Finance Facility for Immunization among the largest. It is as yet unclear what the impact of these vertical initiatives will be. Private donors like the Gates Foundation have established good track records. These forms of funding are crucial in cases where per capita spending in health is less than US$ 10 per capita, as in many poor countries. In the context of this book, however, it is important to reflect on the impact of public policy making more generally, and regarding the sustainability of these initiatives.

In donor-dependent countries, the particular aid modality has important consequences for the balance of power within public policy making. This relates to the availability of resources in particular sectors, and for particular agencies within that, vis-à-vis other sectors. It is likely that international support will remain volatile, and there are questions about the sustainability of many well-funded initiatives (for example, Lancaster (2008), regarding the large increases of funding for HIV/AIDS by USAID). The vertical initiatives may move attention further away from the state as central actor in providing legislative frameworks and standards, toward "a multiplicity of new—and largely unaccountable—actors in the health arena," with public–private partnerships "as potentially radical new systems of global governance" (Poku and Whiteside, 2002: 192).

New Aid Modalities 2: Poverty Reduction Strategies

In 1999, the World Bank and IMF endorsed a new approach for borrower countries to access the Highly Indebted Poor Countries program, or HIPC. This came about partly as a result of the successful NGO pressure on the IFIs, particularly through Jubilee 2000, assisted by the changes in European governments in the late 1990s. This broad movement had argued for more debt relief, and to make this debt relief pro-poor, and address the negative consequences of structural adjustment. The international financial crisis in East Asia—and perceived failure of the IMF, particularly in Indonesia—also had increased the pressure on the international community. Moreover, at the end of the 1990s, pressure had mounted to increase the effectiveness of aid, and the World Bank's conclusion was to emphasize country ownership and good economic management.

The HIPC became an attempt to ensure that the extra funding from debt relief would be beneficial for poverty reduction, and to enhance the national ownership of development strategies. The framework became known as the Poverty Reduction Strategy Papers, or PRSPs, and within just over five years, about 40 countries had developed such a strategy, and "second-generation" strategies (Driscoll and Evans, 2005). The approach was mainly relevant for Africa, but PRSPs were also developed (sometimes simultaneously as Five Year Plans) in Afghanistan, Bangladesh, Bhutan, Cambodia, Indonesia, Lao PDR, Mongolia, Nepal, Pakistan, and Vietnam. Since the mid-2000s, the interest in PRSPs that marked the early 2000s has diminished, as new approaches, emphasis, and indeed new actors appeared on the scene.

The central elements of the PRSP approach are worth highlighting in the context of this book, as many of the principles appear to match well with the social policy framework proposed here. A first objective was to ensure aid relationships would be more country owned. It is acknowledged that the PRSP approach has made a difference to the way donors approach the aid relationship. But the international community has realized that the challenges in getting countries in the "driver seat"—where they are not already—remain substantial. The experiences indicated a strong tendency for donors to apply the approach in a bureaucratic manner, as they did with the governance agenda, with high expectations to solve problems in aid relations. Donors became closely tied to paths set out through the PRS process and disarray set in when the partner government's policies did not follow the plans set out earlier. Of course, the latter is not uncommon, but in the Latin American context, this fueled a debate whether the PRSP approach should be abandoned.[4] In short, donors usually are not well equipped to deal with the politics of public policy making.

A second element of the PRSP approach was the promotion of participation in the formulation of national development plans. A large number of civil society organizations did engage in the donor dialogue, and saw the process as an opportunity to open up the space for political engagement. Nevertheless, and despite large diversity across countries, a common assessment was that processes of participation remained ritualistic. Many NGOs concluded the economic model was a given, even though, as the last chapter discussed, social spending did receive increased attention. Often, participation remained outside the area of mainstream politics, ignoring, for example, parliaments and excluding trade unions and the private sector, as well as women and marginalized groups.

The new approach also included a strong emphasis on results orientation, which was partly a response to the pressure on the international development community to show clearer results. It involved an emphasis on clear costing of PRSPs and expenditure frameworks, and more precision in impacts on poverty. Observers have agreed that the approach has strengthened the focus on poverty reduction, and increased attention to poverty issues across government ministries. However, some observers also have concluded there was no fundamental departure from the policy advice that dominated during structural adjustment. Others have emphasized that poverty analyses have insufficiently informed the development strategy. More broadly, the PRSP was not always found to link strongly to budget processes, plans amounted to wish list rather than being proper proposals, and financial management problems have not disappeared.

Finally, the new modality emphasized comprehensive planning for development and poverty reduction. This ensured that all relevant areas of development were generally included.[5] It included new or renewed interest within the IMF regarding the quality of budgets and sectoral spending, including in health and education.[6] The policy dialogue with donors extended beyond finance ministries and specific sectors, and line

---

[4] Booth, Grisby, and Toranzo (2006); Dijkstra (2005, 2006); Holmqvist and Metell Cueva (2006).

[5] "[C]omprehensiveness is important in order to capture the complementary nature of public actions across sectors" and that "a comprehensive strategy does not mean sacrificing priority setting. In fact, the more comprehensive the strategy, the more important it is to identify its main priorities" (IMF and World Bank, 2005: 16).

[6] After some years, and following evaluations stressing relative large increases in shares of social expenditure, the IMF emphasized its lack of capacity to analyze composition of public spending (Heller et al., 2006).

ministries generally had a role in the formulations of PRSPs. But there were many questions regarding whether the new approach indeed promoted such comprehensive and cross-sectoral policy making. Driscoll and Evans (2005), for example, noted that strategies for the social sectors and for the productive sector were not integrated. Ownership of the plans by line ministries and sub-national governments remained limited. State capacity for effective policy planning and implementation also remained limited, and "hampered by constant inter-ministerial infighting, as well as by the disconnect between key sector ministries and ministries of finance..." (Cheru, 2006: 369). The comprehensiveness also caused difficulties in terms of ownership, as it is practically impossible for governments to be and remain committed to such plans.[7]

With respect to the social policy approach this book argues for, the renewed emphasis on country ownership in aid-dependent countries emphasized in the early 2000s is, of course, welcome. In the poorest countries, there is a need for long-term support to enable cross-sectoral national policy making. Similarly, the enhanced results orientation is important for social policy as it is for other forms of public policy. The focus on social sectors, particularly in terms of spending, remains subject for debate, but the discussion about the links between growth and social sectors including social protection has the potential to take social policy out of its residual corner. The emphasis on comprehensive and cross-sectoral planning and policies in PRSPs is also in line with the approach to social policy as put forward in this book, has the potential to help address the fragmentation of social policy that has accompanied structural adjustment, and has brought often weak social ministries to the table of important policy discussions from which they are usually absent.

But the approach has been largely technocratic. The way pro-poor public policy has been proposed has, by and large, neglected the political economy of such policies, and has paid little or no attention to the constituencies that are essential for progressive policies. There has also been limited reflection on how international support can promote or strengthen such constituencies—in fact, most of the governance literature tends to be pessimistic about promoting progressive forces where they do not already exist, and successful support has tended to drive on existing policy commitments, as China, for example, has demonstrated.

[7] The time pressure behind PRSPs was partly responsible for its shortcoming, and the problems have been openly described by international agencies. Many also have emphasized the need to move away from the blue print approach that marked some of the experiences. And increasing attention has been paid to donors aligning to national plans, and harmonizing approached.

Further, within the emphasis and literature on broad national-level participation in the formulation of PRSPs, there has also been very little analysis of or reflection on different kinds of social policy processes. The participatory processes promoted within this new aid modality seem far removed from the long-term articulation of class and other interests, and how these relate to public policy formulation and implementation. Official donor practices and analysis, as Booth, Grisby, and Toranzo (2006) highlight, is not a good substitute for political analysis, including regarding the way international support becomes associated with particular interests and patronage politics.

Poverty Analysis in the International Development Debate

With the increasing focus on poverty as overarching objective of international development, and dating back to the "social dimensions" focus of the World Bank, analysis of poverty received a big push. The origins of the poverty analysis, particularly in Africa, can be traced to the "Social Dimensions of Adjustment" and the Living Standards Measurement Studies (LSMS), developed to monitor progress in raising levels of living, and to identify the impacts of government policies. These have included various dimensions of household well-being, including demographic, health, and education. Measuring health and education progress also has been supported, through DHS and education surveys.

The initiatives by international agencies, notably the World Bank, rapidly increased the coverage of poverty mapping in Africa. Nevertheless, in Africa, data about trends remained limited, and many of the surveys remained one-off. Even in the early 2000s, when the PRSP approach was at its height, much poverty data on Africa was out of date. This is partly because of the technical difficulty and cost of these types of surveys, but the lack of regular monitoring also suggests that the poverty analysis was only to a limited extent embedded in national policy making or advocacy. Many countries in Asia had longer traditions of poverty monitoring, which also became an area of support and collaboration, even in China, whereas in India the World Bank actively engaged in poverty analysis and debate.

The quantitative poverty analysis also came under critique. It often takes two years for the results of surveys to be available and therefore, it is less useful as an instrument to measure trends and impacts of policies. Much data collection was done poorly, and it was felt to be costly. Poverty analysis became criticized for the strong emphasis on income poverty, neglecting the multidimensional nature of poverty, assets, and, particularly, poor people's own perceptions. Following this critique, participatory approaches to poverty analysis became popular. But as with quantitative poverty analysis, there are concerns about whether Participatory Poverty Assessments (PPAs) and similar instruments do influence policy making—with the work in Vietnam a positive exception (see Box 4.1). The interest in such participatory exercises seemed to have faded somewhat, and there are few examples where they have become institutionalized as part of regular monitoring of well-being or poverty.

For our discussion on social policy, two questions regarding poverty analysis are relevant: has it influenced policy making, and how does the type of analysis influence the conceptualization of social policy? First, as already indicated, many quantitative poverty surveys followed donors' needs, and less has been achieved in enhancing national capacity to undertake such surveys. The comparison of numbers of poor people across countries illustrates the importance for donors, helps them decide aid allocations, and enables cross-country regressions linking economic growth and poverty, for example. But the international poverty comparisons are of less relevance

Box 4.1 Poverty Analysis as Advocacy in Vietnam

The Participatory Poverty Assessment (PPA) in Vietnam has been considered as an example of internationally commissioned research that has influenced policy, through a process of coalition building. International agencies have played an important role in shaping the poverty analysis and policy in Vietnam. As elsewhere, the World Bank has provided long-term technical support, in the form of two poverty specialists—in quantitative and qualitative methodologies. The research in Vietnam was embedded in a global debate around the promotion of participatory methods, with evidence from elsewhere suggesting positive impacts of participation on project efficiency. The PPAs had started to become part of Comprehensive Development Framework (CDF) and PRSP approaches, and participatory assessments around the world formed the basis for the widely-debated *World Development Report 2000–2001* (World Bank, 2000). The PPA, both the research and the policy processes it promoted, was the work of a coalition of organizations. This coalition helped to improve quality of the research, including by providing access to geographic areas which might otherwise have remained limited, and arguably it created the conditions for sustained research impact, in a context where economic growth was high, and was having a sustained positive impact on poverty alongside widespread concerns about increasing inequalities.

Source: Turk and Shanks (2003).

for national policy making. While the PRSP approach enhanced the status of poverty analysis, including that of participatory assessments, and made it more central to debates with ministries of finance and not just in social and welfare sectors,[8] the cases where there was a good link between poverty analysis and planning remained an exception.[9]

Second, the poverty analysis that was promoted focused on the identification and categorization of the poor. Alternative analytical approaches—including those that are mainstream outside the international development debate—have found very little entry into the debate. The dominant poverty analysis has remained weak in terms of "understanding," in the sociological sense, the processes which lead to deprivation. It has conceptualized poverty as an objective state, ignoring the behavior of actors—conscious and merely reproducing—the values and norms that inform these, and how these are embedded in societal structures. Poverty, and inequality, has been conceived mostly in terms of positions with respect to variables ("living below the poverty line"), rather than in terms of relationships between people, thus insufficiently highlighting discriminatory practices and norms embedded in economic and societal structures (Tilly, 1998). This type of poverty analysis has played an important role in approaches to "target" the poor.

Residual Social Policy in International Development: Social Funds

During the 1980s period of stabilization and adjustment, the World Bank started to look for ways in which the impact of economic crises could be ameliorated, focusing on people directly impacted by crises. The main approach to this obtained the name "social fund," which in the 1990s expanded rapidly. Over time, the emphasis of the social funds' approach has shifted from short-term emergency relief toward more general developmental

[8] Poverty and Social Impact Analysis (PSIA) was developed to consider policy options and sequencing of policies, and identify offsetting measures for negative consequences of reform programs (Robb, 2003).

[9] A range of problems have been highlighted in reviews of PRSPs. Conclusions from poverty analyses often were not included in the discussions on policy, and policy priorities sometimes often not derived from the analysis. Poverty analyses often were badly linked to identification of macroeconomic or sectoral policy priorities. Emphasis in many countries remained on income poverty, and other dimensions of deprivation remained secondary. Analysis often remained descriptive, with few attempts to identify and explain causes of poverty.

programs, broader social protection, and proactive strategies of dealing with risk mitigation and risk reduction, and it became closely connected to community-driven development. It has been adopted by regional development banks and was often co-financed by other donors. In 2000, social funds existed in over 50 countries, with total expenditure amounting to US$ 9 billion. They remained a small part of social security activities in most countries, but in some countries, they have been critical, and the approach greatly influenced international development approaches in the social policy arena.

The first fund was the Bolivia Emergency Social Fund (ESF), which aimed to address the social costs of adjustment, focusing on miners laid off after the collapse of tin prices and closing of state-run mines. Social funds in Ghana (Gayi, 1995) and Uganda were set up in a similar vein. In Asia, social funds have been less important, but World Bank social funds have been developed in (in chronological order) Sri Lanka, Cambodia, Philippines, Timor Leste, and Lao PDR (de Silva and Sum, 2008). Similar initiatives have existed elsewhere too, like the Social Investment Project in Bangladesh and (support to) the District Poverty Initiative in India. In Thailand, a social fund was created with a focus on establishing a new economy after the 1997 crisis, and Indonesian agencies share many operational characteristics with social funds.

Social funds are provided as regular loans to countries, usually co-financed with recipient contribution. They form an intermediary that channels resources to small-scale projects for poor and vulnerable groups. The funds do not implement projects, but appraise, finance, and supervise them. They are institutionally distinct from government sectoral policies and services. Organizational set-up varies across countries, from autonomous agencies outside government bureaucracies, to location within ministries or offices of the president. A central administration disburses funds to intermediary organizations, including local government, private firms, and NGOs. They create procedures to overcome the common problems of time-consuming, bureaucratic, and poorly administered public sector procedures. They recruit staff at higher rates than civil service standards, as civil service pay scales are too low to attract the best professionals.

The funds thus support local groups' project, local NGOs, community groups, small firms, and entrepreneurs, within a set menu of eligible and non-eligible projects. This tries to ensure quick and targeted actions to reach poor and vulnerable groups—Box 4.2 describes an example of this targeted approach. The social funds are "demand-led," and use co-financing to ensure activities do have ownership and sustainability. Social funds stimulate

Box 4.2 Targeting in the Egyptian Social Fund

The Egyptian Social Fund for Development (ESFD), one of the world's largest social funds, used a geographical poverty targeting approach. This combined two indices of poverty: a poverty index and an unemployment index. The poverty index was a composite of six variables, measured using data from the population census, weighted by population size. The poverty index range was divided into equal sub-intervals labeled, "non-poor," "poor," "very poor," and "ultra poor." Six variables were used to construct the index: female illiteracy, access to drinking water, access to kitchen in the housing unit, ratio of food expenditures to total household expenditures, relative drop in average annual expenditures, and use of kerosene as sole energy source. An unemployment index, based on the unemployment rate, was proposed as the basis for determining ESFD targeting for unemployment-combating activities. A combined index was then calculated, being the mean of the poverty index and unemployment index, based on an assumption of equal importance of the two targets of alleviating poverty and combating unemployment. Distribution of ESFD funds was proposed on the basis of the poverty, unemployment, and combined indices, but also taking into consideration population size.

Source: Jeremy Holland's analysis, described in Fumo et al. (2000).

participatory development initiatives, and often fund the promotion of processes of participation, and have experimented with a range of community contracting models. The approach to participation has evolved toward facilitating community-driven development (CDD), "an approach that gives control over planning decisions and investment resources to community groups and local governments."[10]

Social funds have been praised particularly for their rapid disbursement, flexibility, and ability to respond to demand from poor communities, and, for example, in Indonesia, it was a very popular instrument of the World Bank's President to ensure improvement of the Bank's performance and reputation in the country. Impact and project quality have varied inevitably, as the approach was implemented in a wide range of contexts.

But there also have been shortcomings to the approach. Experience shows conflicts between efficiency goals and the need for time-consuming and costly processes of community ownership and decision making. There are potential trade-offs between reaching the poor and demand-led approaches, and possibly even a risk that social funds increases corruption. Review of the

[10] See the World Bank social development website. The CDD portfolio in the Bank is approximately US$ 2 billion a year. It operates in many areas of development, and focuses on building the capacity of communities and enhancing their access to information.

District Poverty Initiatives Project in India highlighted that funds to local governance structures catered to the interest of the powerful.[11]

Of direct relevance to the social policy discussion in this book, social funds also have been found to create new structures rather than work to reform existing government institutions, as a reaction to the slowness of public sector reform. This can have a negative impact on mainstream policy and public sector institutions, or at least reduce incentives to address tackling tough issues regarding accountable governments. Establishing funds may displace other sources of funding, as ministries may reduce allocations to areas that are targeted by social funds. The approach manifests a common tendency in the international development community to address problems quickly, setting up parallel structures rather than working with government institutions—a problem that has been more prevalent in Africa than in the larger and less aid-dependent countries in Asia but is not absent there either, and not uncommon to problems with India's centrally sponsored schemes and their impact on state programs.[12]

Social fund adopted and illustrated a distinctive approach to targeting the poor, with much attention to poverty analyses and identification of poor communities, including in evaluations. Not all social funds adopted a targeting methodology; for example, in Thailand, poverty targeting was less important than concerns regarding restoring self-reliance and cooperation. But most funds adopted clear instruments for poverty targeting, and allocation of project funding on the basis of easily identifiable shared characteristic (geographical targeting, targeting against eligibility criteria, or self-targeting). Of course, records of poverty targeting have differed, but social funds have been seen as successful, and targeting performance has improved over time. Against this success, the approach has also reinforced conceptualization of poverty as a residual issue or problem. The poverty analysis focuses on identification of the poor—but does much less in identifying causes of deprivation, on relationships of power and processes of exclusion, and how these can be addressed—and thus, has remained within the residual paradigm of mitigation.

To conclude, the evidence shows that there have been considerable successes with social funds, and that they have successfully experimented with and established models of service delivery to poor people. But at the same

---

[11] Gaiha and Kulkarni (2006). Gaspart and Platteau (2006) criticize the practice of providing cheap aid money for poor communities. Berkman (2008: 135) describes how the World Bank's emphasis on empowerment weakened scrutiny in procurement processes.

[12] The broader institutional implications receive much attention in the recent World Bank review by de Silva and Sum (2008).

time, the isolation of funds vis-à-vis mainstream public policy institutions and its relative neglect of politics remains a concern. The social funds have remained relatively small in many cases, but their impact has been considerable in promoting residual approaches to poverty.

Social Protection and Social Security

As part of the 1990s focus on poverty reduction in the international development debate and as a response to the financial crises of the 1990s and the collapse of the Soviet Union, a concept of social protection has been promoted, by agencies like the World Bank (Holzmann, 2008); research centers like the Chronic Poverty Research Center (Barrientos and Hulme, 2008), Overseas Development Institute (ODI), and Economic Policy Research Institute (EPRI); and NGOs like Oxfam that have promoted a move away from in-kind transfers (Green, 2008: 211). This new approach has a strong emphasis on cash transfers to benefit poor people directly, including pensions and school subsidies. This section briefly considers whether this development has moved approaches to social policy from residual to more proactive approaches, while in the second part of this book we will describe examples of this new generation of social protection programs, for example, in Brazil and Bangladesh.

Different international agencies promoted the new social protection agenda from different angles (Conway, de Haan, and Norton, 2000).[13] The ILO's thinking on social protection, for example, in the context of the "decent work for all" strategy, highlights that more than half of the world's population is excluded from any type of statutory social security protection. Its approach is based in social democratic norms, with a strong emphasis on redistribution and universalism. The ILO approaches have been less influential in the international debate since the early 1980s, though recently, there is resurgence of its influence, including with the financial crisis of 2008–09, and the concept of a "social protection floor" that was initially advanced by The World Commission on the Social Dimension of Globalization in 2004.[14]

Regional development banks also have been promoting notions of social protection. The Asian Development Bank has a strong productive approach,

[13] Inspiration for the attention to cash transfers has come from Latin American examples (see Chapter 5)—it seems that, for example, the Chinese experience has gone largely unnoticed in the international debate, and India has a longer experience recently reinforced with the new National Employment Guarantee Scheme.

[14] Simulations by the ILO suggest that 2 percent of the world's GDP would be required to provide all the world's poor with a basic package of benefits (Cichon, 2009).

emphasizing, for example, labor market policies designed to facilitate labor adjustments and promote operation of labor markets, and social insurance programs to cushion the risks associated with unemployment or work injury, and agricultural insurance.

Among the bilateral organizations, over the last few years, DFID, for example, has greatly increased its work on social protection, particularly cash transfers, and regular and predictable grants provided to vulnerable households which are seen as an important option to ensure that the benefits of growth reach those living in chronic poverty. GTZ sponsored a pilot program, like in Zambia, which provides cash transfers to the poorest 10 percent of the population. This is a targeted but unconditional program, with some success (Schubert, 2005). The *2010 European Report on Development* (EUI and EC, forthcoming) focuses on social protection, hoping to promote a coordinated European policy.

The beginning of recent interests in social protection is often situated in *World Development Report 1990* (World Bank, 1990), which defined "safety nets" as the third leg of a three-prong strategy, alongside economic growth and human development. The social protection emphasis received strong reinforcement in *World Development Report 2006* (World Bank, 2005) on inequality, which highlighted the positive impact of instruments of social protection for economic growth alongside the impacts on poverty and vulnerability. The social protection portfolio at the World Bank grew rapidly during the 1990s, partly through the social fund approach. This was accompanied by reconceptualization of the safety nets approach, toward a cross-cutting "risk management framework," which highlighted the multiple risks all people are exposed to, the poor in particular. The World Bank has recognized the limitations of social policy experiments as the three-pillar approach to pensions in Chile, and the need to focus on coverage of the poorest (Holzmann and Hinz, 2005).

This new international social protection agenda covers a wide range of policies, different elements, categorizations emphasized by different agencies, and conceptual frameworks (Devereux and Sabates-Wheeler, 2007). It differentiates itself from "social insurance," which refers to financing by contributions and based on insurance principle, or protection against uncertain risk by pooling resources. It is stressed that coverage of social insurance is low, and hence there is much attention to non-contributory benefits which are of more relevance to the poor who typically cannot afford to pay contributions. The new concept of social protection thus overlaps more closely with an older notion of "social assistance," which refers to support to the poorest, forms of public action that transfer resources to groups deemed eligible due to deprivation. Many programs are means-tested and/or conditional. Eligibility rules are kept simple: for example, a maximum household income level, and/or beneficiaries undertake a specific action, such as young children attending school, or pre- and post-natal visits for pregnant women or lactating mothers.

A central question with respect to cash transfers programs is their suitability in the context of the poorest countries, even though recent analysis is emphasizing the limited costs of the programs (Cichon et al., 2004, 2009). Cash transfers have enormous potential to benefit the extreme poor, but at the same time, poorest countries tend to have the weakest administrative capacity. Recent experience is mostly not from the poorest countries, although large-scale targeted programs have long histories in South Asia, as we will discuss later. The literature on cash transfers is explicit about the range of implementation challenges. This includes the need to build political support, though it usually provides little indication of how donors can achieve that, and indeed there is the temptation for international agencies to promote social protection instruments to avoid difficult decisions about accountability of government institutions. And the social protection approach has again reinforced a targeting approach, which we discuss in more detail next.

Targeting, and Arguments for Universalism

A key question that new social protection approaches bring to the fore once again, and closely linked to the poverty analysis described earlier, is the role of targeting. As mentioned earlier, targeting became a central feature of the policy debate under adjustment (Townsend, 2004), while also having a much longer tradition, and strongly present in both the welfarist and productivist social policy approaches in Asia that we describe later.

While targeting is key to recent social protection programs around the world, the social policy literature has been very critical of principles of targeting. Mkandawire (2005) highlights that more equal societies have tended to lean toward universalism and fears that policy advice has not learnt from the historical experience with targeting.[15] Tendler (2004) emphasizes that targeting has contributed to a "parcelization" and "projectization" of social policy, including because of the "partnerships" they tend to encourage. But there are significant policy choices involved.

[15] Apart from Mkandawire, critical views are expressed in Tendler (2004) and Deacon (2000), who include the ILO as an agency where targeting gained popularity.

First, there is the cost dilemma. Targeting is a mechanism to reduce expenditure. At the same time, it is generally recognized that there is a cost to targeting: its administration can be demanding and expensive, and "leakage" a common problem. Both costs and leakage vary according to types of targeting: targeting using income criteria is difficult, particularly with large numbers of poor people; self-targeting in employment schemes is considered a good way to reach the working poor; and targeting on the basis of visible and group characteristics (like having school-age children, pregnant women) is less likely to lead to leakage and probably less expensive. At the same time, performance of any scheme and modality is dependent on administrative capacity and commitment.

A second argument about targeting revolves around the social and economic impact on individuals, which, for example, in the US, has been heavily debated, particularly when ethnic or racial categories have been used. Targeting benefits can stigmatize groups of beneficiaries. It singles out a group of people as "poor" and as "beneficiaries," dividing them according to specific programs and group characteristics. This may lower their self-esteem, and as I have discussed elsewhere (de Haan, 2007a), even affirmative policies like India's "reservation" do not necessarily have the emancipatory power that they should have, or are thought to have according to their design. Moreover, because benefits are targeted, they provide little incentive for beneficiaries to "graduate" out of the program, as they would lose the benefit the moment their situation improves. Providing benefits on an universal basis avoids both these problems. However, these issues are very context specific. Targeted benefits can be a "right" and encourage civil society or political mobilization, as in the Maharashtra Employment Guarantee Scheme and the new India-wide employment scheme based on the Maharashtra model that we describe in the second part of this book. And the negative impact on incentives can be addressed in program design: if wages are provided below market level and employment schemes only operate during times when the labor market does not provide employment, beneficiaries will not become dependent on the benefits.

A third question is around political support. It is often asserted that programs for the poor tend to be poor programs, though to my knowledge there is rather little evidence for this. Universal programs would be more likely to be supported by middle classes, and they would be less likely to support programs from which they derive no benefits. However, in practice, targeted programs often are supported by middle classes, for example, under an assurance that the benefits do reach the "deserving poor," particularly if they commit themselves to sending children to school, or when they serve a perceived self-interest like reducing rural–urban migration (even though it is doubtful this is likely to be the effect). In India and Bangladesh, child development and primary health and nutrition programs for the poor are seldom openly opposed by the powerful, and targeting of programs provides an important legitimizing role in communist China and Vietnam (and more broadly, in the "productivist" social policy approach underbuilt by a Confucian ethic).

From a political perspective, targeting and universal approaches may not be as radically opposed as some of the literature has implied. All countries' social policy combines both approaches, though the mix has shifted over time, and the international debate has contributed to increased targeting. The key question is the extent to which the mix of policies—and "targeting within universalism" (Skockpol, in Echeverri-Gent, 1993: 197 ff.)—contributes to the realization of rights of citizens. Moreover, the key analytical challenge is to understand the approaches in countries' historical and ideological context, taking into account deep-seated beliefs around individuals' and states' responsibilities alongside technical efficiency arguments, and the way in which international approaches and debates influence these approaches.

Beyond Residualism? Public Policy and its Politics

Have recent trends in international development approaches taken social policies away from the residual approach that dominated under structural adjustment? What do approaches to poverty analysis and PRSP approaches imply? Have the approaches to social protection, which received higher priority on the agendas of major international agencies since the late 1990s, and the increased emphasis on vulnerability, for example, changed the understanding of social policy? And most recently, what does the renewed attention to vulnerability since the 2008–09 crisis, and, for example, the development of the Global Impact and Vulnerability Alert system, imply for broader development approaches?

With the new social protection emphasis, international development approaches have moved away from the 1980s residual safety net paradigm and focus on crises mitigation. However, the social protection agenda remains, by and large, isolated from a broader social policy agenda. In donor budget support, social sectors and social security in particular, still tend to be seen primarily as consumptive expenditure, and not as investment in productive and cohesive societies. There is attention to inter-linkages between sectors at program or project level, such as beneficial impacts of pensions on education of grandchildren, or of nutrition support on education. But a consideration of such links remain absent at the levels of integrated policy formulation, reform, and implementation.[16] In my own experience, development practices still fall short in strengthening national processes for social policy making and analysis. They need to focus more strongly on cross-sectoral dialogue while recognizing the long-term challenges this may involve. International agencies' organizational divides—within organizations or between World Bank and UNDP, for example—contribute to this. Moreover, the social protection discussion, by and large, has remained at the level of projects and programs, and is thus often not linked to the strengthening of national policy making, of social policy concerns across public policies, or efforts to strengthen national ownership of a social protection agenda.

The social protection agenda, furthermore, has focused on technical aspects, with limited attention to its political economy, and national histories and traditions of social policy (or indeed, the need to create such traditions). The creation of political support for programs is usually thought to be beyond the capacity of international agencies; may be rightly so, but aims to replicate successful Latin American examples tend to negate the deeply political nature of these successes. Graham (2002) rightly highlights the need for "crafting sustainable social contracts," and indeed, in both Latin America and China, as we will see later, social policy reforms and crises responses are clearly part of strengthening legitimacy.[17] Social policies are central to political contestation, elections, and the building up of national unity, including in one-party states. In turn, programs are areas of contestation around extension of rights: the universal pension schemes in Brazil and South Africa which originated under autocratic rule and included motivations to stem migration to urban areas, much later became part of progressive politics. However, much analyses and policy advice on social protection have remained technical, failing to incorporate an understanding of the political economy of such policies.

A depoliticized approach also marks the broader international development approaches around poverty analysis and poverty reduction strategies.

[16] Van Ginneken (2003) stresses the need to ensure linkages between approaches to social security like statutory social insurance, contributory schemes, and tax-financed social benefits.

[17] The IDS research program focuses on "transformative" social protection, and the need to pursue policies that address the power imbalances that create vulnerabilities (Devereux and Sabates-Wheeler, 2004), and build voice, agency and citizenship among marginalized groups (Kabeer, in UNICEF, 2008).

They remain focused on the identification of the poor, to be targeted by specific programs, with too little attention to analyses of causes of poverty, and the underlying structures and beliefs that keep groups of people deprived. While poverty reduction strategies have brought deprivation to the core of the international development agenda, perspectives need to be broadened, beyond the confines of addressing "poverty," and incorporate a better understanding of the political economy that drives policy making for the non-poor as well as the poor. This implies positioning itself more strategically vis-à-vis social policies: the politics of social policies are much more important than the technocratic approaches of international agencies, and donors themselves play a central role in these politics. The second part of this book is dedicated to help build an understanding of the way in which national contexts and histories drive social policy approaches.

SOCIAL POLICY REGIMES

PART TWO

The second part of this book describes social policy regimes, focusing on the principles of solidarity that drive public policies. Such regimes are path dependent. Colonial histories, globalization, and adjustment play an important role, besides national ideologies and political constellations, in prompting public policy interventions. As a central organizing principle, we focus on differences in approaches between East and South Asia, while we also briefly describe dominant approaches in Latin America and Africa where structural adjustment strongly influenced the earlier social policy approaches. Such a comparison, of course, remains a huge research agenda, and the ideas offered here focus on illustrating the potential of a comparative approach.

This comparison draws on the literature of the welfare state, which has filled many pages with comparisons and typologies of national experiences in the OECD context. Esping-Andersen's *The Three Worlds of Welfare Capitalism* (1990) has generated much debate, and his *Social Foundations of Post-Industrial Economies* (1999) re-examines the earlier typology. Two elements are critical for the purpose of this book. First, the typology of welfare regimes focuses on the combined and interdependent ways in which welfare is produced and allocated between state, market, and family, or voluntary or non-profit sector. It is argued here that while there are large differences in this respect between OECD and developing countries, the analytical question of the allocation of responsibilities remains important in all contexts. Second, a notion of decommodification developed by Esping-Andersen quantifies the degree to which state intervention reduces dependence on markets transaction and labor markets. For example, Therborn defined welfare states as those states where more than half of government expenditure was on social policy (Gough, 2004b: 19). In this respect too, differences between countries in the South and richer OECD countries are very large, and data for developing countries are unreliable, but the question itself is of relevance in all contexts.

Esping-Andersen's notion of welfare state regimes focuses on the "historically dominant constellations of collective political mobilization" (Esping-Andersen, 1999: 40–41). He originally distinguished three approaches to solidarity and means of dealing with risks, and three regimes characterized by a different public–private mix of provisions or entitlements, which have continued to cut across a long-term historical trend of increased state intervention. It is important to highlight—and we will elaborate on this later—that the characterization refers to predominant approaches, and are of an "ideal-type" nature, and social policies in each country typically include elements of different approaches.

A first approach identified by Esping-Andersen is of "residualism," the principles of which we have already encountered in the description of social policy approaches in the South, particularly under structural adjustment. A residual approach focuses on limiting assistance to targeted groups, of the deserving poor, and groups like single mothers, the disabled, and the aged. Such assistance tends to be means-tested, and relatively ungenerous, often justified by an argument that the median voter is unlikely to support generous programs for the poor. Such an approach tends to divide society into haves and have-nots, with a group that can obtain private insurance, and a small group dependant on welfare. The welfare state regime that is marked by residualism is the liberal one, which has roots in the 19th century English political economy, and exists strongly in Anglo-Saxon countries which have a relatively strong bias toward targeting of social assistance, a narrow definition of the risks that ought to be covered through state support, and instead a strong encouragement of market mechanisms for social insurance.

A second approach has been labeled "corporatist," and continental European welfare states have maintained strong traits of this approach. In different countries, corporatist solidarities have evolved from histories of collective mobilization, resulting, for example, in a diversity of pension plans or health insurance. Particularly in countries where both liberalism and socialism historically have played small roles, conservative corporatist approaches have remained important. Early social reforms, as in Germany under Bismarck, had a strong authoritarian character, with a strong focus on nation building. Social security in Japan and South Korea has been characterized as corporatist, with status divisions permeating the system. In a corporatist approach, risk is pooled through membership based on professional status or sectoral occupation. Unlike in the market-oriented approaches, such membership is typically compulsory, thus ensuring a corporatist form of solidarity. A male breadwinner bias and centrality of family as care giver—often underpinned by religious norms—are central elements of corporatist regimes.

The third approach identified by Esping-Andersen is the "universalistic" one. This is based on an ideology of national solidarity, and the idea of pooling all risks under one umbrella. Social democratic welfare regimes that emphasize universalism have been central to Nordic countries, and trade unionists have regarded universalism as means to strengthen solidarity across classes. The National Health Service (NHS) in the UK has already been mentioned as an example of a publicly funded universal service, which was set up after the Second World War; in its own words, "[T]he central principles are clear: the health service will be available to all and financed entirely from taxation, which means that people pay into it according to their means."[1] Often, the ideology of solidarity has been combined with practical arguments, like the idea that universalism reduces the need for extensive bureaucracy and limits market distortions, a theme emphasized by Beveridge, for example, and described in Lindert (2004). Under universalist approaches, extensive and relatively generous systems of income transfer programs have been combined with social services and income support for working women, based on strong egalitarian principles, but also in the promotion of productivity and full employment.

Other welfare regimes and approaches have been suggested since the original formulation. For example, while residual approaches are central to welfare provision in Australia and New Zealand, it can be argued that more universal welfare guarantees exist through labor markets and the wage arbitration system. Second, it has been highlighted that clientalism is a key driver of welfare provisions—and bureaucracies—for example, in Mediterranean countries, and as we will see next, in many regions in the Global South. While Esping-Andersen hesitates

[1] Available at http://www.nhs.uk/NHSEngland/aboutnhs/Pages/NHShistory.aspx; the website hosts the animation film that explained the rationale of the new system to UK citizens, as well as the health history of a group of people born in the year the NHS was initiated.

to see this as a defining feature of welfare regimes, clientalism can be so pervasive that an understanding welfare provisions would fall short if it was not taken into account. A third addition to the initial categorization has focused on the productivist orientation of social policies, sometimes also labeled "corporatism without labor." This has been seen as central to the social policies of the "late industrializers" of the Nordic countries (Andersson and Gunnarsson, 2004), and the East Asian social policies, with relatively low government spending, and carefully balanced social and economic policies, as we will describe later.

While these categorizations have found to be of value in OECD contexts, and increasingly in East Asia, it is important to ask the question about their relevance in a development context. Of course, conditions in the South are fundamentally different on many counts (Gough, 2004b: 28–33; MacPherson and Midgley, in Yeates, 2001: 18), including a limited importance of a capitalist mode of production and predominance of broader livelihoods rather than wages and salaries; the importance of exclusion and coercion, and limited state commitment to address these; different forms of political mobilization; and a broader set of actors responsible for the welfare mix and a larger role of the international community. Overall, the role of social policy as a countervailing force has been considered to be much more limited and the institutional context in developing countries much more challenging.

The approach chosen here is a pragmatic one, acknowledging that more formal analysis of "regimes" is desirable for future research. This book uses the categorization as heuristic device, based on the assumption that using an explicit categorization is better than not using any at all (and on the observation that policy makers make comparisons and try to learn from experiences elsewhere anyway). It draws on the OECD literature to highlight the elements that appear useful for understanding social policy in the South. Thus, this part of the book highlights corporatist and productivist approaches in East and Southeast Asia; a move from corporatist to more residual approaches in Latin America; and from post-independence universalist to residual approaches in countries in Africa and South Asia. The comparison, thus, while drawing on Gough (2008), is at the analytical rather than empirical level, using a heuristic device to help improve understanding of the complex and very varied contexts across the South.

First, as mentioned, the focus is on social policy rather than welfare state regimes. This implies a wider notion of public policies than that of the welfare state context in OECD countries from the 1960s onward. This use of a social policy notion is consistent with Esping-Andersen's analysis, which emphasizes that the solidarity principles pre-date the welfare states, and allow for different levels of "decommodification," the extent to which public policies have replaced market transactions in social provisions. The European welfare states are a manifestation of social policy, analytically similar to the way, say, Chinese efforts to build a harmonious society are a manifestation of social policy. Table 7.1 will show significant differences in the role of the state, comparing total public spending and social spending—however, more analysis and better data are needed to understand these differences.

Second, the book's focus of attention is the principles of solidarity rather than categorization of countries and expecting all policies and sectors to conform to the ideal type. Within countries, specific programs are usually based on different principles, reflecting outcomes of historical political conjunctures. For example, in the UK, liberal and market-oriented approaches have predominated, with an emphasis on targeting, but health care has remained based on universalistic approaches, even though the organizational principle has been argued on grounds of efficiency, and the approach remains contested. Further, "corporatist" elements exist in most countries' social policies, including in those who are predominantly universal or predominantly liberal, for example, through benefits for civil service employees. Latin American countries, as described later, have shown features of all three of Esping-Andersen's welfare regimes (Barrientos, 2004a: 139). Therefore, the principal focus of the categorization will be to highlight "predominant" approaches and ideologies within countries, rather than clusters of countries—even though for convenience we describe these by region because of broad similarities in socio-economic histories.[2]

Third, in the South, processes of nation building are relatively recent. Therefore, questions of citizenship and the role of social policies in nation building need to be at the center of social policy analysis. This theme is perhaps less dominant in the welfare state regime debate, though it does feature in US–Europe comparisons, and recent debates on immigration and integration may be driving renewed attention to the citizenship aspect of social policies. Different patterns of integration and ethnic or racial differentiation have contributed to differing norms and public policy practices. The relatively large welfare states in Europe have evolved in the context of relative homogeneity, as in Scandinavian countries, or as in France with its strong emphasis on integration, and with education as a key way of

[2] Abu Sharkh and Gough (2008) provide what is probably the first attempt to a cluster analysis of welfare regimes outside the OECD context, using a combination of "welfare mix" (public spending on health and education, social security contribution) and "welfare outcomes" (immunization, girls' secondary enrollment) variables. This analysis labels South Asian countries except Sri Lanka as "insecurity regimes" and most countries in East Asia as "informal security regimes."

building that national unity. Social policy changes reflect the inter-linkages between social policy on the one hand, and citizenship and national unity or state building on the other, notably in Malaysia (as described by Yusof, 2006) and India (analyzed in de Haan, 2007a), and also, in Africa, as Chapter 6 will highlight. Affirmative action became a key component of post-Apartheid South Africa's social and economic policies, and identity politics have come to play an important role in Latin America too.

Fourth, among the differences between OECD and development contexts, the nature of labor markets is one of the more important ones. Most analysts emphasize the existence of a large "informal" or "unorganized" sector as a major obstacle to expanding social policies, particularly social insurance. However, the distinction between formal and informal is not a natural phenomenon. It is also the creation of public policy interventions and definitions, and in fact, a defining characteristic of corporatist social policy principles. Influenced by modernization theories alongside group interests, categories were created that defined and reinforced difference between those in the "modern" sector, with relatively privileged jobs, and those in the "traditional" sector, characterized by lack of security, low pay, etc. Adjustment and reforms since the 1970s have tried to change this, but usually by reducing employee numbers, rather than changing the relative position of those in the modern sectors, who typically have been in better positions to resist such reforms. The key point for this book is that while labor market constellations are indeed very different, public policy is not absent in labor markets even if they are predominantly "informal." Solidarities are expressed through such labor market policies, and the nature of labor market regulation exerts a direct influence on social security policies.

A fifth point relates to path dependency of public policy. In the OECD context, the categorization has convincingly shown the existence of patterns of social policy approaches, linked to political constellations as well as ideologies, and thus a degree of path dependence. The description in this part of the book is based on an assumption that in the South, too, such path dependency exists, but is less well analyzed, and is, of course, of a dynamic nature. In the South, international influence tends to play a larger role in such path dependency, first through colonialism, and since independence, through the role of international organizations (Davis, 2004; Gough, 2004b) and the increased intensity of exchange of policy ideas. But this impact of the international community does not negate the existence of path dependency. Instead of considering the international context as external to public policy formation, including in terms of taxation, it appears essential to integrate the international context into the descriptions of the political constellations that influence social policies: from the colonial past, through the early periods of independence, up to period of adjustment, and the more recent international approaches that were described earlier, policies are determined in the interaction of such international and national forces.

The focus of the following chapters is Asia, and Chapters 7 and 8 describe East and South Asian experiences respectively. To differing degrees, the period since the 1960s has marked the economic rise of Asia, and we will focus on the accompanying social policy changes. But the same period of globalization was accompanied by relative stagnation in other parts of the South, and social policy changes were no less dramatic. Chapter 5 will describe the corporatist nature of social policy in Latin America as it developed in the earlier parts of the

20th century—with differences across the continent too—and the move toward liberal approaches from the 1970s onward. Chapter 6 focuses on Africa, with the attempts to build up universal systems after independence, followed by a decline in social services through the lost development decade of the 1980s, and accompanying shifts toward targeted and liberal social policy approaches, often under increasing international influence.

5

Latin America
From Corporatism to Liberalism

Within the Global South, Latin America has a relatively old tradition of social policy analysis. This is a direct consequence of the relative early industrialization in Latin America. Following decolonization in the 19th century, many countries followed an import-substitution strategy. From the 1930s onward, Latin American countries put in place strategies to reduce economy's external dependency and promote production of industrialized products, with ideological and theoretical models that emphasized a proactive role of the state. Relatively early industrialization, urbanization, and the emergence of new class interest—alongside the theories supporting the industrialization model—led to comparatively early reflections on the role of social policies.

A dominant theme in the literature on Latin America is the impact of structural adjustment and how this has led to a much more neo-liberal policy regime. This was not unique, and as we will see in Africa, the impact of adjustment on policy approaches has been severe. But Latin America has been a trendsetter, as events in Chile in 1973 were a symbol of global moves toward liberalism, and the "Tequila Crisis" in Mexico in 1994 set a trend for international financial crises. However, in Latin America, the social policy changes happened from an often exclusive or corporatist regime that was built up under interventionist economic policies, while in Africa, this occurred in a context of attempts to build up universal provision in health and education alongside state-led industrialization and rural development.

Moreover, social policy changes in Latin America happened under the influence of deep-rooted and multifaceted inequalities.

In Latin America, toward the later parts of the 1990s, after a period of liberalization which, in many places, was initiated under repressive regimes, new approaches started to emerge. For example, in Chile and Brazil, there are signs that this may have significant impacts on the very high levels of inequality, with more inclusive principles and increased importance of identity politics which find expression at national and international levels.

This chapter discusses the stagnation of Latin American economies in the latter part of the 20th century, the predominant characteristics of its social policies as they had emerged since the 1930s, the changes during the period of adjustment, and recent moves toward arguably more inclusive policies. As in the next chapters, in doing so it focuses on a small sub-set of the continent's countries, representing a diversity of economic and social structures.

Latin American Economies: Lost Development Decades

Latin America's economy, despite a large diversity, has been characterized by stagnation during the 1980s and much of the 1990s, at least as compared to their East Asian counterparts. Within the developing world, Latin America also appears to be the continent worst affected by the 2008–09 economic crisis: while the South as a whole is expected to have GDP growth rates of 1.9 percent and 5.1 percent in 2009 and 2010, the respective figures for Latin America are 2.2 percent and 2.9 percent (Vos, 2009). Three of the countries, given in Table 5.1, experienced negative growth over three decades: Bolivia remains among the poorest countries in the western hemisphere, but also among the most unequal, including inequalities based on identity; Peru, which underwent social and agrarian reforms in the 1970s, and entered a path of liberalization in the 1990s; and Venezuela that remains relatively poor despite the availability of oil resources, and notwithstanding recent progress in poverty reduction.

Compared to other parts of the South, parts of Latin America like Brazil and Argentina industrialized relatively early, while other countries like Bolivia experienced less transformation. The state assumed responsibility for national progress and, according to observers, with long-term transformative impacts and leading to more equal opportunities and outcomes. In many countries, the development of the industry was supported by proactive import substitution, which created an urban working class and a new elite. In Mexico, for example, this modernization was pushed through under the stewardship of the Institutional Revolutionary Party, PRI, from the

Table 5.1 Socio-economic Development in Selected Latin American Countries

	GDP per capita (US$) 2005 PPP	*GDP growth 1975–2005*	*Urbanization % population urban*		*HDI*	*Poverty US$ 1.25/day (2008 revision)*	*Poverty US$ 2/day (2008 revision)*	*Inequality (Gini)*
			1975	*2005*	*2005*			
Argentina	14,280	0.3	81.0	90.1	0.87	4.5	11.3	0.51
Bolivia	2,819	–0.2	41.3	64.2	0.70	19.6	30.3	0.60
Brazil	8,402	0.7	61.7	84.2	0.80	7.8	18.3	0.57
Chile	12,027	3.9	87.6	90.1	0.87	<2	5.3	0.55
Mexico	10,751	1.0	62.8	76.0	0.83	<2	4.8	0.46
Peru	6,039	–0.3	61.5	72.6	0.77	8.2	19.4	0.52
Venezuela	6,632	–1.0	75.8	93.4	0.79	18.4	31.7	0.48

Sources: UNDP (2007); World Bank, World Development Indicators for poverty data, available at http://data.worldbank.org/data-catalog/world-development-indicators (accessed in December 2009).

1930s to 1950s. But while the progress involved movement out of rural areas, the percentage of people absorbed in the formal sector remained relatively low, and even declined in the latter part of the century, after growth during the 1950s and 1960s. Over the time, clashes between old and new elites also emerged, including around land reform.

Latin America's levels of income inequality have traditionally been very high, largely as a result of its colonial history and subsequent failure to break through these established barriers (World Bank, 2003a). On average, the continent has had a Gini coefficient of around 0.50, well above the most unequal OECD countries. This level of inequality has been more or less stable over the last four decades, but most recently, the trend may have been slightly downwards, including in racial inequalities, partly reflecting the political pressure for more equity. In Brazil, the Gini coefficient increased from 0.57 in 1981 to 0.63 in 1989, but then declined to 0.55 in 2007. This decline in inequality has been ascribed to declining inflation, declining returns to education, rural–urban convergence, and increases in social transfers targeted to the poor (Ferreira, Litchfield, and Leite, 2006; Ravallion, 2009). Mexico's inequality declined as well, even though wage inequality increased and the southern part of the country was falling further behind, ending a long-run trend toward regional convergence.[1] In Argentina, inequality increased sharply between 1974 and 1998 (with rising inequality happening at periods of hyperinflation and crisis), and then remained at the same high Gini level of 0.48 till 2006 (Cruces, 2009).

The persistent high income inequality in the region is related to inequalities in access to land and education (Goñi, López, and Servén, 2008). Education indicators have improved consistently in the region, and inequality in education fell in most countries during the 1990s. However, even then the gaps between the top and bottom tended to increase. Health inequalities are severe too. Peru, where inequality has been increasing slightly in recent time, has particularly high inequalities in health outcomes and access to health facilities. A child born in the poorest quintile is nearly five times more likely not to reach the age of five years compared to a child in the richest quintile. The economic crisis of the late 1980s may have widened health disparities (less so in education), and led to significant losses, for example, in infant mortality, particularly among less educated women. Since then, and with expansion of health funding, Peru's inequalities appear to be reducing slowly.[2]

---

[1] Andalón and Lopez-Calva (2002); World Bank (2005: 204).

[2] Medrano, Sanhueza, and Contreras (2006); Paxson and Schady in World Bank (2005: 34); Schady (2005).

Social security coverage in Latin America is highly unequal, with coverage of the employed about 30 percent in the lowest income countries of the continent. While in a few countries there are significant efforts to increase access to traditional social security schemes, such as Uruguay and Ecuador, alternative strategies are explored, including integrating financing sources and subsidizing social security schemes (van Ginneken, 2010).

Inequalities based on ethnic or racial differences are crucially important in Latin America, where 20 percent of the population identifies itself as Afro-descendants and 10 percent as indigenous. Excluded populations suffer from invisibility, higher rates of income poverty, which tend to be permanent rather than transitory, and stigma and discrimination. Women from marginalized groups suffer from multiple forms of deprivation (Buvinié and Mazza, 2008). In Peru, Andinos form 60 percent of the population in poverty, even though their population share is only 45 percent. Levels of income and human development deprivation among Andinos are also much higher than the average, and gaps are not closing (Figueora and Barrón, 2005: 13).

Rural areas, too, have continued to be marked by large inequalities, and the pattern of land reform has been radically different from the East Asian experience where land reform has been considered a precondition for its economic success. The 1950s, the 1960s, and the early 1970s saw increasing levels of organized rural protest, against a context of large land inequalities and exploitative labor relations, and elites moving out of agriculture. The new urban elite saw land reform as a means of weakening the power base of old elites, and as a vehicle for enhancing the domestic market. Land reforms did eliminate bonded labor and reduced land inequality but did not go further. Counter-movements manifested themselves, for example, in Chile in 1973 and in Peru after 1975 (Bebbington et al., 2008).

Latin American Corporatism, with Diversity

The Latin American state has played an important role in the economy and development of the continent, and for some commentators, the development state was a response similar to the Keynesian welfare state in Europe.[3] This is partly reflected in the following table (Table 5.2), which shows total government revenue and spending in different sectors. In terms of total

[3] With respect to Brazil, Amorim (2009) observed a strong response to economic crises of 1930 and 1964, but a "passive" reaction to the crises of the 1980s/1990s (although the elite privileges were not challenged in either of the periods).

Table 5.2 Government Spending in Latin America

	GDP per capita (US$) 2005 PPP	*Government revenue (% GDP)*	*Public spending on education (% GDP)*	*Public spending on health (% GDP)*	*Social security expenditure (% total government revenue)*
Argentina (2004)	10,000	18.1	4	4	17
Bolivia (2003)	3,590	18.8	6	4	10
Brazil (1998–2001)	7,815	22.6	4	3	35
Chile (2005)	12,173	23.8	3	3	6
Mexico (2000–01)	10,966	15	5	3	10
Peru (2005)	6,460	17.6	3	2	9

Source: World Bank, World Development Indicators, available at http://data.worldbank.org/data-catalog/world-development-indicators (accessed in December 2009).

public spending and revenue as part of GDP, Latin America is at the average for middle-income countries, with state spending forming about 18 percent of GDP. Across Latin America, there seems to be less variation than in East Asia and Africa. For example, Argentina is close to the average of middle-income countries, while Mexico's is somewhat smaller, and Chile's is a few percentage points larger. By comparison, and relative to national income, Bolivia's and Brazil's states are fairly large.

Social spending too has been substantial, in terms of proportion of GDP as well as of total government spending, confirming the trends described in Chapter 3. There has not been a general decline in social spending during the period of globalization, but trends have not been uniform. Chile's aggregate and social spending expanded significantly till 1973, and was actively cut back after that. However, Argentina did not cut back in social spending during liberalization (Taylor, 2001). Its total government spending showed a substantial relative increase during the 1990s, probably partly due to the slow growth performance. Social spending (including its financing) has been found to be progressive in Argentina, and has not changed much over time (Gasparini, 2004: 22). Bolivia spends relatively large amounts on health and education, and relatively little on social security. Brazil's social security spending is very high, but this is partly because of its relatively high and regressive spending on old-style pensions, and is thus probably contributing to overall inequality. Peru's social spending is relatively low, as is Chile's.

Latin American social policies have been characterized as state corporatist, highlighting that the power balances that were created under the process of modernization are critical for how social policies have evolved. Pressure group bargaining—rather than the rights of all citizens—has dominated policy-making processes. This has typically had strong biases in favor of urban and modern sector groups, the social classes that formed the core part of the process of modernization. This has contributed to large inequalities in social security. Strong interest groups of civil servants, for example, have successfully resisted reforms and continued to benefit from relatively generous provisions, for example, of pensions in Brazil, while the non-contributory schemes, as we discuss later, emerged as a parallel system of provision. In other cases, fragmentation of interest groups may have contributed to an inability to resist reforms and declines in entitlements.

While corporatism has been a central feature of large parts of Latin America, other social policy principles have existed as well, and different Latin American countries' have followed different principles, as described in detail by Armando Barrientos (2004a). First, aspirations of public universal provision, particularly in health and education, have reflected features of a social democratic regime in many countries. Many labor, education, health, and other social policies were universalist in their aspirations. But in practice, the universalism was "stratified universalism," and groups that were able to voice demands were able to have benefits extended (Palma and Urzúa, 2005: 11–12). The model was also based on the notion of a labor-based society, often accompanied by a male breadwinner model, in principle perhaps universal, but in practice, partial, because of high rates of unemployment and large size of the informal sector (Economic Commission for Latin America and the Caribbean [ECLAC], 2006).

Second, social insurance and employment protection reflects a conservative welfare regime. Like elsewhere, a majority of workers have been excluded from access to social provisions, and from labor market protection. "Instead of developing towards universal coverage, social insurance and employment protection reinforced the segmentation in the welfare mix by excluding more vulnerable groups of workers" (Barrientos, 2004a: 160). Economic instability and the crisis of the import-substitution model, and the related political changes, have reinforced the conservative aspects of the social policy approaches, even though economic policies moved toward liberal principles.

Third, and following from this, low coverage of state welfare provision reflects a liberal or residual principle. The coverage of social policies is not only low, but also has been declining in many areas. Social spending in Latin America has had a relatively poor record in reaching the poor and most vulnerable, due to uneven regional distribution, passive, fragmented, and clientelist providers, and social and cultural barriers. The new social protection agenda, as discussed next, partly reflects liberal principles, with its focus on targeting, but is addressing some of the systemic problems of exclusion of the poorest and vulnerable to crises.

International influences played a very important role in the evolvement of Latin American public policies, both through imposition of northern ideas and the forceful resistance to what are seen as imperialist ideas (as elsewhere in the Global South, the resistance itself is an integral part of policy making, just as resistance to globalization is a critical part of the process of globalization). The United Nations Commission for Latin America had a big influence in the debate on agrarian institutions as barrier to economic growth, and ideas around import-substitution industrialization. In terms of social policy, the southern part of the continent saw a dominance of Bismarckian principles in the introduction of early 20th century social security provisions, with a focus on the coverage of specific occupation groups. In other parts of Latin America, social–democratic approaches and Beveridge's influence were more strongly felt, introducing universalist principles. International impact, again, was strongly felt at the start of the adjustment period, with the US political influence and economic advice leading the post-1973 Chilean development path, along neo-liberal ideology in a "pure doctrinal form" (Mason, 1997: 79), and of course, with the financial crises that came to dominate economic development in the 1990s.[4]

From Corporatism to a Liberal Regime

Most of the features of Latin America's social policies have undergone significant changes since the early 1970s. Observers have highlighted a radical shift from the development state that existed since the 1930s, with its shortcoming and elite domination, to a neo-liberal economic and residual social policy model. The policy shift was fueled by critique regarding fiscal imbalances, lack of state capacity, and inefficient administration, with an active role of World Bank and Inter-American Development Bank (Cortés, 2008). The popularity of the new ideology was fueled by a combination of internal economic and political crises, the impact of rising oil prices and declining commodity prices, dwindling state revenue undermining the populist power like that of the PRI in Mexico, and interventionist US policies supporting authoritarian regimes.

Existing welfare provisions were unable to cope with fiscal crises (Mesa-Lago, 1997). The new ideology highlighted reductions in social spending and targeting besides decentralization. The "social funds," as described in Chapter 4, found entry to the policy scene in many countries, starting with Bolivia's Emergency Social Fund (ESF), which was designed to address the social costs of adjustment process, including the severe unemployment of mining workers laid off due to the collapse of tin prices and the closing of state-run mines. The ESF was followed by the Social Investment Fund (SIF), which had long-term poverty objectives and further, developed community participation and involved local governments (Glaessner et al., 1994).

At the same time, decentralized planning and diversified administration and delivery of services became increasingly important themes in the new model of governance. This drew on wider ideological currents than just a neo-liberal one and experiments in privatization, and included the

[4] At the beginning of the 21st century we witness attempts to share Latin America's recent social policy experiences with developing countries, notably in Brazil through the Ministry of Social Development and Fight Against Hunger (www.mds.gov.br/arquivos/agenda_brasil_africa_ing_21.08.08.pdf), and the International Poverty Centre (www.ipc-undp.org/ipc/africa-brazil.jsp).

grassroots ideology of the 1980s, and Christian and indigenous movements. These changes have also led to new forms of participatory or deliberative democratic experiments (Recondo, 2008), of which the Porto Alegre experience is worth highlighting (Box 5.1).

Chile played "a paradigmatic role in Latin America's welfare regime shift" (Barrientos, 2004a: 161). Its restructuring of economic and social policies happened earlier and deeper than elsewhere—subsequent reforms elsewhere on the continent have drawn on and learnt from Chile's experience and have generally been more moderate. Changes implied increasing reliance on individuals and households for the provision of welfare; targeting of safety nets and social spending rather than benefiting organized labor, professionals, and public servants; reduced labor market protection; decentralization; and introduction of competition and private market in the provision of services.

Like in Chile, welfare reforms in Argentina moved from corporatist/conservative to more liberal. The changes were more complex than in Chile, and happened under a more open political regime. Social policy provisions

Box 5.1 Participation in Local Public Policy: Porto Alegre's Experience

Changes in the 1988 Constitution enhanced the autonomy of Brazil's municipalities in revenues and expenditures decisions. The decentralization of budgetary decisions and the long history of democratic civil society action contributed in Porto Alegre in 1989 to the establishment of participatory budget making. Porto Alegre is the capital of the Brazilian state, Rio Grande do Sul, with over a million inhabitants, after rapid urbanization till the 1980s and increasing gaps in urban infrastructure and marginalization of large parts of its populations.

This new and now well-known democratic institution enables participation of citizens in discussions around budgetary issues. Discussions take place in regional and thematic plenary assemblies, held every six months or so. All citizens are entitled and encouraged to participate in discussions about transportation, education, leisure, health, social welfare, and economic development. From this follows regional or thematic demands and priorities, and the assemblies elect delegates and councilors, and carry out an evaluation of the executive's performance. The councilors have the responsibility to rank the demands, and thus to determine the allocation of funds, and vote on the investment plan proposals of the executive. Inevitably, conflicts have arisen, but studies do show that citizens believe that this new form of policy making has resulted in improved services.

Source: Descriptions can be found in many publications; for a short history see, www.unesco.org/most/southa13.htm (accessed in December 2009).

had expanded particularly during the populist Peronist period of the 1950s and 1960s, with considerable power of trade unions. Structural adjustment from 1989 onward implied reduction of employment protection and reforms of pension and health insurance in the mid-1990s—but with much more resistance than in Chile. Social security spending has been largely tied to the labor market, and poverty programs were limited, with "Trabajar," an important and well-documented innovation, introduced to respond to the country's high unemployment, with pro-poor outcomes (Jalan and Ravallion, 1999). The crisis in 2001 was followed by establishment of an effective cash transfer program covering 20 percent of households, the *Programa Jefes y Jefas de Hogar Desocupados*, but this has remained temporary (Cruces, 2009).

Brazil's recent development are of relevance for a variety of reasons, including because as an emerging economy, it is now rapidly becoming an important global agent, and as mentioned earlier, seems to have some success in reducing inequality.[5] Brazil's economy stagnated during the 1980s and early 1990s, with high inflation and budget deficits. There was modest economic growth since the mid-1980s, but with little impact on poverty, due to the country's high inequality, though growth in the service sector appeared to have been relatively pro-poor. According to Ravallion (2009: 14), the policies after 1994 conformed closely to the Washington Consensus prescriptions of macroeconomic stability, low inflation, trade reforms, and privatization, but this was accompanied by an extension of social policies, particularly cash transfers (but with a focus on targeting, along the emphasis of a post-Washington Consensus), as described next.

Pension reforms have been a marker of the move toward a liberal or conservative social policy regime. The World Bank—that has provided significant lending to pensions reform over the last decades—proposed a multi-pillar system, with publicly managed unfunded, mandatory privately funded, and voluntary privately funded components. Following extensive critique, it has been acknowledged subsequently by the World Bank that the operations that supported pension reforms paid little attention to social assistance for the aged poor.[6] Chile introduced individual retirement plans in the early 1980s: the coverage of pensions increased while individual benefits declined, while the transfer between systems generated huge

[5] Martin Ravallion (2009) recently published an interesting paper on poverty reduction in Brazil, China, and India, inter alia highlighting Brazil's relatively large capacity for redistribution of income.

[6] Gill, Packard, and Yermo (2005); Holzmann and Hinz (2005); World Bank (1994).

demands for additional subsidy. Bolivia was one of the countries that tried to emulate the Chilean model of pension reforms, but with unique features, including its direct link to the privatization (capitalization) of state-owned enterprises (SOE). While opposition to the plan was defused fairly quickly, it was unsuccessful because of financial constraints and political instability (Barrientos, 2004a: 164–66).

The privatization trend existed in other sectors (including in infrastructure provisions) and countries too. Peru implemented labor market reforms in the 1980s, and the informal sector expanded rapidly. Peru and Mexico now have significant numbers of individual retirement plans, and in both countries, social insurance coverage has decreased rapidly in the two decades after 1980. Mexico also abandoned many of its older policies supporting the rural poor (Berg and Taylor, 2001: 3), thus solidifying a trend toward greater reliance on market mechanisms. In Peru and Mexico, reforms in the late 1990s also provided conditions for expansion of private health insurance providers.

While many economists have celebrated the conditions for economic growth created under the new liberal regime, from a social policy perspective, the impacts of the changes to a liberal regime are generally felt to have been negative, similar to the way adjustment in Africa has been perceived. Assessments of new social policy instruments show mixed pictures. For example, evaluation in Peru suggests that programs to enhance access to health through public insurance during the 1990s did not reduce inequalities (Medrano, Samhueza, and Contreras, 2006), though the (real) increase in public expenditure during the 1990s may have contributed to a reduction in disparities in health (World Bank, 2005: 34). The World Bank-sponsored social funds have obtained good reviews regarding targeting and outreach, but the impact on overall levels of inequality remains unclear and probably has been quite small.

The paradigmatic change has been widely felt, even though class interests that were based in the old rural development, and early industrialization models continue to exert a large influence. Both privatization in social and infrastructure sectors (such as the privatization in the water sector in Bolivia, which was reversed in 2005) and targeted anti-poverty and social fund approaches have clearly marked a move toward a liberal model, with a greater reliance on individuals' ability to negotiate market forces. But over time, both economic stagnation and crises, and the continued inequalities, led to new policy developments, with greater concern for the poor.

The New Social Protection Agenda: Latin American Innovations

Much attention has been given recently to the new forms of cash transfers and non-contributory schemes, many of which originated in Latin America, and governments like Brazil's have become keen to share their experiences with the rest of the world. The workfare program, Trabajar, was an innovation in Argentina in the 1990s, and is now widely known. The *Bolsa Escola* started in Brazil in the mid-1990s, in the city of Campinas, was extended to several other localities, and nationally, in 2001. In 2006, 12 countries in the region had introduced similar programs, like the *Plan Familias* in Argentina, *Bolsa Familia* in Brazil, and *Oportunidades* in Mexico, which has been expanded to almost a quarter of the country's population. While non-contributory, and thus directly relevant for the poor that were previously excluded from social policy provisions, particularly social security, many programs are means-tested and conditional, with simple rules for eligibility (as described in Chapter 4).

Similarly, non-contributory pensions have received much attention, and have been praised for reducing inter-generational inequality, providing benefits on a broad basis rather than based on contributions, and at relatively low fiscal costs. For example, there are now two non-contributory pensions in Brazil, following social security reforms which started in 1991: a rural old-age pension that benefits men from age 60 and women from age 55 who worked in informal employment without required earnings or inactivity tests; and the less developed, social assistance pension in urban areas.

Non-contributory pension schemes in Brazil, while now playing an important redistributive and anti-poverty role, originated under autocratic rule (as they did in South Africa), and included motivations to stem migration to urban areas (HelpAge International, 2003: 20). Barrientos (2008) describes how the emergence of these programs were influenced by social mobilization, like the rural social movement in Brazil, which helped create the conditions for reform-minded policy makers to design such schemes. In Brazil (as in South Africa), a "renewal of the social contract was…key in the extension of non-contributory pension programs…" (Barrientos, 2008: 180). Details of the new pension schemes are described in Box 5.2. Bolivia also has made efforts to introduce a social pension program, starting in 1996, and revamped after the election of Evo Morales

Box 5.2 New Social Policy in Brazil: Non-contributory Schemes

The two new non-contributory pensions followed Brazil's social security reforms which began in 1991, with the rural scheme being developed much more and earlier. The rural old-age pension, *Prêvidencia Rural*, benefits men from age 60 and women from age 55 who worked in informal employment. The reforms thus extended entitlement to all qualifying workers, and expanded coverage to female rural workers who were not heads of household. The value of the pension benefits was raised, to the level of the minimum wage. The scheme is non-contributory, but pensioners need to show proof of economic activity. In 2000, 4.6 million beneficiaries received the old-age pension, and fiscal cost was estimated at 1 percent of GDP.

A new social assistance pension, the *Beneficio de Prestação Continuada*, was introduced in January 1996, following a scheme set up in 1974. This pays the minimum wage to disabled and elderly people aged 67 years and above, living in urban or rural areas with a household income less than a quarter of the minimum wage. Conditions for entitlement under this are thus much tougher than under the rural pension scheme. In 2000, there were 0.4 million beneficiaries, and 0.3 under the old scheme, and fiscal costs was probably around 0.2 percent of GDP.

Source: Barrientos (2008).

and replaced with Renta Dignidad in 2008, a non-contributory scheme for all citizens over 60 years of age.[7]

The move toward these non-contributory schemes, thus, partly signifies a continued trend toward liberal principles of targeting, similar to the emphasis given in the Third Way approach of New Labour in the UK. This includes an emphasis on social policies as a form of productive investment, while at the same time, highlighting fiscal affordability—but without a systematic discussion on the place of the schemes in broader social policies and modes of financing (Bastagli, 2009). These innovations were accompanied and fueled by a critique of the contributory schemes and privatization that had marked the neo-liberal wave across the continent since the mid-1970s, including of the problems of efficiency, financing, and equity that characterized these new programs, and carried out under a new form of populist leadership emphasizing more inclusive national unity, as discussed next.

In 2008, at the time the financial crisis was started to be felt across the world, the reversal away from neo-liberal models seemed to be reaching a

[7] Available online at http://www.helpage.org/Researchandpolicy/PensionWatch/Bolivia (accessed in May 2010).

new phase, with Argentina's President proposing to nationalize the private pension funds which were set up in 1994 (Venezuela, for example, also nationalized steel and cement industries, and as indicated earlier, privatization experiments in water in Bolivia had been reversed). Unlike during earlier financial crisis, many countries now have substantial reserves, but of course, it is too early to judge what the impact of the crisis on social policy trends will be.

A "Third Way" in Latin America?

A key question with respect to Latin America is whether we are witnessing the emergence of a new model of principles of solidarity, alongside a resurgence of nationalism in countries like Venezuela and Bolivia.[8] After the move toward liberal principles during the 1970s and 1980s, there have been signs of a newly emerging social contract, for example, in high inequality countries like Brazil, with the expansion of new forms of social protection and affirmative action. As highlighted in Barrientos, Gideon, and Molyneux (2008: 763), "it is striking how visible and contested social policy has become. National elections, parliamentary debates, and social mobilization are increasingly focused on social policy issues." The Economic Commission for Latin America and the Caribbean, ECLAC, in its 2006 report on social protection, calls for social protection instruments to be embedded in social rights, and fostering social citizenship.

The new social contract is manifested clearly in the case of Chile where outward economic policies have been combined with increasing access to opportunities for all and specific programs for the most marginalized (*Chile Solidario* for the poorest, and the Regime of Explicit Health Guarantees, AUGE). Chile's new approaches indicate that social provisions and rights and citizenship can be mutually reinforcing. *Chile Solidario* aims to

> move from a formal to a more real, active citizenship, capable of defending its rights and complying with its corresponding duties. The most important of these duties is the "family contract", which commits the State to deliver the goods and services to which the participant family is entitled, and commits the family to carrying out the tasks assigned by the family support monitor in order to meet the minimum conditions. (Palma and Urzúa, 2005: 33)

[8] The nationalism is usually anti-US, and was most recently expressed particularly by Venezuelan leader Hugo Chávez, who, at the first meeting with new US President Obama, presented him with a copy of Eduardo Galeano's book *Las Venas Abiertas de América Latina*, and at the Copenhagen climate summit quipped "it still smells of sulfur here," after Obama had left the podium.

The new model is also based on the idea that economic growth and justice are compatible. In the words of Brazilian President Lula (Lula da Silva, 2009):

> [W]e have grown and enjoyed economic stability. Our growth has been accompanied by the inclusion of tens of millions of Brazilian people in the consumer market. We have distributed wealth to more than 40m who lived below the poverty line...The expansion of our domestic market has not happened at the expense of exports—they have tripled in six years. We have attracted enormous volumes of foreign investment...All this has enabled us to accumulate $207bn in foreign reserves and thereby protect ourselves from the worst effects of a financial crisis...

Moreover, racial and ethnic differences are becoming a central part of public policies and electoral politics, as highlighted in Bolivia in particular, where a recent new constitution grants greater power to its indigenous majority. As summarized in Green (2008: 31–33), who highlights Bolivia's example as an illustration of a new social contract based on more active citizenship and more effective states, until the 1980s, Bolivia's Chiquitano people lived in near-feudal conditions, having survived some of the worst impacts of colonialism. An indigenous identity began to emerge in the 1980s, when Chiquitano began to identify themselves as indigenous, forming the first organization on that basis. In 1995, they presented their first legal demand for title, and they won parliamentary recognition, and over time, continued to build national alliances. The 2005 municipal and presidential elections saw an enormous rise of indigenous leaders, including of course, Evo Morales.

Slavery and the colonial domination of Afro-descendant and indigenous groups, and subsequent historic denial of culture and identity perpetuated in various ways, are critical to understanding the contemporary economic, political, and social exclusion processes (Hopenhayn, 2008). Affirmative action does not have a long history in Latin America, but recent political events signal the articulation of a new element of its social policies. Forms of affirmative action can be found in Colombia, Chile, and Brazil, in areas of education, integrated local development, access to land and capital markets, labor markets, and access to justice. In Brazil, until recently, severe racial inequalities, particularly relating to 80 million Afro-descendants, were not officially recognized—Brazilians were made to believe there were no black or white Brazilians. But a high-level secretariat has been created with a mandate to prepare all forms of public administration for racial equality—without programs for economic empowerment as in South Africa.[9]

Experience with the new forms of affirmative policies is still very limited (Buvinić and Mazza, 2008). The extent to which the emergence of indigenous movements, for example, has contributed to reducing the severe inequalities equally is not very large, as Lucero (2008), for example, describes for Bolivia and Ecuador. But the critical issue is that social policy making has distinctly changed in most countries in the region, with a combination of the targeted cash transfers effectively reaching many poor people; a new kind of leadership like former union leader Lula in Brazil and Bolivia's indigenous leader, Evo Morales; and new approaches to inclusive policies and citizenship.

Are there Lessons from Latin America?

What is the relevance of the lessons from Latin America for experience elsewhere, and what does this very short overview contribute to the social policy framework proposed here? In the first place, for different reasons, the Latin American experiences have been driving much of the global debate, and have become symbols of critical moments in the development of globalization. Structural adjustment combined with authoritarianism was introduced early on the continent, and social policy changed rapidly accordingly. The events in Chile in 1973 marked the start of the neo-liberal areas, the financial crisis in Mexico in 1994 the start of a period of global financial instability, and the new non-contributory schemes have been leading the recent debates on social protection. Chinese policy makers, moreover, have shown a keen interest in Latin America because of its high levels of inequality and in the lessons this provides for its own efforts to establish a "harmonious society," and Brazil has shown interest to share its experiences with African and other developing countries.

In the context of the social policy framework proposed here, the Latin American experience demonstrates three main issues. First, Latin American history shows how social and economic policies are inextricably linked. The models of import substitution in the earlier parts of the 20th century that led to modernization also entailed the development of the corporatist models of social policy. In the neo-liberal model with its emphasis on

[9] Presentation by the vice minister at a UNDESA session of the United Nations Educational, Scientific and Cultural Organization (UNESCO) conference in Buenos Aires, February 2006.

reducing state responsibility, social provisions were increasingly targeted, and an idea of individual responsibility became central to social provisions and other public goods. Finally, new models of social protection—yet to be fully articulated—are promoted under political regimes that simultaneously promote economic openness and internal justice, and only time will tell whether these schemes will become part of broader inclusive social policies.

Second, the description in this chapter shows the importance of path dependence, and of structures and institutions created much earlier—in this case, under state-led modernization—for subsequent evolvement of social policy. Among other things, the high socio-economic inequalities continue to exert a deep influence on public policies, for example, illustrated in the continued regressive funding for pension for civil servants, with new "social" pensions being created alongside the old systems. While there were earlier attempts at poverty reduction in both urban and rural areas, the recent innovation have been explicit attempts to include parts of the population that were earlier excluded from social policies.

Finally, Latin American experience shows that social policies are deeply political. Class and other interests continue to drive existing institutions, whether public or private. The public institutions and even new governance models often reinforce old inequalities, but are also challenged by new political realities and the emergence of new interest and pressure groups, such as in the form of identity politics and rural protests. Latin America's new politics are behind the recent interventions that are starting to address old divisions of ethnicity, race, and gender, and at least in some cases, declining levels of inequality suggest that more inclusive development models are being formed.

6

The Short Era of the Developmental State in Africa

While Latin America has been marked by relatively early industrialization followed by crisis, the history of development in Africa is one of relatively late decolonization after the scramble for Africa of the late 19th century which divided the continent into about 50 countries with artificial borders. Independence was followed by a mere two decades of relatively good progress in economic and social indicators.

However, the 1960s and the 1970s were succeeded by two decades of deep economic crisis and structural adjustment, and in many cases, severe development regressions, notably in health indicators, and with the devastating impact of HIV/AIDS. Very few countries have escaped the downward trends. Botswana has been one of the exceptions. It is a small country, with unfavorable conditions for economic development at independence in 1966, but with a stable democracy since, in which the availability of diamonds did not become a "resource curse" but instead a solid social contract has been maintained. Mauritius has been the other country, regarded as among the few exceptions, showing sustained development.

Moreover, soon after independence, and often fueled by the Cold War, a number of countries descended into civil and/or external wars. Corruption and the siphoning of funds away from the continent has been a major factor in the post-colonial history of Africa, with dictators like Mobutu in Zaire, Mengistu in Ethiopa, and Abache in Nigeria among the most corrupt and often, also violent.[1] Uganda was another example of a country devastated by civil war, with Idi Amin's regime (1971–79) responsible for the violent death of between 100,000 and 500,000 people, and the expulsion of Asians; but the country has experienced considerable progress since, recently under multi-party democracy with a strong leader, but with continuing regional strife.

Since the 1990s, there has been economic progress in large parts of the continent, and recently, a number of years of decent economic growth above the average of OECD countries, partly because of the stimulus provided by the economic success of China. Recent growth has been, to a large extent, the result of increase in commodity prices, signaling the continued export dependency of economic growth. The impact of the crisis of 2008–09 on Africa is still unclear, but the dependency on commodity prices and resulting fluctuation in growth rates suggest the impact will be significant.[2] In any case, the continent continues to be marked by the worst economic and social indicators. The selection of countries in the next table (Table 6.1) highlights the continued state of deprivation in many parts of Africa.

Despite exceptions and recent progress, sub-Saharan Africa continues to be marked by a dominant primary sector of agriculture and mineral resources, low domestic capital formation and direct foreign investment, and indebtedness and dependence on aid, with official development assistance (ODA) forming more than 20 percent of gross national income (GNI) in countries like Malawi, Mozambique, and Rwanda (see Annexure). Many countries are marked by high unemployment or underemployment and a large informal sector, and continuing high levels of poverty. States have "limited developmental capacity as the political leaders are unable to mobilize and foster mutually-interlocking relationships between the state and various social, political and economic interests" (Edhigeji, 2005).

---

[1] Moyo (2009) in her account of the failure of international aid in Africa emphasizes the willingness of donors to realize the dictators' dreams. A corruption index is included in Table 6.1, suggesting a wide variety across the African continent. More recently, the numbers of civil conflicts have decreased.

[2] Weeks (2009), who argues for proactive fiscal policy in African countries, including through employment schemes. Holmqvist (2009) too shows that the immediate crisis impact was felt through collapsing commodity prices, while the impact through aid and remittances are harder to ascertain (Holmqvist, 2009). UN projections (Vos, 2009) indicate GDP growth rates of 5.6 percent in 2008, a projected 1.6 percent in 2009, and 4.3 percent in 2010 (slightly below the average of developing countries).

Table 6.1 Socio-economic Development in Selected African Countries

	GDP per capita (US$) 2005 PPP	*GDP growth 1975–2005*	*Corruption perception index 2008 score (rank in brackets)*	*Urbanization % population*		*HDI 1985*	*HDI 2007*	*Poverty US$ 1.25/day*	*Inequality (Gini)*
				1975	*2005*				
Botswana	12,387	5.9	5.8 (36)	11.8	57.4	0.58	0.69	31.2 ('93)	0.61
Ghana	2,480	0.7	3.9 (67)	30.1	47.8	–	0.53	30.0	0.41
Kenya	1,240	0.1	2.1 (147)	12.9	20.7	–	0.54	19.7	0.43
Malawi	667	–0.2	2.8 (115)	7.7	17.2	0.38	0.49	73.9	0.39
Nigeria	1,128	–0.1	2.7 (121)	23.4	48.2	0.43 ('90)	0.51	64.4	0.44
South Africa	11,110	–0.3	4.9 (54)	28.1	59.3	0.68	0.68	26.2	0.58
Tanzania	744	1.4	3.0 (102)	11.1	24.2	0.43 ('90)	0.53	21.5	0.35
Uganda	1,454	2.4	2.6 (126)	7.0	12.6	0.39 ('90)	0.51	51.5	0.46
Zambia	1,023	–1.8	2.8 (115)	34.9	35.0	0.50	0.48	64.3	0.51
Zimbabwe	2,038	–0.5	1.8 (166)	19.9	35.9	–	–	–	0.50

Sources: UNDP (2009b); World Bank (2008) WDI data revision; CPI scores; available at http://www.transparency.org/news_room/in_focus/2008/cpi2008/cpi_2008_table (accessed in December 2009).

Moreover, absolute deprivations are coupled with often high inequality even in countries where urbanization has remained very low, and of course, in South Africa, where after the political transition from Apartheid rule, inequalities do remain extremely marked.

> Results from recent surveys reported by a number of countries in sub-Saharan Africa confirmed…that income inequality is indeed considerably higher than had been thought…in Africa despite low level of per capita income and predominantly homogeneous livelihood systems. (Okojie and Shimeles, 2006)

This indicates that development approaches that focus on poverty reduction may be neglecting a critical aspect of the challenges these countries face, and as indicated earlier, economic growth is both less likely to be benefiting the poor than in more equal conditions, and the inequalities are likely to cause serious obstacles to economic growth and enhancing productivity. Some authors have attributed part of the differences between East Asia's and Africa's economic growth to the larger gender inequalities in the latter.[3]

Unlike Latin America, there is much variation in African countries' inequality. South Africa, of course, has the reputation of being highly unequal, following the racist divides established under colonial domination, and income inequality at a Gini of 0.58 and changing little since the end of Apartheid despite various forms of affirmative action (Gelb, 2003; Jenkins and Thomas, 2004). Other high inequality countries with a Gini of 0.50 or more (according to World Development Indicators) include the settler economies of Namibia, Lesotho, and Zimbabwe, but also the poor landlocked nations, namely, Central African Republic and Niger. Medium inequality countries include Uganda, Kenya, and Ghana—though they may still inadequately reflect deep-seated inequalities, for example, between Ghana's north and south (Aryeetey and McKay, 2005), and between ethnic groups and genders. At the other end, there are countries—but surprisingly few, and fewer than assumed until recently—where income inequality is low: Tanzania with a Gini coefficient of 0.35 and Benin with 0.37.

Non-income dimensions of well-being also highlight stark high levels of inequalities, often particularly in rural areas. A Gini coefficient for asset ownership calculated for 12 African countries varied from a high of 0.75 in Niger to a low of 0.43 in Tanzania. And an indicator of asset inequality in seven African countries showed low inequality in Ghana, followed by Senegal and Zimbabwe, Kenya, Mali, Tanzania, and Zambia (Okojie and Shimeles, 2006), thus partly but by no means completely reflecting comparisons in

[3] Blackden and Bhanu (1999), Blackden et al. (2006); see also Klasen (1999 and 2005).

income inequality, and highlighting the need for policy approaches to be sensitive to inequalities as much as absolute measures of deprivation.

Because of the lack of household survey data, knowledge about changes in inequality in Africa is still limited, and often restricted to short periods. Short-term increases have been found during the 1990s, for example, in Ghana, Senegal, and Ethiopia. Cramer (2003) found a rapid rise in inequality in Rwanda, possibly contributing to the conflict.[4] Economic growth and poverty reduction in Uganda, during the 1990s, was accompanied by rising inequalities due to unbalanced growth between sectors—inevitable perhaps but calling for renewed policy attention.[5] Kenyan inequality also has been reported to be on the rise, but during economic stagnation and worsening of human development indicators and governance crisis. Declines in inequality are hardly ever observed, except for Zambia during 1991–98, but this was during a period of decline in GDP.

While in Latin America ethnic and racial deprivations are well documented, the development literature on Africa has not been equally explicit about group inequalities, though ethnic diversity has been described as a main cause of political and national instability.[6] As the given data shows, high levels of income inequality are found in the "settler" regions in the southern part of the continent, notably but not only South Africa and Zimbabwe, while more complex ethnic diversity characterizes, for example, Ghana and Nigeria—in all cases, these differences have become core to political and administrative settlements (Bangura, 2005; Ibrahim, 2006). Ethnic differences in Tanzania appear to have been maintained as a result of explicit nation-building policies under the post-colonial socialist regime (Mamdani, 2005), while the group differences that were fueled under colonial rule erupted in Rwanda in the 1994 genocide (Mamdani, 2001). The violence in Kenya in 2008 shows that the impact of group inequalities is very hard to predict, and that the challenges of various forms of inequality continue to exist across the continent.

[4] The link between changes in income inequality and conflict is far from direct: low levels of income inequality according to surveys do not exclude protests, as shown in Indonesia and in China, where protests tend to be much more related to corruption and incompetence than directly related to the rise of overall income inequality.

[5] Balioumune-Lutz and Lutz (2004) analysis of rates of economic growth in rural and urban areas in Africa concluded that sectoral inequalities were on average increasing, but rural–urban disparities were decreasing.

[6] The colonial origins of such social differences are discussed for example in Mamdani (2001) and Moncrieffe (2008).

Social Policy in Africa?

While the early industrialization and urbanization in Latin America led to a long and continued tradition of social policy analysis, in Africa this tradition has been much weaker, and marked by lack of continuity. In general, the literature on social policy in the world's poorest countries is very limited, with the work of Jimi Adésínà and Tada Akin Aina as main exceptions. Much of the development literature is critical of an application of the notion in Africa. We already mentioned the critique emanating from the IDS research program, for example, that highlighted that a social policy notion neglected the lack of formal labor markets and multidimensional livelihoods of the majority of populations. While generally being more receptive of application of a social policy notion in the South, contributions in Gough and Wood (2004) too, by and large, deny the usefulness of using the concept in African contexts. Bevan (2004: 248) is rightly concerned that a social policy notion is a western concept. She finds the notion inadequate to understand insecurity in Africa, illustrated in emergency situations of Sierra Leone in the 1990s, and the humanitarian crisis in Sudan in the 1980s—many other examples could be quoted. Data scarcity, moreover, makes analysis of public policy more difficult.

However, a tradition of social policy analysis is not absent among African academics, and it has recently been given new emphasis, notably by the African Union that defines social policy as a set of actions, programs, and projects "designed by governments in collaboration with relevant stakeholders to promote social development through improvements in the quality of life of citizens irrespective of class, gender, race, ethnicity, religion, political beliefs, national origin and geographic location" (African Union, 2006: 12). Within the UNRISD research program, Adésínà (2006, 2007) has made a forceful argument for applying a social policy notion to the African context, focusing on health and education, and stresses the radical break brought about by structural adjustment. Aina in the introduction to a CODESRIA publication on social policy, applies a concept to analyze the relationship between ordinary people's lives and globalization and its "identical twin" structural adjustment, stressing how "globalization has not only generated so much anxiety, insecurity and resistance; it has generated an almost unanimous perception of polarization, pain and greater inequality along with the feeling of almost insurmountable threat to ordinary people's livelihoods and cultures" (Aina, 2004: 5). In my view, a notion of social policy is important to conceptualize socio-economic changes over the last decades. The contention here is that a social policy concept that focuses on principles of solidarity and its relation to economic policy can be helpful—however, the fragmentation of social policy has, in many cases, severely hampered the articulation of such principles.

It is important to discuss the reasons why a social policy notion is often though to be less applicable to Africa. It is commonly argued that it is less relevant in the context of rural societies, with extensive poverty. This was the subject of discussion of the introductory chapter, but here some of the points need reiteration. As shown earlier, Africa is not just marked by poverty, but also by very high levels of income and asset inequalities. Africa is urbanizing, though, of course, at very different rates across the continent. And demographic changes are reshaping the conditions in many countries, of course with respect to HIV/AIDS but also the growing numbers of young people, which is expected to increase pressure for job creation and risks of growing exclusion, for example (World Bank, 2009). While admittedly, the social policy discussion as originated in the OECD discussion appears less useful in a poor rural context, it is important that the problems that social policies address exist too. Alongside moral commitments, and increasingly integrated societies with better communications, the pressures for such policies are present and increasing, and the shape such policies (including in the way this is driven by global frameworks) take can have a significant impact on social relations and processes of exclusion and inclusion, as Christiansen and Whyte (2008) demonstrate, for example, with respect to child support in Uganda.

Moreover, though not explored in-depth in this book, a concept that focuses on the political project of social policy provisions also has the potential to inform debates about post-conflict reconstruction or peace building. This question is of particular relevance for the African continent, as it has experienced about half of the world's conflicts in recent times.[7] Most of these conflicts have been civil conflicts (rather than international, though many with cross-border implications), and are closely interwoven with questions of access to natural and political resources. A large number of the world's "bottom billion," as defined by Paul Collier (2007), live in the countries marked by conflicts, which are often linked to dependency on mineral extraction. While a social policy agenda in such areas is of course very different from countries with stable political institutions, elements of

[7] Between 1997 and 2002, according to the African Development Bank (2008), Africa has experienced a decline in numbers of conflicts. Recent conflicts include those in the Democratic Republic of Congo (DRC), which has claimed five million lives, Darfur, Chad, and Kenya.

a development agenda—particularly around transparency and stakeholder dialogue—show large overlaps with the framework as described in the concluding chapter of this book. Box 6.1 illustrates this.

Box 6.1 Public Policies in Conflict Context

Conflicts are responsible not only for direct human suffering, but also indirectly: OXFAM has estimated that 50 percent of food crises in Africa can be explained by armed conflict and consequent human displacement (Green, 2008: 200). As described in the recent African Development Report, addressing post-conflict situations requires a combination of measures of economic management, political participation, and regional integration (African Development Bank, 2008). Michael Ross (2008) describes ways that can reduce the likelihood of conflict in high-risk settings of mineral dependency and weak institutions. Rent sharing is often not successful. In conditions where resources are regionally concentrated, central governments can set up mechanisms to ensure affected regions receive a larger share of the rents from natural resources than other regions. This has been done for oil producing regions in Nigeria, but special arrangements did not manage to stop the violent conflicts that have disrupted election and oil production. However, transparency can help, in the sense that it can help restrain government corruption, and reduce misperceptions—Chad adopted measures to this extent in 1999 but the success of these are as yet unclear. Beyond financial transfers and transparency, an ongoing dialogue among the various stakeholders—and promotion of this by firms and NGOs—is critical, for example, to formulate ex-ante guidelines on ways incomes will be spent. Neglect of local concerns is not only unjust but also unsustainable. Finally, the conditions of mineral extraction necessitate additional attention to human rights and security, including avoiding abuses by security forces, and intensified dialogue with local communities.

Sources: Green (2008); Ross (2008).

Despite large social–political diversity across the continent, the broad recent history of post-colonial development provides an important starting point for a discussion of social policy regimes. The countries, by and large (and with exceptions like South Africa), have much in common regarding a recent elite-driven attempt of nation building, and explicit attempts of simultaneous economic modernization and providing redistributive justice, trying to forge a new social contract. States have taken a predominant role in changing the country's development, and this was often strongly supported by the international community (models that are now often considered failures—such as Nyerere's socialist model in Tanzania—found relatively widespread acceptance).

These social policies emerged out of its colonial predecessors, which were "selective, discriminatory, and exclusionary, geared to protecting and advancing colonial interests and those of white settlers" (Aina, 1999: 76). As late as 1972–76, the ratio of Zimbabwean government expenditure on education for black and white children was 1:12 (Osei-Hwedie and Bar-on, 1999: 93). Post-colonial social policies—often aimed at addressing this historical injustice—have had a strong focus on redistribution rather than productive investment, and a key issue to consider is the centrality of a residual approach to social policy in the continent, and how the crisis and adjustment have reinforced this.

Various factors that set these countries apart are important for the discussion on social policy.[8] In the first place, the large differences in levels of inequality.[9] The settler economies of southern Africa show very high levels of income inequality. Mainly in South Africa, social policy trends since the end of Apartheid are a direct response to inequalities, particularly the main racial divides. Ghana, which was not a settler economy, provides an intermediate case in terms of overall income inequalities, but regional differences are large and greatly influence the public policy sphere, similar to Nigeria where the federal state is a direct response to regional differences. Tanzania, for example, has had much lower levels of income inequality, following the public policies of the post-colonial period.

The way ethnic and racial identities have been incorporated into post-colonial social policy frameworks has been central to the development of nation states as well as articulation of interests of minorities or deprived groups, and of course, this too forms a central constituent of the articulation of social policy. In South Africa, Apartheid—much stronger than in other countries—enshrined and codified racial differences and categories into public policy framework. In post-Apartheid South Africa, affirmative action for the ethnic or racial majority became a key component of social and economic policies, similar to the way identity politics have come to play an important role, particularly in Brazil (though, of course, Brazil did not

[8] To my knowledge, few studies exist that describe histories of colonial social policy and how these influenced approaches after Independence, and the differences between, for example, Anglo- and Francophone countries' social policies (for example, a stronger emphasis on insurance approaches in Francophone countries). Manji (2000) provides a short sketch for the African context.

[9] See the foregoing discussion; qualitative studies include Anderson and McKay (2004); Milanovic (2003); Nel (2003); World Bank (2005).

experience the dramatic policy reversal of South Africa). Box 6.2 describes the reforms in South Africa's pension scheme, how the current universal scheme emerged out of its racially based predecessor.

Box 6.2 Social Pensions in South Africa

In South Africa, social pensions are paid to men aged 65 and above and women aged 60 and above. The entitlements are means-tested on the income of the individual beneficiary and the spouse. In 1993, there were just above 1.5 million old age pensions being paid, with 1.2 million being paid to blacks, and this grew rapidly through the 1990s. It reaches poor rural areas, has had an impact on poverty, and has redistributed income. It is funded through general taxation, absorbing 60 percent of social security expenditure, and 1.4 percent of the GDP in 2002.

Social pension were introduced in South Africa in 1928. These were means-tested old age grants for whites and coloreds, and blacks were explicitly excluded. The entitlement was extended to blacks in 1944, but with lower entitlements and with stricter conditions. After the end of Apartheid, the racist principles were of course abolished, entitlements became equal in 1996, and parity achieved through a range of measures, including tightening means test for whites. Interestingly, in South Africa, this social pension with its origins under Apartheid, and not without contestation, has been looked upon as a basis for the development of a comprehensive social security system.

Other African countries with a social pension program include Burkina Faso, Cameroon, Mauritius, Namibia, Botswana, Lesotho, Swaziland, and Kenya, many with high coverage of the population (80–100 percent), and many universal. Costs as percentage of GDP vary between 0.5 percent in Botswana and 2.4 percent in Lesotho. Many of the schemes use modern bank transfers, to bank accounts and commercial ATMs.

Source: Barrientos (2008); Casey and McKinnon (2009); Cichon (2009).

In other countries too, social policies and ethnic differences are closely interlinked. Tanzania's *ujamaa* strategy was part of a project of nation building, creation of nationalism, and cultural decolonization. In Rwanda, affirmative action became part of the politics leading up to the extremely violent inter-ethnic strife (Mamdani, 2001). In Nigeria, 470 ethnic groups, and the long-standing inequalities between south and north, form the heart of the Federal Character Principle, the constitutional provisions for power sharing and protection of disadvantaged groups (Ibrahim, 2006). Distribution of access to bureaucratic jobs and resources still plays a key role in the fragile nation state, in which federal institutions must reflect its federal character. Zimbabwe's social policies of the 1990s (during growing inequality and increasing gaps in financial capacity) need be understood in context of the 1980s which tried to reduce racial gaps in living standards, and focused on transfer of income rather than wealth. Even Zimbabwe's recent crisis and Mugabe's increasingly despotic rule can been seen as a result of the recent nature of nation building: according to Mamdani (2008), it is conceivable that Zimbabweans will see the period 2000–03 as the end of the settler colonial era.

A further reason why social policy analysis is relevant for Africa is because of the size of the state or public expenditure, as was discussed in Chapter 3. Public spending as part of GDP in Africa is substantial, partly under the influence of aid. Domestic revenue has shown a significant rise over the last decade: from 15 percent of GDP in 1997 to 19 percent in 2006 (Cichon, 2009).

Levels of spending also show large cross-country variety, with, according to existing data, little change during the 1990s. The unequal economies of southern Africa have large states, and, for example, South Africa clearly indicates how state intervention historically has been related to elite capture, which after the end of Apartheid has been transformed to enhance equity. The social pension scheme described in Box 6.2 is an example; this is often described as part of the new social protection agenda, and the relevance for poorer parts of Africa remains to be tested, but in itself, it is an important case of how social policies evolve. In comparison, Uganda in particular has much lower state spending. This may be linked to its pattern of adjustment, but another country that has followed adjustment, Ghana, has a much larger state. Spending figures by themselves tell us little about public and social policy, and probably very little about poverty and human development outcomes, but serve mainly as an indication of the enormous variety across the continent, and justification for further investigation of the determinants of public policy in the South.

As elsewhere, the African continent shows much variation in spending on the different social sectors, with comparable data being relatively scarce and showing year-to-year fluctuation, and with donors playing an important role in determining patterns of spending, particularly in (among the countries listed in Table 6.2) Malawi, Uganda, and Zambia. The South African state is relatively large, as are Zimbabwe's and Ghana's. As elsewhere, public health spending generally has been low, notably in countries like Nigeria and Kenya. Education receives somewhat more attention, for example, in Kenya and Uganda. Social spending is high particularly in Malawi, according to available data, and particularly high in health—but of course, with the low levels of GDP, total spending remains very low and

Table 6.2 Public and Social Spending in Africa

	GDP per capita (US$) 2005 PPP	*Government revenue (% GDP)*	*Public spending on education (% GDP)*	*Public spending on health (% GDP)*	*Social security expenditure (% total government revenue)*	*ODA (% GNI)*	*Aid allocated to social sectors (% total aid) 2007*
Ghana (2004–05)	1,119	23.8	5	2	n.a.	9.2	46
Kenya (2005)	1,346	20.2	7	2	0	4.1	18
Malawi (2003)	630	n.a.	6	10	n.a.	21.4	48
Nigeria (2005)	1,731	n.a.	n.a.	1	n.a.	11.4	39
South Africa (2005)	8,478	30.8	5	4	2	0.3	63
Tanzania (1999–05)	1,049	n.a.	2	3	n.a.	14.5	31
Uganda (2004–05)	846	12.6	5	2	n.a.	16.7	51
Zambia (2002–05)	1,183	17.2	2	3	0	14.6	58
Zimbabwe (1997–2001)	n.a.	29.5	5	2	3	11.7	51

Sources: World Bank World Development Indicators, available at http://data.worldbank.org/data-catalog/world-development-indicators (accessed in December 2009); UNDP (2009b) (last 2 columns).

it is likely that a very large proportion of the social spending is from donors (20 percent of Malawi's GNI is international aid). Social spending in Zimbabwe also appears to have been relatively high, but with increasingly poor human development indicators with the country's descent into civil and political strife.

The Post-colonial Project: Dualism and Universalism Competing

Social policies in many countries in Africa (like elsewhere) obtained a strongly dualistic nature. This manifested itself along a number of axes. A first form, created under colonial rule, was between urban and rural areas. For example, in Malawi and Zambia (but much less so in Tanzania) there was a strong urban bias, toward higher level, urban-based curative facilities in their health sector expenditure patterns. Within the agricultural sector, a strong dualism manifested itself through the support to modern, often export-oriented large enterprises. Malawi's support focused on coffee and estate agriculture (disrupted by the economic shock of 1979), and maize production did receive some support too. This bias was still felt to exist in 2002 (Government of Malawi, 2002). Similarly, in South Africa,

> the legacy of exclusion and discrimination in South African agriculture…[poses] the challenge…to improve participation in all facets of the sector and rid it once and for all of the many entry barriers rooted in its historical dualism. (Department of Agriculture, South Africa, 2001)

Within the urban sector, a clear dualism was created between what came to be known as the formal and informal sectors. Welfare provisions were made available to employees in larger enterprises, in public and private sector—which in most poor countries never formed more than 10 percent of the working population. Even recently, only 3 percent of Kenya's elderly population received any pension benefits, and 5 million of a total of 7 million workers had no coverage at all (Kakwani, Son, and Hinz, 2006). Attempts to extend provisions outside the formal sector have remained limited.

Extension of social security is considered particularly problematic in Africa, and seen as a key element of the development failures that manifested itself during the 1970s and 1980s (ISSA, 2008). At present, usually not more than 5–10 percent of the workforce of African countries is covered by social insurance, though new policies emphasize national social security plans, community-based schemes, and tax-financed social pensions (van Ginneken, 2010).

There has been little social mobilization for extension of provisions outside the formal sector. Trade unions, by and large, have restricted their activities to large-scale enterprises (in India, as we will discuss in Chapter 7, the advocacy activities of SEWA highlight the difficulties of stepping outside the boundaries of operating within the formal sector). For employers in the formal sector, the introduction of provisions tend to be an incentive to try reduce numbers of employees, including women, or to try to escape registration of economic activity altogether. The key point for the argument about the application of a notion of social policy with respect to labor markets in the poorest countries is the following. The informal–formal distinction is not just a sign of underdevelopment, but is also policy induced. It reflects a dualistic approach to social policy which restricts benefits to a segment of the population, even if unintentionally (for example, extension of traditional social security mechanisms is technically difficult and administratively costly). But the distinction also reflects the continued aspiration of the modernization thinking, expecting absorption of workers in the formal or modern sector. This has proven increasingly elusive, as since the 1960s and the 1970s, the percentage of workers in the modern sector has usually stagnated or declined, but arguably, the hope of extension of a modern sector has held up a search for alternative mechanisms (which the new social protection agenda now provides).

While it is often argued that the most important social policy change in the last decades has been toward targeting, and refinement of that targeting, using the poverty analysis and social funds discussed earlier, it is important to emphasize that the principles of targeting are by no means new. They fit within particular historical traditions, as much as universalist and insurance principles do. Africa—as well as Asia, as we discuss later—has long traditions of targeted programs. Tanzania, by and large, avoided the urban bias of other countries in the region. But its forced *ujamaa* villageization can be described as a regional targeted anti-poverty intervention, to provide inputs, education, and health to the remote rural poor, continuous with colonial policy.

Targeting also played a key role after independence, with economic as well as political arguments. The post-colonial project with modernist ideologies and inward-oriented development reinforced—even if unintentionally—an economic and social dualism that was established under colonialism. Social policies in many African countries obtained a strongly dualistic[10] nature,

[10] This, thus, also has characteristics of corporatist principles, but the term dualist seems more appropriate, to emphasize the state-driven nature of the divide between a modern and traditional or informal sector.

despite a strong universalistic and often rights-based approach to welfare. And with economic crises, and adjustment and globalization, an increasing number of workers fall outside the modern or organized segment of the labor force, highlighting the increasingly large need but also enormous challenges for ways of extending social policies beyond the boundaries created through the earlier dualist approaches. The focus on targeting and the poverty analysis that has supported this in the later period, while reaching out to the poorest, have contributed to further segmentation of the population as receivers of social services.

During the 1960s and 1970s, thus, moves from dual to universal systems were significant. After independence, provisions for health and education expanded rapidly, often in explicit response to the stratification created under colonialism. In Zimbabwe, free education was committed overnight, and over 5,500 schools established in six years, and massive infrastructure was put in place to enhance access to clinics. In Zambia, 880,000 new school places were created between 1964 and 1984 and the number of health centers grew by more than 160 percent by 1988 (Osei-Hwedie and Bar-on, 1999: 93). Zimbabwe became "a human development success story" in the decade after independence in 1980, with a sharp reversal during the early 1990s (Watkins, 2001). In South Africa, after the end of Apartheid—with much better fiscal conditions than other African countries—a similar push toward universalization was made. However, in most of Africa, this progress ended abruptly with the onset of adjustment, and the gaps have been greatly deepened with the outbreak of HIV/AIDS, and political leaders' failure to address this as in the case of South Africa (Green, 2008: 235), which not only challenged health systems well beyond its limits but also impacted health personnel itself.

As in Latin America, the dualist focus on provisions for the minority of workers in the modern sector has been combined with universal provisions in health and education. Most countries developed national health care systems and compulsory education, often constitutionally enshrined. Of course, high proportions of private out-of-pocket spending, particularly in health, indicate significant deficiencies, which were worsened at least during the earlier phases of adjustment. As mentioned earlier, fiscal constraints and efficiency came to dominate the social policy debate, notably in discussions on user fees.[11] Notwithstanding the emphasis on adjustment, donors have continued to emphasize universal provision of health care and education. In fact, the debate around user fees in the 1980s highlighted the

[11] Appleton (2001); Gilson and McIntyre (2005); Thobani (1983); Watkins (2001).

strength of arguments for universal approaches, in response to externally imposed experiments. Approaches, again often donor supported, have been increasingly on provisions at primary levels, which according to some, neglects the role of higher education, including as a precondition of a developmental welfare state. Recent "vertical" donor initiatives, including by now very significant private organizations like the Gates Foundation, are given a renewed push to the health provisions—though arguably with limited attention to the needs for a broad approach to strengthening the capacity of health systems.

The universalist aspirations of the post-colonial governments were only very partially achieved. As discussed, the period of adjustment—with increasing international influence, though this too has contained different ideological influences—had a strong emphasis on targeting, which even the more recent approaches in the area of social protection continue to support. What remains to be seen is if this can become part of a broader universalist agenda, including of "targeting within universalism," and whether institutions like the African Union and, of course, African governments can revive the earlier aspirations, which were greatly disappointed under the influence of conflicts and structural adjustment, to which we turn next.

Structural Adjustment and Beyond?

The impact of structural adjustment on social policy has been significant in most countries on the continent, as was already discussed in the first part of the book, and much more so than in Asia (and less in South Africa than elsewhere in Africa). As highlighted by Aina (2004) and Adésínà (2006), the onset of structural adjustment implied a sharp break in trends in ideas, and health and education service provision, which had seen considerable improvements during the 1960s and 1970s. In the same period, civil unrest and wars in many countries—often fueled by the Cold War—brought an effective end to the experiments of the early years of independence. As Osei-Hwedie and Bar-on (1999: 98) stress,

> [N]ewly constructed schools, clinics and hospitals could no longer be maintained...transportation, water delivery, and electricity supplies also staggered or, more often, degenerated...large numbers of trained personnel left for greener pastures, undermining the delivery of existing services and the development of new initiatives.

The short period of the developmental state was not able to overcome the dualism that had been created under colonialism and reinforced after independence, and adjustment marked the end of the short experiment, pushing the agenda toward further cost reduction and targeting of services and benefits.

Since the 1980s, there has been a forceful critique of structural adjustment—with Cornia, Jolly, and Stewart (1987) probably the most-frequently cited (and followed by many others) critique of the social impact of structural adjustment. It is beyond doubt that the 1980s and 1990s reversed many of the positive trends of the earlier decades after independence, but it remains a matter of debate whether an internationally imposed structural adjustment program was responsible, and whether it is justified to attribute a large impact of structural adjustment on poverty (Killick, 1999), or whether it was the economic crisis and policy failures that were responsible for these reversals (and for the need for adjustment, and a search for new donor approaches). The international community, including the World Bank, did respond to international critique and events following adjustment programs in Africa, with the emphasis on poverty monitoring to measure the impact of adjustment programs, and the introduction of social funds, initially in Ghana, then spreading to a large number of African countries—but both initiatives, as we demonstrated earlier, reinforced residual approaches to social policy.

While most countries in sub-Saharan Africa have been marked by two decades of stagnation, the patterns have not been uniform of course. There is a group of countries marked as failing states, with the largest concentration of chronically deprived people and groups,[12] and large part of the world's "bottom billion" (Collier, 2007). In areas of civil conflict, the preconditions for inclusive social policies are absent, and besides kick-starting economic growth, these countries are typically challenged to create a social contract alongside the basic functions of nation-states. Structural adjustment did not lift these countries out of the crisis, and some of the policies since adjustment have worsened their predicament (such as the relative neglect of agriculture), but many of the problems are not directly attributable to adjustment.

But there is also a group of countries that has done relatively well over the last decade or more. For example, Ghana which seems to have followed the path of adjustment promoted by international institutions has had relatively stable economic progress, while maintaining relatively strong and

---

[12] Chronic Poverty Research Centre (2008: 9–15). The number of chronically poor people in sub-Saharan Africa is estimated to be as large or slightly larger than in South Asia. About 40 of the 76 "chronically deprived countries" are in sub-Saharan Africa (not all of which are "failed states," like Tanzania).

democratic institutions. It reduced the size of the public sector during the early 1980s, but spending in health and education has remained substantial. It introduced a National Health Insurance Scheme in 2001, to replace out-of-pocket fees (Agyepong and Adjei, 2008). Ghana's leadership did use donor resources, to build up political alliances, but also with relatively good results in economic and social development. The proportion of spending has remained fairly stable since the 1980s, and is seen, by some international agencies, as relatively large, in relative and not in absolute terms of course.[13]

Uganda is often quoted as a more recent success story, though currently with much weaker institutions than Ghana. It emerged from a civil war in the mid-1980s, but has remained involved in regional conflicts. Notably, it became one of the darlings of the donor community, as the documentary, *Our Friends at the Bank* (First Run/Icarus Films), very well demonstrates, and a leading example of the PRSP approach described earlier (but see Dijkstra and van Donge, 2001), creating a stable economic environment and fairly stable economic growth during the 1990s. This included significant investments in social sectors, much of it financed by the international community, including through the additional funding that became available through debt relief. The governance agenda that the new aid modalities promoted implied a support to democracy, but at the same time, strong support to strong leaders like Museveni in Uganda.

At least till the onset of the 2008 crisis, many African countries experienced significant economic recovery, and in many countries, this happened under relatively democratic regimes. Donors remained very important in a large number of these countries, and many of them did prioritize policies in health, education, and increasingly, the new generation of social protection instruments, including cash transfers such as the recent program for children in Kenya as described in Box 6.3.

For the foreseeable future, the economic and social development in many if not most African countries cannot be seen in isolation from international aid. In the TV documentary, *Addicted to Aid* (BBC One, Monday, November 24, 2008), Sorious Samura asks a group of Ugandan economics students about their career plans, and a majority indicate plans to work for international aid organizations (as opposed to Ugandan companies). One of the key challenges for a social policy agenda is the development of new traditions of social policy which are rooted in local contexts. No doubt the international community—in its great diversity, including through the

[13] Aryeetey and McKay (2005). World development indicatorse show an increase of government revenue as percentage of GDP from 18 percent in 2001 to 24 percent in 2004.

Box 6.3 Cash Transfers in Africa: The Example of Kenya

Kenya has a variety of social protection programs in place. A WFP-supported School Feeding Program operates in slums in Nairobi and food-insecure districts. An Emergency Food-Aid program reaches around 1.8 million people in arid and semi-arid areas. A Hunger Safety Net Program (HSNP) is a pilot program being implemented by the government with DFID support. A national drought contingency fund is supported by World Bank and the European Commission (EC). Labor market and public works programs are limited, while pension systems cover only half of the employed in the formal sector.

In 2009, DFID, UNICEF, and the World Bank approved support worth US$ 73 million for the project Cash Transfer for Orphans and Vulnerable Children Project (CT-OVC). This aims to provide protection for orphans and vulnerable children, of which there are an estimated 2.4 million in Kenya. It provides a social safety net access for extremely poor households, through expansion of the existing government-financed program, and hoping to increase government capacity for social protection policies with the Ministry of Gender, Children and Social Development developing a National Social Protection Strategy.

Source: World Bank, Kenya, 2009.

critique of aid like those by Moyo (2009)—will continue to exert great influence on finance and ideas. It will be essential that new public policies are carved out of this international exchange, and that the international community creates the space for the development of national capacity and policy traditions. Aid can help development, but it does so only under specific conditions, notably local capacity and commitment that channels aid in the right directions—a condition that to a large extent has been absent.

Fragmentation of Social Policy Formulation

In Africa, social policy formulation has been fragmented, particularly since the 1970s. Experts that discussed the "integration of social and economic policies" in 2001 noted that the narrow policy focus of the 1980s still existed, and highlighted an imbalance in power between finance and social ministries.[14] The international community has played a key role in this, including through the strengthening of finance ministries and not social

[14] de Haan, Huber, and van der Heever (2001); this argument is probably less true for health and education sectors, where sector-wide approaches have done much to support capacity.

sector ministries, donors' sectoral approaches, and through the unpredictability and short-term nature of aid flows. And it runs the risk, in my view, of missing opportunities to promote constructive dialogue on enhancing social policies—including about how they can promote economic growth—through institutions like the G20 and the African Union.

As described earlier, the impact of structural adjustment on social sector spending is not as clear as much critique has suggested. While total funding for health and education in most countries is clearly inadequate, and adjustment policies and sector reforms have emphasized spending efficiency, the trends in spending as share of overall spending or GDP do not show a clear downward trend under adjustment. Recent trends, particularly under debt relief, show a clearly upward trend. But as mentioned earlier, there is a great amount of volatility. For example, in Malawi, significant fluctuation in percentage shares to poverty-reducing areas have been observed, which have been attributed, partly, to levels of donor funding (Government of Malawi, 2002: 15). Box 6.4 demonstrates this with respect to Ghana.

Box 6. 4 Social Policy Financing in Ghana

Aryeetey and Goldstein (2000) highlight the lack of articulated social policy in the case of Ghana, a country which has been relatively stable in political and economic terms, and a relatively string civil service (Agyepong and Adeji, 2008). Policy during the 1960s and 1970s focused on rural development and higher education, but state capacity soon started to weaken, while donor influence increased. Ghana followed a path of fiscal compression early on with state expenditure plummeting from 25 percent of GDP in 1976 to 8 percent in 1983 (Herbst, 1994).

Rapid changes in government social sector spending can be seen as an indication or even cause of fragmentation of policy making. Social sector spending as share of total government spending increased during 1960–65, then fell, rose to 46 percent in 1975, fell to 33 percent in 1981, rose during the 1980s, and fell again to about 35 percent in 1996 (Aryeetey and Goldstein, 2000: 295–301). Even in post-reform Ghana, expenditure patterns are driven largely by revenue flows and political expediency, and do not appear to follow clear commitments to policies and expected outcomes (Aryeetey and McKay, 2005).

Sources: Aryeetey and Goldstein (2000); Aryeetey and McKay (2005); Herbst (1994).

Such fluctuations, and a lack of coordination among funders, are compounded by a disconnect with democratic processes. With a strong influence of donors, welfare funding decisions are largely made outside the domestic political system. The PRSP approach, even with its emphasis on broad participation in policy formulation, to some extent reinforced the apolitical nature of policy making in aid-dependent countries. Donors have put a lot of emphasis on enhancing the accountability of aid, but this has tended to focus on accountability to the tax-payers in donors' countries (de Haan, 2009c), which does not necessarily reinforce the accountability mechanisms from citizens to states in the recipient countries. The modality of donors funding has tended to limit the development of feedback mechanisms that followed from the political dynamic of group interests, social stratification, and political mobilization described by Esping-Andersen and Lindert. While such a disconnect may make budget execution more effective and less contested, it does not promote the development of a sustained social contract; instead, it runs the risk of reinforcing charitable state–citizen relationships.

A predominant role of international NGOs has reinforced fragmentation. While the US social policy models include sustained contributions to core welfare provisions by civil society organizations, NGOs in developing countries are not or much less home grown. The focus of NGOs, or the principles of solidarity that they purport, varies considerably. Their programs with developmental objectives play a role in delivery of universal basic services like education or rural development, through microfinance programs, or targeted poverty programs, and humanitarian aid. A key question in contexts where NGOs play an important role is how they combine their programs with government provisions, or under government regulation, and whether this adds up to a coherent national social policy, or—particularly in the case of external funding—neglects the development of local accountability and even fuels patronage politics. This is not to underrate the importance of NGOs and civil society, but an argument to incorporate them into a broader public policy analysis, and consider their impact—through project implementation and the global debate on aid, particularly in the social sectors—on enhancing state capacity.

Despite considerable attention to social sector programs, and most recently social protection, the argument here is that these have not added up to coordinated well-articulated social policy. The PRSP approaches we discussed earlier had the potential to build toward these, moving away from the projectized approach of earlier development "interventions," but their promises materialized only very partially, and donor dependency is only very slowly being reduced, with international aid in many African countries still forming more than 20 percent of the public finances, and an increasing number of donors further complicating policy making. In this context, social policy analysis should include a focus on the reasons for the gap in the articulation of social policy and how the international community influences this, and how this particular mode of public policy implementation impacts citizens' well-being and opportunities to shape public policy.

What is the Role of Social Policy in the Poorest Countries?

Of course, the development of a comprehensive social policy framework is not seen as the panacea for Africa's development problems, but social policy is a critical accompaniment of economic growth and efforts to promote this. The potentials of extending social security are severely hampered by demographic as well as economic constraints. In many countries, the political and institutional preconditions for adequate social policies barely exist, and recent attempts to promote social protection, while valuable, merely scratch at the surface of the broader development problems (see Adésínà, 2010). These constraints are intensified under globalization: while histories of East Asia and India, as described later, show the central role of public policies in managing the diverse aspects of globalization, countries in Africa are likely to benefit from current globalization "only if they possess what most of them manifestly lack—sound institutions" (Eyoh and Sandbrook, 2003: 244–45). Continued donor dependency, among other things, continues to hinder the creation of the social contract that is an essential element of any social policy. The recent financial crisis may not have affected Africa most, but it—and of course, the preceding crisis in food prices—once again highlights the external forces over which African countries have no control but do have to adapt to.

The point in the context of the framework proposed in this book is that even in the world's poorest continent, there is both political and analytical value in applying a notion of social policy. Elites in Africa, after independence, engaged in a political project of modernization and addressing historical inequalities. In most cases, these projects failed with the onset of economic crisis and adjustment. An expansion of social policy was hampered by continued economic stagnation, and very limited urbanization and industrialization (and hence, broadening of political alliances)—but at the same time, the social policy agenda was succeeded by a "poverty agenda" and attention to social sectors never waned, and has been reinforced, most recently, by a new social protection agenda which many analysts believe to be affordable and has the potential to be development oriented, but is no panacea for the deep-rooted poverty and institutional problems.

The development of social policy in Africa cannot be seen in isolation from the development of the basic institutions of state functioning more generally. While there is not one "model" of governance, the expansion of services needs to be accompanied by the strengthening of capacity and accountability. However, it is important to highlight that this does not necessarily impose a trade-off, but that social policy development itself can be, and historically, has been part of the development of social contracts. The multiple internationally imposed crises of 2008–09 reinforce this once more. The strengthening of broad social policy approaches, as proposed by the African Union, can and should play an important role in this. Though aid dependency is declining in quite a few countries, donors will continue to play an important role in influencing development priorities, and it is critical that they create the policy space for an integrated social policy agenda.

7

East Asia

Social Policy's Role in Economic Success

The literature on social policy in East Asia has seen rapid growth over the last two decades. Overwhelmingly, this has characterized social policies in the region, with all its diversity, as predominantly corporatist, with a very strong "productivist" focus, and intentional congruence between economic and social policy. Most countries in Asia have proactive—but selective—social policies, designed to play a key role in its patterns of economic growth and globalization. Countries in the region introduced welfare policies at a lower level of development than OECD countries, and with clearly articulated strategies to learn from international experience.[1]

East Asian social policies have played a key role in nation building. Egalitarian norms have been centrally important, often under authoritarian practices, vis-à-vis labor and citizens' rights. Emphasis has been on equality or equity focused on productive opportunities, with social spending remaining low, confirming Pierson's (2004: 15) thesis that the welfare states of late industrializers have been smaller and less redistributive. Benefits have tended to be skewed to sections of the working population, and liberal residual notions can be traced in ways programs for others have been formulated.

Of course, social policies in the East Asian region are not uniform. They vary across the more developed economies of Japan and South Korea, to the

[1] Hort and Kuhnle (2000); see Holliday (2000), Gough (2004a), and Kwon (2005a), among others, for analysis of East Asian social policies.

emerging economies of China and Thailand, to the low-income countries of Vietnam and Cambodia. In countries like Japan and Korea, social insurance schemes have been central to the welfare states, while provident funds have been dominant in Singapore and Malaysia. China's social security systems is still relatively young, but probably rapidly expanding even after the 2008 financial downturn. Vietnam and China share historical similarities of state socialism and continued party control, leading one observer to suggest the notion of a Marxist–Leninist welfare regime, which included a drastic process of commodification of social provisions in the early stages of reform (London, 2009).

This chapter, similar to the next one, describes East Asian policies along thematic lines using the framework of Ian Gough describing the main drivers of social policy change in this rapidly developing region, with a focus on the emerging economies of China and Vietnam.[2] It begins with a description of levels of public spending.

Public Spending: Investing in the Future

In terms of quantitative importance of the state, according to the simple indicators used in Table 7.1, East Asia shows considerable variety. The states in Malaysia and Thailand are relatively large. South Korea's state remained relatively small in proportion to its GDP, but now seems close to the average. China's government expenditure forms 11 percent of GDP according to the international data. Total government expenditure showed an increase since 1980, then sharply declining till 1995, and again increasing after that.[3] The low and declining spending during the reform period was not accompanied by the emphasis on a small state as the Washington Consensus highlighted. The state has maintained a strong steer of social policy along-side economic policy, and has strengthened this in response to macro-level transitions and crises.

Social spending in the region has remained relatively low, but also with much variety across the region. Social policies in the region have expanded during periods of economic growth as well as after economic crises,

[2] This is based on the joint paper with Gita Sabharwal, and I owe most of the insights into Vietnam's social policies to Gita. For China, see, for example, Hussain (n.d.), Zhang Xiaojiang, and Salazar (2007). The impact of crises is discussed more extensively in de Haan (2010).

[3] Central government revenue declined from 31 percent in 1978 to 15 percent in the early 1990s (Leonard, 2008: 37). According to Song Li (2009), inclusion of extra-budgetary revenues would lift the fiscal revenue number above that of many OECD; and fiscal revenues doubled from 10 to 20 percent between 1998 and 2008.

Table 7.1 Social Expenditure in Asia

	GDP per capita (US$) 2005 PPP	*Government revenue (% GDP)*	*Public spending on education (% GDP)*	*Public spending on health (% GDP)*	*Social security expenditure (% total government revenue)*
Bangladesh (2004–05)	1027	10.0	2	1	n.a.
Cambodia (2004–05)	1440	9.7	2	2	n.a.
China (1999–2005)	4088	9.6	2	2	n.a.
India (2005)	2230	12.6	3	1	0
Indonesia (2004)	3078	18.4	3	1	3
Malaysia (2003)	10803	23.7	8	3	n.a.
Pakistan	2184	13.0	–	–	–
South Korea (2004–05)	21273	23.3	5	3	16
Thailand (2005–06)	7378	20.2	4	2	5
Vietnam (2005)	2143	n.a.	n.a.	2	n.a.
East Asia and Pacific (2005)	3893	11.0	–	–	–
South Asia (2005)	2077	12.7	–	–	–

Source: World Bank, World Development Indicators, available at http://data.worldbank.org/data-catalog/world-development-indicators (accessed in December 2009).

where in the case of South Korea, the expansion happened partly as a result of civil society pressure to expand social security. In China, expenditure on social services as percentage of total government spending has gradually increased. However, China's data exclude spending through state enterprises and individual workers (Guan, 2005: 251–52).

East Asian countries like South Korea introduced social welfare policies earlier than OECD countries at similar levels of development (for example, in terms of levels of urbanization) but social investments were selective, with relatively high shares of health and education rather than safety nets, and benefits were often limited to workers in the formal sectors (with social insurance in large firms), and with little targeting to or benefits for the poor. South Korea's social policy was very closely linked to a policy emphasis on enhancing growth and productivity, and in line with the nationalist emphasis of public policies, and the strong interventionism in markets (Kwon, 2005b, 2005c). After the 1997 crisis, that instrumentality is thought to have been weakened somewhat. According to Schmidt (forthcoming), relatively high public spending on education is an expression of the future orientation of all East Asian welfare regimes, notably in Hong Kong, Singapore (where education spending is second only to defense), South Korea, Taiwan, and Japan—though private spending is equally important in most cases.

In the 1970s, "Indonesia was unusual in being able to invest heavily in both infrastructure and human capital in the early stages of its development because of financial support from donors and then from oil revenues" (Timmer, 2004). Currently, Indonesia's state size is about average according to our simple indicator, with very low social spending shares. Indonesia's experience can possibly also be categorized as Bonapartist and productivist, has been beneficial to the poor, under a repressive and centralized policy regime. While public investment contributed to a rapid spread of access to health and education, investments in health and education, and certainly social security, remained low. Indonesia's experience shows the importance of non-social sectors for poverty reduction, including rural finance, and investment in agricultural infrastructure promoting labor intensity under a low-wage regime. The 1997–98 crisis brought some dramatic changes to the social policy orientation, alongside political changes, and has probably increased social spending, with a range of immediate measures in response to the crisis and the establishment of a nation-wide decentralized targeted social safety net.

Vietnam's state is large according to indicator of public revenue and spending, as is Malaysia's, but for different historical reasons. In Vietnam, social spending, according to the international data, has been low, but levels have been increasing, and national-level data provide higher figures. World Bank data showed a decrease in government health spending from 5 percent to 3 percent between 1994 and 2002, and increase in education spending from 8 percent to 10 percent; more recent trends show the share of health spending remaining about the same, and education spending going up. Social security spending is at about 11 percent of government spending, and regressive, while targeted poverty programs take up about 3 percent of the government budget.[4] Efforts in Vietnam to reposition the targeted poverty reduction programs into a comprehensive and universal social protection system, prioritization of universal health insurance, and (at slower pace) universalization of old-age insurance, similarly reflect the potentials of social policies in a global economy.

Social expenditure in Thailand is substantial as proportion of total government spending, though this does not amount to a comprehensive system of social policy (Kwon, 2005b: 19), and only 19 percent of the workforce was covered by social security (Suwannarat, 2003: 228). While family and community responsibility form a key part of traditions of welfare provisions, the government's role in social services started to expand during the 1970s, with emphasis on equitable access to education and health, and gradual extension of a universal health insurance system, reinforced during economic crises. In Thailand, as in Indonesia, the 1997–98 crisis brought significant changes to the social policy orientation, including through expansion of health care provisions and pensions for the poor.

The Great East Asian Transformation

Social policy changes in East Asia are driven by at least three sets of dramatic changes at a macro level. First, urbanization is happening at great pace, highlighted by the 150–200 million migrants (or "floating population") in China, and similar proportions in Vietnam. Second, rapid industrialization and expansion of tertiary sector is accompanied by a managed process of privatization of former state-owned means of production, and equally carefully managed reforms in agriculture (with great similarities between China and Vietnam). Third, particularly in China which implemented a vigorous one-child policy, the great transformation is accompanied by a rapid ageing of the population.

---

[4] Klump and Bonschab (2005); data from the government and World Bank provided by Gita Sabharwal, DFID, Vietnam.

Each of these developments has demanded rapid development of social policies—and indeed arguably, the successes have greatly benefited from the rapid social policy responses.[5] Urbanization in China, combined with the job losses from privatization, has demanded the development of a minimum income program, restricted to urban residents (that is, those with an urban *hukou* or registration), alongside the macroeconomic policies that explicitly have targeted the creation of 7–9 million jobs per year (hence, the target of at least 7 percent GDP growth per year). The *di bao* program is described in the next box (Box 7.1).

Box 7.1 China's Urban *di bao*

The new social assistance program Minimum Living Standard Scheme was piloted in Shanghai in the early 1990s, and has been extended rapidly since the late 1990s, including different categories of poor urban households. Initially focused on income transfers, at the level of the difference between a household's income and the minimum living standard, it has been broadened to education, health exemptions and housing. It is administered by the Ministry of Civil Affairs, and as other schemes is operated on a decentralized basis with local governments having space for experimentation and regulation, including the setting of the minimum standard of living. The decentralized nature of the program and the public finance difficulties of province and county administrations have led to much lower levels of spending in the poorer parts of the country.

The program has been considered successful, even though coverage remains too low and is only slowly expanding, and impacts vary across localities because of the decentralized implementation. One of the key reasons for success has been the administrative capacity to implement and target the program, and ensure that negative impacts, like on labor supply, are kept to a minimum. There are clear though locally varying rules for eligibility, using a multiplicity of factors (household income, asset tests, sometimes work requirements). Neighborhood communities play a key role and provide much of the human inputs in administering the schemes. For deciding on eligibility—as is common in many sectors in China, and commonly accepted—lists of beneficiaries are publicly displayed with possibility to appeal against inclusion.

The *hukou* system greatly influences the new social policies like *di bao*. Registration remains key for accessing health care and education, and migrants remain excluded from the urban *di bao*. But there are exceptions, such as in Nanjing that integrates rural and urban *di bao* policies.

Sources: Chen, Ravallion, and Wang (2006); Gustafsson and Quheng (2007); Ravallion (2009).

[5] The wide range of China's social security policies is described in the White Paper of 2004, published in English; available at www.china.org.cn/e-white/20040907/index.htm (accessed in May 2010).

While in the OECD literature urbanization and industrialization are seen as key to development of social policy, in the South social policy also focuses on rural areas, as we will also discuss for India in the next chapter, and the new social protection agenda, including in Africa, demonstrates. In the case of China, in the 1980s and the 1990s, public policies came to focus on enabling moving out of agriculture, through relaxation of restrictions on migration (though most migrants still face exclusion from services in urban areas, as described next), and a range of training programs for potential migrants. During the 1980s, the macroeconomic reform strategy was complemented by a focused poverty strategy. In 1986, 15 percent of the country's counties were designated as "poor counties," and the State Council established a Leading Group for Poverty Reduction in 1986, which has managed an annual budget of about Rmb 10 billion since.[6] Current health and social security reforms also have strong rural components, while primary education was made free, aiming to reduce rural–urban differences, and through the gradual introduction of the New Cooperative Medical Scheme (NCMS), and efforts to increase public health spending, particularly in poor areas. Reforms were given a push in 2009 as part of the economic stimulus package following the economic crisis, as described in the next section.

In the case of China, the transformation was accompanied by a remarkable discontinuity in social policy. The economic reforms implied a radical privatization of the economy, and collapse of the social services previously provided through communes and state-owned enterprises. China's policies during the 1980s focused on privatization and economic growth, while accepting increasing inequality. During the 1990s, the forces for strengthening the role of government in public services started to grow, resulting in reforms in education, health, and social security. However, the gaps that were created continue to be significant. In particular, the privatization of health services has led to very large out-of-pocket expenses. This has contributed to very high rates of private savings, and health expenditure is one of the main causes of people falling (back) into poverty.

Another remarkable social policy aspect of the transition in China as well as Vietnam has been the continuation of restrictions on migration,

[6] Provision of credit for development projects has been among the most important forms of support. This targeted approach has been relatively successful in terms of targeting and promoting economic growth, but it has not managed to reverse the national trends of growing inequality, and researchers have pointed at problems of targeting and inefficient project design and fund allocation (Rozelle, Zhang, and Huang, 2000). Moreover, taxation of farmers (till recently) and inflation have been identified as significant factors behind the relative stagnation of rural areas, possibly more important than the opening up to external trade (Ravallion and Chen, 2004).

through the registration system that was created during the pre-reform period, continuing to pervade all aspects of public policies, administration, and surveys. In China, a *hukou* is obtained at birth, and a migrant with a rural *hukou* (and their children) is unlikely to be able to avail of social services in urban areas, or be able to obtain a job in the formal labor market. It is widely recognized that this system needs an overhaul, and there are many areas where local experiments do give migrants access to essential services. Migration has also been recognized as a key element of China's economic growth, and indeed, there are many policies that promote training of and labor market information for migrants, and public policies were put in place to support returning migrants during 2008. Nevertheless, the complete overhaul of the system (including of statistics collection) is likely to be a process of decades rather than years, and the dual system continues to exist.

Demographic changes in China have been particularly dramatic, and will continue to influence social policy over the decades to come. The one-child policy has had an enormous impact on family relations. The rapidly declining dependence ratio arguably has provided an economic stimulus. But over the coming decades, population aging will provide significant challenges for social policy provisions, while the "demographic dividend" is coming to an end. In East Asia as a whole, the population of older people is expected to increase from 11 percent in 2000 to 21 percent by 2021 and 31 percent in 2050 (HelpAge International, 2007: 8), with the Chinese transition being particularly fast. According to a recent OECD report, for a sustainable financing of China's pension system, contributions to pensions should be close to 50 percent of earnings (OECD and World Bank, 2009). The lack of pensions, alongside health, continues to be a major reason for high levels of private savings (and the impact of the economic stimulus is thus not likely to change the propensity to save very quickly).

The Impact of Crises

Economic crises have been crucial for evolving social policy responses in the Asian regions (Kwon, 2008).[7] The crisis of 1997–98 brought very significant changes in the social policy regimes in South Korea, Thailand, and

[7] In one of the early contributions to the East Asia social policy literature, Hort and Kuhnle (2000) describe that countries in the region had introduced welfare policies at a lower level of development than OECD countries, and that these expanded during the growth period as well as after economic crises. Evidence presented here confirms that pattern.

Indonesia, while in China, it reinforced resolve to enhance exports and reserves. Political systems came under pressure, including regarding levels of inequality, particularly the wealth of and corruption among the richest.

While maintaining productivity and international competition remained important, the 1997–98 crisis elicited varied responses. For example, Singapore and Hong Kong maintained the basics of selective welfare provisions. Reforms in both South Korea and Taiwan led to more inclusive approaches (and enhanced democracy), with introduction of employment and health insurance schemes.

> [A]lthough social policy reform in Korea and Taiwan was triggered by the need for economic development, the newly elected governments carried out the reform with a social consensus and established the idea of social rights as the main rationale of the welfare state. (Kwon, 2008: 8)

South Korea increased its social expenditure after the 1997–98 crisis, from low levels and using its strong fiscal position, continuing a trend started earlier during the 1990s (You and Lee, 2001: 306). In terms of organization of its social policy delivery too, reforms that had been on the political agenda for decades were implemented after the crisis in South Korea, particularly the integration of fragmented health funds (Kwon, 2005b). The reforms imply greater inclusiveness, alongside an emphasis on international competitiveness. Besides the strategy for technology development, the Korean government put in place institutional arrangements for structural adjustment, for example, providing benefits and training for people outside the large companies (which started in the mid-1990s). In 1998, the new president established a tripartite committee of employers, employees, and government, which enabled the forging of a new social consensus (Kwon, 2005b: 13). Labor market policies too changed substantially, under pressure from civil society, toward greater inclusiveness from what used to be essentially a dualist system, under the banner of "Productive Welfare." During 1998–99, public works were put in place, forming the largest single budget item (Yi and Lee, 2005: 161). A Minimum Living Standard Guarantee was introduced in 2000.

Thailand government's role in social services started to expand during the 1970s, with emphasis on equitable access to education and health, and gradual extension of a universal health insurance system (Tangcharoensathien, Teokul, and Chanwongpaisarn, 2005). During the crises of the early 1980s and 1997, social programs continued to receive attention, and they formed a key driver of their expansion. In response to the crisis, Thailand put in place schemes to support laid-off workers, provisions for employing vulnerable workers, student loan schemes and scholarships, and support to the elderly (Teokul, 2009). Thailand has a universal health insurance system, which developed from restrictive insurance provisions for civil servants and formal sector employees. In response to the crisis, it put in place a scheme that allows health care costs for individuals not covered under insurance schemes to 30 baht per visit. It achieved universal coverage in 2002, following crisis and the electoral success of the Thai Rak Thai Party which had universal coverage as a commitment during the election (Tangcharoensathien Teokul, and Chanwongpaisarn, 2005).

Like for Thailand, the impact of the 1997–98 crisis on Indonesia was very severe, with among the worst economic contraction, exchange rate collapse, liquidity crunch, banking and corporate sector bankruptcies, and common assertion of a failing IMF response. Compared to other countries in the region, Indonesia's reform process started earlier, and ethnic tensions played a role in policy change. Shortly after the crisis, and with rapidly developing evidence of the negative impact on the populations, Indonesia expanded its social expenditure, with targeted subsidies in health, for schooling, and rice (which helped to promote a global interest in a social protection agenda), arguably moving a little toward a more welfarist regime alongside a process of democratization.

China (as India) was relatively sheltered from the 1997–98 crisis, but reinforced its emphasis on export orientation to enhance fiscal reserves (China did draw very important lessons from events in the 1990s, and the Japanese stagnation). The Government of China's response to the 2008 financial crisis was evolving as this book is written, and some of the details are provided in Box 7.2.

Interests: Nation Building and Elites

An understanding of the productivist nature of East Asia's social policy regimes leads us to focus on the various interests underlying the development models. Gough (2000) uses Holliday's welfare typology of "productivist welfare capitalism"—in which social policy is subordinated to economic policy—and distinguishes three aspects of the "Bonapartist" nature of East Asian social policy: its role in nation building, in securing the loyalty of elites (or "corporatism without labor"), and in helping to legitimize undemocratic regimes. Moreover, in the implementation of social policies, and public policy more generally, East Asia states had the ability to shelter officials from social groups with vested interests, which has been characterized as "embedded autonomy" (Brett, 2003).

Box 7.2 China's Social Policy Response to the Crisis

The impact of the global financial crisis started to be felt in China very quickly, through the closure of export-oriented factories (with sources mentioning 670,000—mostly small—factories). With predictions of a slowdown of economic growth, Premier Wen Jiabao announced a stimulus plan of over US$ 500 billion, to maintain China's economic growth and thus, also support the global economy. The plan includes spending in 10 major sectors, including low-income housing as well as rural infrastructure. The plan included relaxation of the austere fiscal policies which have contributed to China's enormous financial reserves. The way the plan was formulated suggested a continued focus on maintaining steady and relatively fast economic growth, and increase investment efficiency alongside supporting consumer spending.

While expectations that the decline in exports would be a long-lasting phenomenon were taking firmer roots, ideas quickly emerged that China needs to move toward a much stronger inward-oriented development path, with redeployment of resources previously devoted to exports, and a stimulus of domestic consumption, including a rapid expansion of social security. In early 2009, the State Council announced a US$ 123 billion plan for extending universal health care to be established by 2011. This was intended not only to provide basic medical security in both urban and rural areas but also contained a hope that—alongside other measures to stimulate demand, such as vouchers—it would reduce people's needs for high savings.[8]

Many commentators pointed to the structural challenges that stimulus of personal consumption implied (as well as lack of knowledge of reasons for high savings rates). Huang Jing (2009: 8) noted that "when people have to count on their own savings as their safety net, consumption is more a luxury than a necessity." Policies also included measures to reduce labor cost and social insurance contributions (Gong Sen, 2009). Further, most of the stimulus package focused on promoting infrastructure, possibly enhancing already existing over-capacity, and possibly, also increasing corruption.

Source: de Haan (2010a).

Indonesia's development model under Suharto (between 1967 and 1998) provides one illustration of how authoritarian rule has provided economic growth that did benefit the poor. This strategy was designed and implemented by highly skilled economic planners (the "technocrats") at the direct urging of President Suharto (Timmer, 2004). It occurred under a repressive and centralized policy regime, following a violent coup, based on and actively crafting an alliance with rural inhabitants.

[8] A survey in 2007 by Tsinghua University found that in areas where government sponsored health insurance was introduced, people were spending more and saving less (Wong, 2009).

In the words of Timmer, Indonesia's "pro-poor performance" till the mid-1990s was based on a conscious strategy that combined rapid economic growth with investments and policies that insured the growth would reach the poor. This strategy integrated the macro economy with the household economy by lowering the transactions costs of operating in the markets—factor markets and product markets—which provide links between the two levels of the overall economy. Income inequality has remained, and was consciously kept low (Gini of 0.33). Public policies have contributed to a rapid spread of access to health and education (possibly because of a perceived preference for infrastructure with more immediate benefits), even though investments in health and education remained low. As described earlier, the financial crisis of 1997–98 led to radical political changes alongside reforms in welfare provisions.

Malaysia's social policy regime is another example of the "East Asian" model where social policies are carefully matched with economic and efficiency concerns, and managed under strong nationalist leadership. Malaysia's welfare state approximates the Singapore type of exclusive welfare state (Kwon, 2005b: 18), yet our simple indicator of government interventions suggests it has a larger-than-average state (alongside high levels of urbanization), with particularly high public spending in education. Its unique feature is no doubt the affirmative action program introduced in 1970 under the New Economic Policy—a year after severe ethnic riots, and introduced under emergency rule.

Malaysia's New Economic Policy has been a major exercise in social engineering, in which education has played a central role, inculcating a sense of Malaysian-ness and patriotism (Brown, 2005a). It aimed to eradicate poverty independent of race and ethnicity, and break the links between race/ethnicity with economic status or function, particularly reducing the differences between *bumiputera* (Malaysian) and non-*bumiputera* (Chinese and Indian). It included explicit targets for employment and capital ownership rather than income inequality (Yusof, 2006). The policy's "implementation and subsequent adjustments radically recomposed the class structure of Malaysian society, altered the balance of power between different economic and social groupings, and entrenched the role of the state in the economy" (Khoo Boo Teik, 2004: iii). The policy has been considered successful, with group inequalities having been reduced, alongside rapid economic growth and urbanization. As in India, as described later, but unlike in Indonesia where regimes sought to suppress such forms of identity, in Malaysia these identities became central in the political structure (Brown, 2005b).

Political interests and dynamics are clearly central to the development in Chinese social policies, with a continued underlying tension between economic reformers and the Left that has wanted to maintain some of the egalitarianism of the communist period. If the debates on reform of the health sector have been any guide, reforms of social policies are as much a battle of ideas as a reconstitution of power balances, with, as indicated earlier, the crisis as exogenous force. With health care privatized, to a large extent, in the immediate post-reform period, discussions were about the forms that social provisions would take (national health care versus social insurance), in turn shaping the relationship between states and citizens (at present, with a focus on insurance principles but with additional support for poorer areas and people). While some of the economic reforms like dismantling of state-owned enterprises (SOE) make directions of restructuring of provisions inevitable (for example, experimentation with urban *di bao*), the policy debates show that ideas can play a relatively independent and crucial role—for understanding the evolvement of social policies it is central to chart the articulation of these ideas and underlying premises, and how these interact with vested interests.

The basics of China's political system may have remained unchanged—at least comparatively in the face of the collapse of the Soviet Union—but policy makers are clearly responding to political and citizens' pressure. While reform of the social security system involves addressing the needs and political pressure of various segments of the workforce, the focus on inequality and the creation of a "harmonious society" is a political project, geared toward maintaining national and political stability.[9] As in Indonesia, while much of China's growth was highly "pro-poor," levels and trends in inequality have been crucially important. While protests against extreme inequalities were central to policy changes in Indonesia, in China, after two decades of accepting rising inequalities, the harmonious society idea became the centerpiece of public policies. Social policy reforms under the harmonious society banner are the Party's response to fear of social unrest, even thought the protests are probably less the result of rising inequalities than perceived injustice around corruption or environmental disasters. Health crises like SARS in 2003 in particular, also have led to a big push for more effective public policy. The recent effective government responses to the May 2008 earthquake and the financial crisis of late 2008 illustrate a similar point, with its leaders reaffirming authority and the country's unity.

[9] Chinese officials are aware of the country's vulnerability that caused the collapse of former communist countries, and the official media had discussed the "Latin Americanization" of China, referring to the possibility that growing income inequalities could lead to upheaval (*Economist*, 2006a: 5). See also de Haan (2010b).

Institutions Adapting under Globalization

In terms of economic development, East Asia's institutions have been somewhat of a miracle for the international development community. While much of the governance literature expects a certain degree of congruence between institutional and economic development, growth in the region, for many observers, appears to have outpaced the development of strong institutions. In the literature, moreover, the region used to be thought to be a social policy free zone—but as the following paragraphs show, institutions for social policy have evolved as part of the East Asian miracle.[10]

While the region is not homogenous of course, the focus on integration into international markets has been fairly uniform, with Vietnam and China fairly late but very proactive examples. In many cases, this integration has happened under what has been termed "authoritarian developmentalism," of proactive economic development with emphasis on integration into the East Asian market (Ohno, 2003a), with development of Suharto's Indonesia as a prime example. Typically, this form of developmentalism emerged under threat—real or perceived—of national security or unity, and often was established by military coup which replaced a weak government. Economic growth functions to legitimize such regimes, though over time, its own success may undermine legitimacy and may lead to transition to multi-party democracy (South Korea, Taiwan; crisis also often plays a role, as in Indonesia). According to Ohno, high performance in East Asia was not accompanied by transparency and accountability, which he concludes may not be necessary for "initiating" growth (Ohno, 2003b), but many observers have argued that this was partly responsible for the 1997 financial crisis.

Writings since the early 1990s on China show a clear picture of how new institutions emerge and evolve while economic growth takes place. Economic reform in China has been seen as a partial reform strategy, characterized by continued institutional innovation, from rural reform (while maintaining an emphasis on food self-sufficiency and promoting migration) to rural industrialization to export promotion, and in the 2008–09 crisis, as suggested earlier, toward a more inward-oriented development path. A centralized policy system drives modernization, building in regional experimentation, as a conscious response to the size of the country and based on the long-established wisdom about limitations of centralized rule. Local officials have strong incentives to have a developmental outlook, as they need to compete for markets and are strongly dependent on local revenue generation.

[10] The varying social policy frameworks in the region confirm the thesis by Pierson (2004: 15), who noted that changes in the global economy impact upon ranges of policy options, but do not undermine the viability of welfare regimes.

Linda Yueh (2008) showed that in the development of legal institutions (property law, corporate law), China, in fact, does not fall behind other countries at similar levels of development, and its path of development of these institutions is not dissimilar to the pragmatic way in which such institutions emerged elsewhere, and combining formal and informal ways of regulating the markets. Policy making is evidence based and development "depoliticized," and there are strong incentives for learning, though arguably, practices for assessing success remain weak (Dollar, 2008; Ravallion, 2007; Zhang, Fan, and de Haan, 2010). With opening up, notably with the accession to WTO, forms of regulating the market have come under increased scrutiny as well, thus continuously driving institutional change.

In terms of China's welfare or social security system, it is of course important to understand the provisions and institutions that were created soon after the foundation of the People's Republic, then at very low levels of income. China's communist state has had remarkable success in improving human development indicators, and the subsequent free market economy—remaining under continued political control—benefited from the earlier state investments in human development (Drèze and Sen, 1989). The Rural Five Guarantee Schemes introduced in 1950 supported the poorest through collectives. Provisions were inclusive, but much more generous social security was created for state sector employees. In the pre-reform period, social policy was inclusive, but had a strong dualistic character too. In particular, urban inhabitants benefited from much better provisions. The dualism was enforced through a strict registration system, which continues to pervade public policies till today.

With the start of the opening up of the Chinese economy, the emphasis on social security disappeared, but arguably, the basic system and channels of provision did not, or very gradually. The reform of the state-owned enterprises has been a very gradual process, continuing for over 30 years, with new programs like the urban *di bao* helping to address the consequences. And the rural–urban disparities have been maintained, and rapid urbanization with growth of slums, as witnessed elsewhere in the developing world, avoided through the administrative *hukou* system. The social policy reforms from the late 1970s onward aimed to facilitate marketization and the state as regulator rather than single provider, moving toward the East Asia type of developmental welfare state, while maintaining the stability of the political order (Guan, 2005).

While a large part of the basic system of delivery has been maintained, most of the provisions in health, education, and social security available during the pre-reform period were, by and large, allowed to collapse.

In education and health, provisions were started to be rebuilt during the 1990s and with increased urgency after the change in top leadership in 2002 and the SARS crisis in 2003. Concerns about social stability led to addressing the inequalities that were felt to be increasingly unsustainable, the decline in rural health services began to be addressed after 2000, and the existence of the "floating population" recognized in public policy. New national primary education policies have made education up to nine years free of charge. The medical health insurance is currently rolled out with all counties developing their own decentralized system, and reform of and policy for the rural health service has only recently been agreed. A voluntary pension system was introduced in 1986, pilots (including in rural areas) and regulation introduced during the early 1990s—but these stagnated during the 1990s. In line with the gradualist and decentralized nature of China's policy reform, local experiments (to be scaled up when successful) have dominated the social security developments.[11] As mentioned, the debates on reform of the health sector showed how reforms of social policies are as much a battle of ideas as a reconstitution of power balances, and through these reforms, institutions evolve, which in turn reshapes the social contract between the state and citizens.

In China, thus, the evolvement of social provisions is closely intertwined with the development of broader policy institutions, including the articulation of rights and citizenship. While many international observers have commented on China's incomplete institutional transition (for example, Hutton, 2007), social policies have evolved in tandem with the very rapid institutional changes that are taking place. These include the interaction of public and private spheres, as a result of opening up of markets (for example, entry to WTO, which also has been used as an instrument by national policy makers to drive through institutional reforms); the power balance between ministries, like health and civil affairs in the reform of health services; decentralization, including of public finance that came to make the funding for social provisions regressive (Zhang and Fan, 2007); and the gradual reframing of rights for migrants workers breaking through the dualism (manifested in the *hukou* system) created during the pre-reform decades.

The opening up of the Vietnamese economy posed many questions similar to China's developments (Suwannarat, 2003: 205). During the 1990s, poverty declined rapidly, even though better-off households benefited more

[11] For example, in Baoji, as described in the HelpAge International publication by Zhang Wenjuan and Tang Dan (2008).

(Glewwe, Gragnolati, and Zaman, 2000). Over the past 12 years, Vietnam's poverty fell by 42 percent, and by 2010, fewer than 10 percent of the population is expected to be poor, according to the Vietnam Development Report (quoted in Sabharwal, 2008). The country has managed to avoid the rising inequalities of China[12]—arguably, with a much smaller country, achieving more equitable growth is less challenging though as we will see effective public policies have been key. Initially, ethnic minorities and the upland and forest areas fell behind the more dynamic areas, but in the second half of the 2000s major increases in inequality appear to have been halted, with poverty declining in the poorer northern areas too (IMF, 2006: 17).

The enterprise-based system of benefits was dismantled, but without signs of a weakening of the state, as reflected in increasing internal revenue generation. Decentralization has been central to the reform strategies. Pre-reform Vietnam had followed a universal model in the delivery of social services, and the conditions created by past policies and communist ideology thus contributed to relatively equal growth patterns (Klump and Bonschab, 2005). In the 1980s, this model translated into land entitlements for all households, as in China. Additionally, every commune got access to primary school and health center. Basic infrastructure including roads, electricity, and drinking water are now increasingly scaled up to achieve universal coverage by 2010.

Vietnam is moving to a system of contributory social insurance, addressing previous regressive benefits for politically designated groups (Evans and Harkness, 2008), thereby making its welfare regime more redistributive than China's (London, 2009). Social policy changes in Vietnam since the reforms have been defined by the high rates of economic growth and the growing aspiration of the Communist Party to be a developed nation by 2020. The growing economy complemented by rapid reductions in poverty and donor support is resulting in social policies—which experienced a period in which targeted programs dominated, and which also were biased toward public sector employees and war veterans—that aim for universal and comprehensive coverage. The new plans for social insurance have received a good deal of attention. With a leg in the formal sector, it prioritizes the poor and provides a benefit package equitable to all, as described in some detail in Box 7.3. Moreover, as in China, the regional disparities brought about by a liberalized economy have been of concern to the government,

[12] Between 1993 and 2002, the Gini for income inequality rose from 0.34 to 0.42, but there was no rise in the Gini for consumption inequality. Most recent data suggest a stable Gini coefficient, though the ratio of top to bottom quintile continues to increase.

Box 7.3 Universalizing Social Insurance in Vietnam

The 2006–10 Socio-Economic Development Plan repositions its targeted poverty reduction programs into a comprehensive and universal social protection system, with an underlying vision of shared growth and inclusion for all. It is still covering only a minority, but legislation aims at extending provisions beyond the formal sector. An overarching law on social insurance was approved by the National Assembly in 2006 (the law for Health Insurance was scheduled to be approved in 2008). The legal framework provides for a universal package with a differentiated approach for reaching the poor, near poor, and the well off.

Formal sector insurance has been made compulsory through a contributory mechanism. This includes public sector employees (who are already covered) and domestic and foreign private sector firms (constituting 20 percent of the labor market). For those working in the informal sector (55 percent of the labor force), social insurance is voluntary: they can choose to buy health and old-age insurance package. For the poor who constitute 16 percent of the working population, social insurance is an entitlement that is subsidized by the government and delivered through a non-contributory mechanism. There are institutional challenges to universalize social protection. Universalizing social insurance will require a unified management information system, for which the government is carrying out pilots. Institutional fragmentation with different ministries owning different elements of current insurance provisions will need to be addressed in order to promote rapid universalization. Finally, social insurance is being made "portable," which will allow people to carry their contributions with them when they move into formal sector employment or from rural to urban areas.

Source: Sabharwal (2008).

and there is explicit recognition of deprivation of, and substantial support for, ethnic minority groups, through the Commission for Ethnic Minorities and Mountain Areas.

Vietnam's Communist Party is committed to rapidly industrialize and catch up with the rest of Southeast Asia, while using the social and economic policy experiences from countries like Singapore and Korea. Despite opening up of the economy and the drive to grow faster, the government has protected social sector expenditure, specifically for education, health, and social protection. Over the past years, social sector spending has increased with a significant rise in education budgets. The move to a comprehensive and universal social protection system appears in line with the policies being implemented by other developed countries in the region, but Vietnam's drive to universalize social protection is carefully managed to balance economic and social objectives. As mentioned, it has created an enabling legal framework which institutionalizes a universal and comprehensive social insurance mechanism. The sequencing of universal programs with old-age pensions following health insurance is designed to be financially sustainable, with resources coming entirely through state budget, even though international agencies are providing support.

Economic and political interests and priorities dictate the direction of Vietnam's social policy. Like in China, in Vietnam, too, there is much emphasis on the consistency between economic and social policy. Social sector investments are seen as instrumental to maintain high economic growth and meet the growing demand for skilled labor. The Communist Party is keen to maintain social solidarity and ensure that the poor are able to access basic services, and are protected from risks and vulnerabilities—which serve as a key driver to universalize social protection in Vietnam. In Vietnam, policies are driving institutional change, and policy makers are clearly responding to political and citizens' pressure. Technical assistance is being leveraged from international donors to support the process of building modern institutions to deliver universal social policies at the national and provincial level.

While national histories clearly determine the institutions that underlie East Asian social policies, and there is a major difference between the models under continued communist party rule and those without, there are some significant similarities in the institutional constellation that drives social policies. China's integration into the global economy and society (including in the WTO) is accompanied by a wide-ranging and complementary set of social policy reforms (Nielsen et al., 2005). Vietnam is following a similar reform path, under one-party rule, possibly moving a little quicker to universalizing social protection. While the underlying ideology, of course, is very different from the rest of East Asia, the patterns of economic integration and emphasis on nation building confirm that the notion of productivist welfare state does provide a useful concept to understand the emerging welfare states in communist East Asia too.

As highlighted by Gough (2008), the evolvement of social provisions is closely intertwined with the development of broader policy institutions, including the articulation of rights and citizenship. In contrast to ideas about incomplete institutional transitions in countries in the region, social policies are evolving in tandem with the very rapid institutional changes that are taking place, including the interaction of public and private spheres, as a result of opening up of markets, in the power balance between ministries, and in the gradual reframing of rights for migrants workers breaking through the dualism created during the pre-reform decades.

Ideas: Productivism under Socialist Guise

As anywhere else, the social policies in the region are informed by different ideas and ideologies. For our description here, the most relevant appear to be nationalism, the productivist orientation behind social service provisions, and authoritarianism, while the Vietnamese and Chinese communist legacy distinguishes itself strongly from the valuation of the capitalist system elsewhere. Further, the Confucian value system and patriarchy have been central characteristics behind the evolvement of social policies, similar to how Christian values influenced many of the European and US regimes, as the next sub-section describes.

First, nationalism is a central driver of social policies across the region, as it was in much of Europe. In Hong Kong, social spending—which had started to expand during the early 1990s—continued to increase under the first executive, Tung Chee-Hwa, who—like many post-colonial leaders before him, and as open admirer of Singapore's Prime Minister between 1959 and 1990, Lee Kuan Yew—"felt the need to demonstrate strong leadership and give people the vision of a better future" (Lee, 2005: 125).

In China, nation building is a central consideration of its social policies, and probably a unifying force in the fierce debates between left and right within China. Public policies have played an important though, of course, contested role in the integration of remote minority areas. Extension of services is often extensively described in public statements, particularly with respect to the Tibet Autonomous Region. During the first 15 years of the reform period, public policies allowed if not encouraged the development of huge disparities across the country. But over the last 10 years, a more even development path has been promoted, including through the promotion of investment outside the coastal zones, and expansion of social services promoting a "harmonious society." National identity was not only promoted through the central government but also eastern provinces that have organized—on the urge of Deng Xiaoping (Cao Hongmin, n.d.)—support for the poorer western provinces (local governments' as well as private support for the 2008 Wenchuan earthquake relief and reconstruction also was very substantial). While NGOs in the western sense do not play an important role in China (and in Vietnam have been introduced mainly under the banner of international cooperation), collective action and mass organizations are important in both practical and ideological terms.

Second, the way links between economic and social policies are conceived, and integrated into public policy making, shows clear signs of the "productivist" orientation of social policy. Public spending, including in sectoral allocations to social sectors (to some extent seen as "non-productive"), is tightly controlled—with, as we discussed earlier, typically crises playing the role of loosening the tight policies somewhat—and the role of private providers is welcomed.[13] In China, public policies around, for example, capacity building, and emphasis on adjustment to enhance returns from policy (for example, in the approach to poverty alleviation programs), emphasize the productivity of public investments, rather than seeing it as merely residual spending, which in turn can lead to a bias toward beneficiaries with stronger capabilities, those, for example, that can repay program loans.

The focus on social insurance schemes has been central to the productivist welfare thinking. Kwon (2005a) describes how Taiwan and Korea introduced mainly insurance-based welfare arrangements, while Singapore followed the British model of Provident Funds (in both Singapore and Hong Kong social development was seen as subordinate to the overall economic development strategy). China, while so far having created a very low level of social security, has opted for insurance-based health schemes. With health care to a large extent privatized in the immediate post-reform period, discussions have continued about the forms that social provisions will take, resulting in the mixed scheme for health care as described earlier.

A further common characteristic of the social policy regime of most if not all East Asian countries has been the way it has been embedded in an ideology of authoritarianism. Egalitarian norms predominate in public debate, but often under authoritarian practices and with a focus on productive opportunities. The authoritarianism of the successful states has been of a particular kind, which has been illustrated by the very different responses to the natural disasters in 2008 of the Burmese and Chinese governments, with the latter earning a reputation of being more responsive to the Wenchuan earthquake, including through the benevolence of its rulers as well as capacity of strength of its state apparatus, than the democratically elected US government in response to the 2005 hurricane, Katrina. While in financial terms, the East Asian experience appears to conform to a Washington Consensus, in ideological terms, the East Asian state continues to be seen as the guardian of public welfare.

[13] See Wu and Ramesh (2009), who argue that two decades of market-oriented health reforms have proven the failure of the model.

Of course, this ideology has not been without disjuncture and contradictions. China's post-1978 free market phase tended to be marked by a perception that opposed social welfare to economic growth, and even now many see the welfare state as encouraging dependency and idleness, thus providing the underlying ideology for minimizing unproductive welfare expenditure, a "residual" policy of the richer East helping the poorer West, for example. Ideological differences within the Party continue to exist, moving public policies between left and right. But even then, and remarkably, the socialist ideology never lost ground, even though equality of opportunity has been more important that equality of outcome. Over the last few years, a strong socialist ideology of equality, social justice, collective action, and an ideology of "welfare state on a lower income" (Guan, 2005: 212) has been reaffirmed, even as inequalities continue to increase.

The combination of capitalism practices and socialist ideology can appear paradoxical, but it is a central feature of the development of social policy in both China and Vietnam. Despite the focus on economic growth, like China, Vietnam retains a socialist and inclusive orientation. The central leadership seeks to maintain its legitimacy and power in the changing socio-economic context of the country, including through the integration of Vietnam into the economic world order and the growing aspiration to become an industrialized country. The Party is responding to this change by being more responsive to the needs and interests of the workforce at large, and the move to universalize social security is one of its outcomes. The socialist ideology is very closely linked to nationalism (and some would argue that in China, nationalism may be replacing socialism as the overarching ideology), with the Party or nationalist leaders as the patriarch over the "harmonious society" and "family"; the gender implications of this we discuss next.

Confucianism and Gender

Confucianism has been a central motive behind the development of social policies in the region, bringing some authors to propose a concept of a Confucian welfare system. Vietnam's social policy, for example, is premised on a Confucian tradition, with the family seen as a main contributor to service provisioning, alongside and typically limiting the role of the state. The role of the community is equally important: for example, labor contributions have been and continue to be an essential building block for most basic infrastructure investments and maintenance, in both Vietnam and China.

The focus on the family leads to a consideration of gender, which includes some remarkable similarities and differences with South Asia.[14] On the one hand, forms of gender discrimination are common across Asia. Foot binding and girl infanticide were among the most extreme expressions of patriarchy in Asia, till the end of the 19th century. The declining sex ratio in both China and India is a major sign of the discrimination of women existing well into the 21st century. Violence against women and female suicide—China being the only country where registered women's suicide is higher than men's—are further signs of continued patriarchy, with parental control over marriage serving to reinforce deep-seated patriarchy (Therborn, 2004: 107 ff.).

These forms of gender discrimination cut across the main religions of the region, including Confucianism in East Asia, and Hinduism and Islam in South Asia. Of course, variations do exist. Southeast Asia provides a different picture, with, for example, bilateral inheritance and later marriage more common (Therborn, 2004: 123–26). The deeply rooted gender discrimination is an entrenched pillar of the perception of the family as main provider of welfare, commonly seen as a central Confucian value. Singapore's great leader and patriarch Lee Kuan Yew summarized this in an interview in 1994: "[T]he fundamental difference between Western concepts of society and government and East Asian concepts…is that Eastern societies believe that the individual exists in the context of his family" (Zakaria, 1994). This idea in turn continues to play a very important role in the perception of limited state responsibility for welfare provisions (Cook and Kwon, 2007), similar to the perception that a return to rural areas continues to be a safety net for migrants in urban areas and export-oriented industries.

At the same time, there is a significant difference between South and East Asia. The economic role of women and their place in the public sphere is much larger in East Asia than in South Asia. In China, the "victory of the Chinese communists in 1949 meant…a full scale assault on the most ancient and elaborate patriarchy of the world…," including a Divide the Family Campaign, a new Marriage Law, equal rights in the land reform, and very rapid expansion of women's and men's education.[15] Women's extra

[14] Therborn (2004) provides a unique comparative overview of patriarchy globally, and its changes and continuities since the 19th century, including under the influence of colonialism.

[15] Therborn (2004: 93–94, 262). Relatively high literacy characterized early 20th century East Asia, but with large gender differentials. In China the main change took place after the revolution. In India, by contrast, literacy remained low and gender disparities continued to exist throughout most if not all of the 20th century. Therborn (2004: 270) notes that in developmentalist states fertility has tended to decrease fast.

domestic employment became very high, constituting a major difference with South Asia. In the beginning of the 21st century, the rate of female economic activity is 83 percent of that of men, compared to 42 percent in India, for example. The reform period has had contradictory effects on women's economic role. The process of privatization has led to a relative decline in female employment. At the same time, migration by women is significant, constituting a reported 40 percent of the total migration labor force. Simultaneously, the one-child policy has enabled higher female labor force participation, and possibly increased the urgency for work outside the household because of concerns about care in old age, with pensions being highly inadequate and health care costs proving a major threat.

International Influence

The absence of colonial domination cannot be used as an explanation of social policy regimes, but the absence of colonial domination in the forms it took in South Asia, Africa, and Latin America is an important factor that sets much of the region apart. A key feature of policy development in the region has been the proactive attitude toward learning from experiences elsewhere, and adapting these to local circumstances. Yeates (2001: 18) highlights how development of social policy in Japan, Taiwan, and Korea was influenced by models and/or thinking from the West. There is clear evidence of public policy transfers or learning within the region, including in Vietnam that looks at China's model besides working closely with the international development community.

International influences are clearly evident in the way Chinese social (and other public) policies are evolving.[16] In the mid-1950s, the Soviet model became an important example for the design of economic and social policies. As elsewhere, the opening up of the Chinese economy, including in WTO accession, have contributed to a need to respond to new demands created by the market economy, often leading to more proactive social policies. For example, China's signing of ILO Conventions have gone hand in hand with addressing rights of migrant, child, and bonded labor. And international collaboration is proactively sought in all economic and

[16] Interest within China for European social policy has grown since the mid-1980s, but has a longer history (Zhou, 2004). There is currently a large project of cooperation on social security with the EU, and in early 2009, DFID collaborated with the Development Research Center to ensure global experience of crises responses inform State Council policy making.

public spheres. Donor projects (for example, in education, poverty, and migration) are seen as important in experimenting with new approaches, and line ministries have set up international departments to liaise with international agencies, and bridging language barriers. The recent openness with which China sought international collaboration after the Wenchuan earthquake—as compared to the response after the 1976 Tangshan earthquake—consolidated this trend of openness.

Vietnam provides an exceptional picture in terms of international influences on its national policies. As in China, its entry into WTO is accompanied with clearly set out policy reforms, including the move toward universal social protection. In doing so, Vietnam has been strategic in using international donor resources to pilot new mechanisms to respond to social and political change. In Vietnam, there is also a clear interest of learning from China, for example, in the context of social security reform.[17] For example, subsidized health insurance for the poor has emerged from donor pilots in selected provinces. Privatization of health care and evidence, often provided by international research of growing pressure on poor households to meet health care expenditure also influenced the government to scale up free health insurance for all poor and vulnerable.

Conclusion: The Relevance of Social Policy Analysis in the Asia Miracle

The story in this chapter suggests that a notion of productivist social policy, within a comparative framework, is useful to describe main features of the way social policies in East Asia have evolved over the last 30 years, and as the next chapter will argue, this can be usefully compared and contrasted with the more welfarist approaches that have been more dominant in South Asia. Productivism is marked by states that focus on enabling market processes, create the preconditions for such markets through social policies, tend to be inclusive of the entire population, and focus on complementarity of social and economic policies.

[17] Rural reforms in Vietnam during 1979–81 were comparable with China's in the same period, even though there was much political tension between the countries at the time including the 1979 border war (Heerink, Spoor, and Qnu, 2007: 19–20).

The East Asian experience did not conform to the free market model as sometimes portrayed. Most countries in Asia had proactive—but selective—social policies, designed to play a key role in its pattern of economic growth. The description supports the conclusion of recent UNRISD and other research that East Asia has been far from a social policy free zone, and Lindert's (2004) suggestion that developments in East Asia fit into general patterns of expansion of social policies. If there is an East Asia model, its key characteristic would be its developmental nature, shaped to enable the entire population to participate in economic growth and mainstream development. This implied strong directions around the role of social policy vis-à-vis economic growth and nation building, including in responses to crisis.

Social policies have been an active accompaniment or part of the rapid economic transformation, and are responding to the new challenges that emerge out of the process, such as the transfer from a strong rural–urban dichotomy toward universal coverage. Crises have initiated remarkable changes in the region, sometimes through the creation of new social protection instruments, and sometimes, through the deepening and universalization of systems of social security that were created earlier. Further, social policy changes follow the institutional reforms undertaken in these countries, with a strengthening of voice in the authoritarian states of South Korea and Indonesia, and remarkably successful efforts of the communist parties of Vietnam and China to contain protests within the existing political frameworks, and social policies as a key instrument for maintaining that stability.

At the same time, while some of the economic reforms like dismantling of state-owned enterprises in China and Vietnam made directions of restructuring of provisions inevitable, the policy debates show that ideas can play a relatively independent and crucial role. For understanding the evolvement of social policies, it is central to chart the articulation of these ideas and underlying premises and national traditions, including the interaction with international influences, including in economies in transition.

East Asia, thus, shows that social policies are a central element of integration into global economies, that social security systems are being introduced at relative low levels of development, and that there is a variety in ways reform of social policies can be achieved. Degrees of commodification (or relative size of state budgets) vary significantly, and not all late industrializers have been marked by a small welfare state. Moreover, there is variance in approaches, for example, between a focus on insurance principles and universal state-funded systems. Countries' paths are not straightforward, notably with China showing a relative neglect of rising inequalities and loss of basic services, which subsequently need to be—and are actively—being addressed. But in many of the cases, successful economic developments and transition have been accompanied by proactive social policies.

8

South Asian Welfarism

This chapter describes the main characteristics of social policies in South Asia, in comparison with the East Asian trends described in the last chapter, and using the same framework developed by Ian Gough (2008) that was used as organizing framework of the last chapter as well. While there is of course much variety across the region, notably with Sri Lanka and the state of Kerala for long being regarded as a positive outlier in terms of providing social services at low levels of economic development, and with Bangladesh for long being regarded as a basket case, there are also remarkable similarities across the region, which this chapter tries to summarize under the term welfarism.

Main characteristics of welfarism include the following.[1] Social security is typically perceived as residual, with a strong emphasis on targeted safety nets, even in the case of recent rights-based policy like the employment guarantee scheme in India. Inclusive provision, including universal primary education, has been very slow to emerge, except in Sri Lanka. Recent health and nutrition indicators show extremely poor implementation of public services, except again in Sri Lanka, which before 1950, introduced general public health interventions and after 1950, also modern obstetric interventions which brought down maternal mortality. Behind the approaches lies a strong historical legacy, and in many of the food programs, for example, one detects clear traces of colonial and perhaps pre-colonial traditions. Social spending,

---

[1] Contributions in the 1991—and still very relevant—volume edited by Ahmad et al. provide overviews of social security in South Asia, emphasizing the limited scope of social security in the western term (and the need to focus on how public policy in the broad sense can contribute to eliminating vulnerability), and the dependence on land, family and other resources.

or government spending more broadly, as shown in Table 7.1 in the previous chapter, has remained surprisingly—given the public attention to social services—low. Public spending on health and education is very low in Pakistan and Bangladesh, though increasing rapidly during the 1990s in the latter. Spending in India increased during recent years, particularly in education, and was protected during the period of adjustment (as discussed in Box 8.1), but has remained low, notably in the health sector.

Box 8.1 Social Spending in India

It is commonly asserted that social sectors spending in India declined during the period of liberalization. However, while there is anecdotal evidence that policy makers' interest did move away from traditional social concerns (Mander, 2004), patterns of funding have experienced remarkably little change. In the Indian context, it is important that there has been a continuous and very open public debate about changes in poverty, and the findings that poverty was increasing in the early 1990s as response to the crisis and adjustment of 1991 probably increased spending for anti-poverty purposes (Dutt and Rao, 2001, even though according to these authors, its political leaders failed "to cultivate the complementarity between economic growth and social opportunity" [p. 214]). Research suggests that there may have been some decline on overall government spending, but not in the social sectors.

The relevance of these trends is highlighted in the case of Orissa, which during the 1990s, gradually became the state with the highest poverty incidence and increasing state budget deficits. During the 9th Plan period, state social sector spending was well protected, with a high share of education, and rural development falling behind. The increases in spending in Orissa were faster than elsewhere, with an increasing share of central government contributions, and to a large extent, following hikes in civil service wages following the Fifth Pay Commission. Social sector spending was often higher than allocations, which is surprising given regular reports of underutilization of funds.

What these trends imply remains a matter of debate. Increased social spending is desirable given Orissa's high poverty rates. But at least three trend questions need to be considered. First, as elsewhere globally, increased social spending seems to have been accompanied by declines in equally important spending in rural development, an issue that is now gradually being reversed. Second, the increased share of social spending happens in the context of increased dependency on central (and possibly international) funding, and sustainability is thus a pertinent question. And third, an increasing part of spending is recurrent as opposed to developmental expenditure, and teachers' salaries may be one of the main reasons for the rising shares of education, leaving little for new investments.

Sources: Dev and Mooij (2002); Joshi (2006); Shariff, Ghosh, and Mondal (2001); World Bank, South Asia Region (2003).

These social policies in South Asia have evolved in a parliamentary setting (though less so in Pakistan), in parliamentary terms, and also, with significant efforts toward decentralization. The way this particular form of democracy interacts with social policy needs further analysis, but the overview here suggests that it has reinforced residual approaches. In India—and in Nepal as well but more recently and to a much lesser extent—affirmative action has played an important role in these dynamics, also with a great deal of continuity from the colonial period, and have provided a particular and, in India, at times, deeply contested form to the social contract.

Electoral without Substantive Democracy

While people's lives in East Asia have been radically transformed, including in much of the most remote areas, the South Asian picture is fundamentally different. Over the long run, India has experienced substantial rates of economic growth and poverty reduction. Rural poverty declined from 47 percent in 1983 to 28 percent in 2004 (Lanjouw and Murgai, 2008), though the share of agricultural employment did not decline dramatically: from 74 percent in 1972–73 to 57 percent in 2004–05.[2] Bangladesh, too, showed substantial progress in terms of economic growth and poverty reduction, starting also in the 1980s. Progress has remained much more limited in Sri Lanka and Pakistan, with both countries deeply and increasingly engaged in internal conflicts of different kinds, and the first having witnessed a dismantling of the welfare state which was followed by outbreak of civil conflict, as described in Box 8.2.

Even in India, progress has remained much behind the transformation of East Asia, even though it has managed to keep levels of income inequality low alongside impressive economic growth. While economic reforms have led to changes in employment structures, they are not nearly as radical as in China or Vietnam, both because the "formal" sector never was very large in India and because the policy reforms have been more gradual. The slow decline in poverty headcount with population growth has meant that the total number of poor people have not declined. Research shows large intra-country variation in both rates of economic growth, and the rate in which the poor benefit from economic growth.[3] Moreover, yearly surveys have

---

[2] Bhalla (2008). Kundu (2009) discusses the rates and patterns of urbanization in Asia, inter alia warning against alarmist perspectives on rising rates of rural–urban migration.

[3] A stable Gini coefficient marks significant diverging trends, in income and human development indicators, across and within states, pervasive gaps between social groups that

Box 8.2 The Dismantling of Sri Lanka's Welfare State and the Conflict

For long, the social policies of Sri Lanka were held up as an example—alongside Kerala in India—of the possibility of high levels of social development at relatively low levels of GDP. This was brought about by an interventionist state, with roots back in the colonial period of the 19th century and in response to threats from the political left. The social policies cemented a strong social contract with its citizens, so much so that for long it was thought that the welfare state could not be touched.

This social contract came to an end in the election year 1977, when Sri Lanka started to pursue policies of economic liberalization. The explanations of this reversal are predictably subject of debate—for example, around the level of budget deficit and unaffordability of the welfare state, and the possibility to enhance revenue because of terms of trade—but it is likely that the "subsequent cuts exposed the underlying fault lines in Sri Lankan society" (Dunham, 2008: 96). Government investment in social services have declined, food subsidies phased out, with reductions in health and education and health spending dwindling more gradually, with the "civil war…as a convenient distraction."

Source: Dunham (2008).

suggested important fluctuations. The low Gini coefficient has not stopped the public debate around the country's large inequalities: for example, in 1992, public debate and increased public policy attention emerged because of increases in food prices and cutbacks in public expenditure (even though spending in social sectors was protected). The large inequalities and idea that the poor had not benefited from the economic growth model was seen as major reason for the political change in 2004, as discussed next. Remarkably poor nutrition indicators and health records have been observed for India, leading to a label for India as "economic powerhouse and nutritional weakling" (Haddad and Zeitlyn, 2009).[4]

India's social disparities are very large and deeply rooted. They overlap to some extent with regional disparities, which are increasing across the country, with implications for public policies as demonstrated for Orissa in Box 8.3, and arguably, related to political and institutional configurations in Indian states (Harriss, 1999; Harriss and Kohli, 2009). In India, average

show little sign of closing (de Haan, 2008), a very large proportion of the world's "chronic poor" (Mehta and Shepherd, 2006).

[4] According to James (2008), while there have been improvements in health in India over the last decades, child health has been getting worse, and immunization status has not seen much improvements even in India's better states. See Deaton and Drèze (2009) for a description of recent consumption trends in India, and how these relate to health and nutrition indicators.

Box 8.3 Inequality Traps and Public Policy in Orissa

State-level analysis for Orissa shows that social disparities are at least as severe within India's poorest regions as they are in India as a whole, and that the various forms of disparities overlap and mutually reinforce each other. In the case of Orissa, which had the highest level of poverty among India's major states in 1999–2000 and 2004–05, inter-state regional disparities are extremely high and social group and gender disparities higher than the Indian average. Extreme disparities continue to exist between populations in the tribal upland (in itself highly unequal) and coastal and higher caste elites. These are deeply rooted in inequalities in access to natural resources; and the socio-economic disparities find mirrors in unequal access to public policies and institutions, and in the perennial conflicts, notably around investment in mining.

These socio-economic inequalities, in turn, contribute to inefficiencies in poverty schemes such as for the "KBK region," the poorest area in "tribal" southern Orissa. The patterns of political representation are directly related to the formulation and implementation of social policies. The lack of success of many programs in the areas where they are most needed can be attributed to the emergency type of responses to destitution, which are now challenged by rights-based approaches that have emerged at central level. Moreover, the nature of public policies and the likelihood that they are effective are directly informed by limited or ineffective political representation of the interests of marginalized groups, despite their numerical significance. Moreover, potentials for progressive policy are hampered by weak decentralization, in which Orissa has a remarkably poor record. And finally, civil society and NGOs have also not been able to play a large role: despite successes of NGOs in development projects, few organizations have deep roots in local realities, and the averse relations with government appears to have limited progressive potential, with the recent appointment of a major NGO leader as the state's ombudsman a promising development.

Sources: de Haan, 2008; de Haan, Dubey, and Sabharwal (2009) extend the analysis of Orissa to a comparison with West Bengal, where poverty is lower but regional inequalities severe too.

per capita income of so-called Scheduled Castes (SC) and Scheduled Tribes (ST) at the all-India level is about one-third lower than that of non-deprived groups. Headcount poverty in 1999–2000 among non-deprived was 16 percent, while it was 30 percent for minorities (largely, Muslims), 36 percent for SC, and 44 percent for ST. Deprived groups suffer from human development disparities too, with typically much worse illiteracy, neonatal, post-neonatal, infant, child, and under-5 mortality indicators for socially excluded groups. Despite public debates and policies, these disparities have shown very few signs of being reduced, particularly with respect to the ST categories, alongside agricultural and urban casual laborers.[5]

Finally, inequalities in land and education are large, much more so than in China and East Asia more generally (Bardhan, 2007). The Gini coefficient of land distribution in rural India is 0.74, much higher than in China, which not only indicates poor access to opportunities among poorer groups, but also a continued elite focus on power in rural areas—though with different degrees of transformation across the country. And educational inequalities are large too. Measured by distribution of years of adult schooling, inequality is higher in India than in most Latin American countries. While in China broad-based education was critical to the phase of nation building, notably under early communist rule, Pakistan has lagged much behind, and in India, a similar effective commitment did not materialize until the 1990s, while in Bangladesh, NGOs played a major role in improvements since the 1980s. Arguably, the failure to address inequalities in access to education can be seen as a contributory factor to the differences in economic growth between South and East Asia, particularly under more open economic policy regimes.

Interests: Fragmentation in Social Services

Social policies in the region continue to be shaped by the relatively low levels and slow rates of urbanization, and despite decent economic growth, relatively slow sectoral transition out of agriculture. But this has not meant a vacuum in terms of social policies for its rural population; in fact, the numbers of programs are large, seemingly ever-growing, each creating their own vested interests. In India, a wide range of poverty programs have existed for a long period of time, including the food distribution system which became a targeted program in the 1990s (absorbing significant shares of public funding), and examples of rural social insurance programs. Bangladesh, too, has a history of well-developed poverty interventions, often evolving from the food and nutrition programs following flood and famine, and with a strong emphasis on population control. The role of large NGOs in Bangladesh is well known. They have played a critical role in provision of education and other services in rural areas. Davis (2004) has thus rightly emphasized that analysis of social policy regimes needs to

[5] de Haan and Dubey (2003); Sundaram and Tendulkar (2003); research by Deshpande and Newman (2010) shows that discrimination also exists among educated and middle classes.

take account of a wide range of policies and interaction of actors, NGOs, donors, and customary cultural institutions, and the international influence on the national politics driving welfare provisions.

While growth and economic reforms since the 1980s have led to changes in employment structures, they are not nearly as radical as in China or Vietnam. Reform of state-owned enterprises is not unimportant, but affects a much smaller part of the economy and working population than in Vietnam and China. While exports have been growing in South Asia too, a much larger part of the economy has retained an inward-oriented focus, and an important part of the white-collar labor force has remained insulated from reforms, or impacts of crises (for example, demonstrated by the strike of financial sector workers in India October 2008). In labor market terms, South Asia's formal sector was never very large, and reforms have tended to be much more gradual.

The extension of social security has, to a large extent, remained limited to a "labor elite," that is, people (mostly men) working in the formal sector with regulations from which the informal sector has remained excluded. In India, commitments to extend benefits to the informal sector have never been very significant, as SEWA has experienced when for long it had to fight merely to be registered as a trade union, as described in Box 8.4. The strong advocacy for extending rural poverty policies usually have not impinged on the older social security programs for the formal sector. Programs like the Maharahstra Employment Guarantee Scheme was promoted by an urban elite which was also concerned to reduce rural–urban migration, but such concerns have never been very significant. Like the extension of primary education to the masses, much of the advocacy has come from an influential but relatively small part of India's elite with a concern for the poor.

As in Latin America, the dualism also has implications for the politics of reform. Liberalization—and particularly labor market reform—in India has been a fairly slow and well-managed process, partly because of resistance within core sectors, of nationalized industries and public sector enterprises. The form this has taken is to some extent the result of the way interest groups are structured and fragmented, and advocacy for the interests of people outside the formal sector has remained much more limited—the case of SEWA is the proverbial exception proving the rule. The politics of extension of social security and other provisions appear as important as the technical difficulties of reaching out to a large and rural poor population, as discussed next.

Box 8.4 Dualism and Advocacy: SEWA

The Self-Employed Women's Association, SEWA, based in Ahmedabad, aims to organize women workers: to achieve full employment, with security of work, income, food, and social security (health care and child care in particular); and for women to become autonomous and self-reliant in their decision-making ability. It sees itself as an organization and a movement, of self-employed workers, combining elements of the traditional labor movement, the cooperative movement, and the women's movement, and is primarily a movement of self-employed workers, now with about 700,000 members, and aiming to expand to other states in India.

The SEWA is a trade union, and was as such registered in 1972. It grew out of Ahmedabad's declining trade unions in the textile sector, but was ousted from the main union in 1981. Its members are part of the unprotected or unorganized labor force (which constitutes 93 percent of India's labor force; 94 percent of women workers are in the unorganized sector). In Gandhian tradition, SEWA perceives their activities to be directed against the "constraints and limitations imposed on them by society and the economy, while development activities strengthen women's bargaining power and offer them new alternatives," including new ones imposed by globalization and labor-displacing technology.

In SEWA's history, advocacy for recognition and extension of provisions that are available to the formal sector has been central. It took till 2005 before SEWA was recognized as central trade union, after years of advocating, and after the Delhi High Court finally overruled objections against the application. It has been a key advocate in debates on extension of social security, notably in the context of the 2003 draft legislation around universal health insurance, life insurance, and pensions. In the words of Ranana Jhabvala, contributory social insurance schemes are thought to be more empowering, as they facilitate greater accountability vis-à-vis officials.

Institutions: The Political Nature of Social Provisions

South Asia's political democracy, and how this has evolved since the late colonial period, has provided a particular shape to the evolvement of social policies. India's social policies are a constitutive part of its broader public policy institutions. As in China, its federal structure is crucially important: both India and China have heavily centralized state institutions, with clear responsibilities for state and lower level bureaucracies.[6] But in India,

[6] Comparisons between India and China are attracting increasing attention, and have the potential to help understand different development outcomes. Following earlier work on

incentives for performance seem to be less effective, probably partly because of public management structures and fiscal decentralization, and partly because Indian state-level elections provide a greater deal of autonomy, also allowing poor public policy performance in states like Orissa.[7] Moreover, the number of social and anti-poverty policies is large, often with overlapping objectives and weak evaluation. Extension and universalization of social protection remains subject to the strengthening of public institutions, particularly in India's lagging regions.

The performance, or non-performance, of public institutions is subject to intensive public debate. In Bangladesh, large and influential NGOs have been at the forefront of the debates on social policy. As described by Davis (2004: 269), the consequence of this is that welfare funding decisions are largely made outside the domestic political system. This, in turn, may reduce the feedback mechanisms that follow from the political dynamic of group interests, social stratification, and political mobilization described by Esping-Andersen.[8] But NGOs have not replaced the state. Even in Bangladesh, where NGOs are unusually strong and "homegrown" funding to NGOs forms only 17 percent of total aid (Davis, 2004), donor importance is gradually declining.

In India, during the 1990s, long and sustained advocacy of individuals and groups from various backgrounds led to renewed attention to primary education. This happened against a poor record of development outcomes and non-performing schools, particularly in poorer areas, with weak administrative capacity. Lack of elite commitment played a role in the limited success in universalizing education, while the immediate post-colonial education policies focused on education of the elite, which has had considerable success in terms of providing opportunities for that elite in global markets of software, for example. Recent changes in provision of education show renewed emphasis on universalization, with a targeting approach to reach the poorest in remote areas. Donors have provided support to pilots

China and India by Drèze and Sen (1989: 204 ff.), Saith (2008a) highlights the differences in rural development and the role of China's mass mobilization, with the Communist revolution breaking the feudal mould, thus creating the conditions for capitalist development, compared to much stronger and continued institutional rigidities in India.

[7] de Haan (2008); Swaminathan (2008); the early evidence on the National Rural Employment Guarantee, as described later, show very similar patterns of policy effectiveness in states like Orissa.

[8] A predominant role of NGOs may reinforce fragmentation, but not necessarily so, as, for example, North American social policy models include sustained civil society contributions to core welfare provisions.

and the national program. The national program, Sarva Shikhsa Abhiyan, focuses on ensuring primary education reaches the children of poor families, often in remote rural communities, where community planning and community management form key features. Much debate has emerged over the appointment of village teachers, and whether this would create a dual education system; however, the aim remains to bring all students into the mainstream system at higher levels of education.

The 2004 reversal from the Shining India model toward the Inclusive Growth model has been interpreted as the verdict of the population against the previous government's policies benefiting urban areas and India's better-off—though the nature of that verdict was more complex, with the dissatisfaction with the religious politics of the Bharatiya Janata Party (BJP) playing an important part. Toward the end of the tenure of the coalition United Progressive Alliance (UPA) government, there was disappointment about the impacts of the Inclusive Growth model, though subsequent elections reaffirmed the position of Congress. The coalition UPA government promised a pattern of broad-based or "inclusive growth," and a Common Minimum Programme. One major initiative has been the extension of social security to the informal sector, which in the words of Guy Standing, approximates a proposal for social assistance rather than universalizing benefits.[9]

One of the other major, more recent, initiatives of the new government was the National Rural Health Mission, also introduced with donor support and international advise, including by a "Columbia mafia." This followed recognition that India's health situation is extremely poor, that the health system that had dominated since the 1943 Bhore Committee had not led to sufficient coverage and had remained urban biased (Sathyamala, 2008), and that—like in many other countries—a very large proportion of health spending is now out-of-pocket. The new mission focuses on improving records of infant and maternal mortality, and promoting institutional birth, including cash benefits to mothers. At the same time, health insurance in India is expanding, as the monopoly of the public sector has been broken. Various agencies have entered the field, large private and multinational companies, governmental, and NGO schemes. Many people are likely to share Vyasulu doubts whether the growth of health insurance can make up for the fact that the state "has failed spectacularly in providing

[9] Comments and discussion during the International Conference on Universalizing Socio-Economic Security in South Asia, February 17–20, 2008, New Delhi, where Arjun Sengupta presented ideas of the National Commission for Enterprises in the Unorganised Sector.

health care" (Vyasulu, 2008: 17). As in China, it appears that diversity of providers and systems of health care will continue to dominate the health sector in future, and one of the key questions will be how universalism is or can be achieved and monitored in the context of such diversity.

As flagship of its pro-poor orientation, the UPA coalition government introduced an ambitious employment scheme at national level, strongly advocated for by a section of the country's civil society, with universal and rights-based objectives, but in practice is a targeted program for the poorest people without labor. A bill for the National Rural Employment Guarantee (NREG) was passed by the Parliament in August 2005. The NREG has set legally enforceable employment norms. The scheme is regarded as marking a move toward rights-based approaches, with a legal guarantee that every adult has a right to basic employment opportunities at the statutory minimum wage, and The Right to Information Act, as a way to ensure transparency in the implementation of the NREG. It aims to end food insecurity, empower village communities, and create assets in rural areas. One member of every poor rural family is guaranteed 100 days of work at the minimum wage. Further, it is stipulated that one-third of the beneficiaries must be women, and there are commitments to provide child care. A few years into implementation, reviews, predictably, show a mixed picture, often with poorer performance in poorer states.[10]

Against the knowledge of programs with different performance in different states and areas, the recent initiatives in education, health, and employment all emphasize community involvement and decentralized management, building on pilots such as in primary education in remote areas of Rajasthan. The last decade has witnessed a growing movement to strengthen accountability at higher levels as well, building on advocacy by activists like Aruna Roy and the People's Union for Civil Liberties, among others. National movements regarding Right to Information and the Right to Food (Dev, 2008: Chapter 5) are civil society-led efforts to strengthen mechanisms of accountability of implementation of government social policies. At the same time, following the 73rd Constitutional Amendment Act, state governments have been transferring powers to Panchayati Raj Institutions, with strongly varying results in different states.[11]

[10] See, for example, Bhatia and Drèze (2006); Comptroller and Auditor General (2007); Dutta et al. (2010).

[11] See Rajaraman and Sinha (2007) on a comparison of functional devolution in four of India's poorest states.

Box 8.5 A New Social Contract in Nepal?

While Nepal has not been undergoing the transformation of other parts of Asia, it has also not been stagnant. Poverty fell from 42 to 31 percent between 1995–96 and 2003–04, and other indicators of well-being improved as well, inequality increased rapidly, with the Gini shooting up from 0.34 to 0.41. This took place in the midst of serious conflict, thought to be associated with lack of opportunities and deprivation, which has since subsided, and a democratic government was elected in May 2008. The increase in remittances (constituting 12 percent of GDP in 2003–04) was among the major factors contributing to poverty reduction. But geographic disparities in Nepal remain large, as do the differences between social groups, with poverty rates of Hill and Terai Dalits, Hill Janajatis and Muslims being much higher than of upper castes, and progress more modest.

Much more recently than in India, new policy frameworks and social movements are emerging that challenge the social disparities. Social movements have been advocating movements for, among other things, equitable representation and to remove discriminatory legal provisions. Nepal's Eighth Plan—the first under a democratic government—was the first to address issues of caste and ethnic groups, while it was only in the Ninth Plan that there was explicit reference to Dalits and *Adivasi* Janajatis, while the Tenth Plan is regarded as a comprehensive statement regarding exclusion and inclusion. The census and household surveys now record no less than 103 social groups, with schedules enshrined in law—thus, apparently following the Indian examples of registration. Recommendations for affirmative action have been made at high levels. But so far, there has been limited concrete government action, in the form of affirmative action, for example, and how the social differences become embedded in Nepal's social policies will become clear over the coming years.

Sources: Bennett (2008); Brown and Stewart (2006); World Bank and DFID (2006).

One particular key element for social policy evolvement in India's political and social structure is its fragmentation along caste and "scheduled tribe" lines—which has been central to the nature of the Indian secular state and its social policies, and the social compact after independence. The Indian public policies vis-à-vis "historically marginalized groups" have, within South Asia's context, the clearest articulation, and they are also critical to the more recent policy evolution in Nepal, as summarized in Box 8.5. The Indian policies emerged out of acute political need, with the differences between Mahatma Gandhi and Dr Ambedkar playing a key role in nation building in the late colonial period. While in Sri Lanka special electorates became the mode of insertion of deprived groups, in India, and against the desire of Dr Ambedkar, reservation of political seats was introduced. After independence, a wide range of affirmative actions—reservation, promotion, and protection—were put in place, initially with a short time frame, but they continued to be part of public policies, and recently—in India's version of a new social contract—with advocacy efforts to extend to the private sector.

While much of these group differences are as "invented," as ethnic or racial categories are elsewhere in the world (de Haan, 2007a), the differences have become a defining element of political and administrative structures. In the long run, the impacts have been political democratization without corresponding social and economic transformation, and the language of reservation may have reinforced caste-based identities. The renewed discussion on reservation under the UPA government, for example, with respect to reservation in the private sector, continues this tradition of affirmative policies against the longer term goal of universalism.

In the previous chapter, we highlighted patriarchy as a common characteristic across East and South Asia, one that cuts across religions, and how this has tended to reinforce a notion limiting state responsibility for social welfare. In South Asia, patriarchy is as strong as in Eastern Asia, with varying expressions (such as *sati*, the self-immolation of widows), and specific ways of intersecting with social differences, and variations also between the southern and northern part of India, with *purdah* thought to be primarily a northern phenomenon.

Since the middle of the 20th century there has been a significant divergence, at least in terms of the economic position of women. Although Gandhi supported equality for and rights of women, he did not promote social transformation—neither with respect to gender nor vis-à-vis caste and tribe—and nothing like an assault on patriarchy that happened in communist China. The constitution came to refer to non-discrimination on the grounds of sex, but no uniform civil code was instituted because of the communal tensions around Partition, and even progressive Hindu legislation did not, for example, touch the issue of freedom of marriage (Therborn, 2004: 96).

Female labor force participation has been much lower in South Asia than in East Asia. This is only partly a continuation of "traditional" patterns: the percentage of women working in large-scale factories actually showed a decline during the 1950s, a trend that was reinforced by patriarchal attitudes of the male breadwinner. The growth of the new export industries has changed this somewhat, but as they employ mainly young women, it is unlikely this is part of a sustained move toward rewarding female labor force participation outside the household. As elsewhere, much labor regulation has remained gender blind, and different models of providing social services are seen to be minimalist models with respect to women workers.[12]

South Asian developments, thus, not only highlight how important it is to analyze the interaction between the nature of political systems and the provision of social services, and how this interaction can impact the efficiency of programs, but also the way in which identities and group interests are shaped. While India's economic growth proceeds, old inequalities remain and new ones are opening up. These changes are pushing at the fundamentals of the institutions that have shaped its social policies since independence (and before). Because of its political structure, reforms will be very gradual, and a key question is whether new growth models and public policy initiatives will be able to break out of the old barriers and push harder toward universalization of social protection. The quality and inclusiveness of institutions, clearly, is as important as the modality of providing social services, whether this is about contributory insurance versus non-contributory, targeted versus universal, or supply side versus cash transfer approaches.

Ideas: The Long Tradition of Welfarism

The dominant social policy approach in India has been one—in Esping-Andersen's terms, and partly through its colonial links—of welfarism or residualism, which aims to limit social protection to a small part of the population, the "deserving poor," and considers funding as a cost and not investment (for example, in human capital), and as a "safety net" (Dev, 2008: Chapter 6). While during the last two decades there has been a move toward targeting of social policies (notably, the Public Distribution System [PDS]), the principles of targeting are by no means new. In South Asia, targeted interventions like public works existed under Mughal and British rule. These continued to be dominant in a variety of food distribution and microcredit schemes, and became the basis of a well-developed system of categorization, of social and economic categories. One of the key questions will be the extent to which the "inclusive growth" model of the UPA government has been able to change this deeply rooted approach, but as already indicated,

[12] Long-term changes in labor force participation in India are discussed in de Haan (1997, 2005), while Chhachhi (2008) emphasizes labor regulation.

the disappointment that appeared to have set in toward the end of its tenure suggested the limitations to the potential for transformation.

In India, targeting has been a common element of a wide range of social policies, carried out on the basis of a well-developed system of categorization, of social (SC, ST, Other Backward Castes) as well as economic ("Below the Poverty Line") categories, and on the basis of the post-colonial pact with businessmen that realized the need for anti-poverty programs. Targeted provisions exist in the PDS, housing subsidies, pensions, etc. One of the best-known examples has been the Maharashtra Employment Guarantee Scheme, which provides rural employment on the basis of "self-targeting," in which wages provided are low enough so that better-off would not apply for the scheme. Similar to the public pressure for education, the role of the middle class has been extremely important in the promotion of employment schemes—in the case of Maharashtra, this was partly driven by urban elites who accepted taxes for a program that would keep the poor in rural areas. The scheme in Maharashtra has been the example for the recent national employment guarantee scheme in India's poorest districts, as described ealier. Also, as discussed earlier, beyond principles and choices for targeting or universalism, administrative capacity is key: Kapur, Mukhopadhyay, and Subramanium (2008) argue in a discussion of India's food distribution and employment schemes that rather that targeting, the root cause of the problem is "the culture of immunity in public administration and the weak capabilities of local governments."

Food distribution or subsidies have played a very important role in many countries, particularly where food security was a major concern, and because of many donors' preference for food aid (Subbarao, 2003). Food aid played a big role in the 1974 famine in Bangladesh, and while the amount of foreign aid has gradually declined, together with government resources, food aid has been used for a range of fairly successful targeted relief programs. Targeting has continued to be dominant in Bangladesh in a variety of food distribution and microcredit schemes (Davis, 2004), the latter being NGO driven, who also espouse strong targeting principles. In India, self-reliance played an important role in the development of the food distribution scheme, and both workfare and nutrition programs have been key parts of the residual social policy approach. In the early 1990s, the food distribution scheme moved from a universal to a targeted scheme. It is often assumed this was under pressure from international organizations, but the politics of this were complex; in any case, the move toward a targeted scheme has not affected the interest of farmers as suppliers, while access to, and corruption in, delivery are central to local politics and advocacy efforts.

Old-age schemes have not found wide application across the region, but do exist in some Indian states, and in Bangladesh, and also have a strong focus on targeting. In Bangladesh, an Old Age Allowance Scheme was introduced in 1997–98 (Barrientos, 2008), with a separate program targeting poor widows and destitute women established later. The first pays a monthly allowance of around US$ 2 per month to the 10 oldest and poorest members of each ward, and the second adds five beneficiaries per ward. Annual budget allocation for the programs amounts to a mere 0.05 percent of GDP, with about 600,000 beneficiaries. Coverage is consciously kept low, with the ward committees selecting beneficiaries on the basis of the age, economic, and health status, targeting the extremely poor and destitute. Evaluations suggest that the programs are well received by local communities and they are reasonably well targeted, but are insufficient in number to cover all poor.

International influences have been important for South Asia's social policy development. This is not a new phenomenon. British ideological influences of course shaped approaches, and India's membership of the ILO similarly had a big impact on the shape of its social policies, and particularly, labor markets. In Bangladesh, particularly following the war and natural disasters, international organizations have played a large role, with a big impact on targeted food distribution schemes, and the support to "national" NGOs.

Gradual entry into global markets mean international practices increasingly influence national public policy, but this has been a very gradual process, particularly in large countries like India. It remains a question how much international organizations have influenced policy changes like the targeting of PDS, approaches to education of the poorest, or support to the elderly. Over time, international organizations will be less likely to determine South Asia's national agendas, but ever-deeper economic integration will continue to push an agenda of reform of social policies.

Conclusion: Universalism in South Asia?

This chapter has described main driving forces of South Asian social policies, and the way these differ from those in East Asia. The political differences between South and East Asia, of course, are very large, with the tradition of parliamentary democracy remaining very strong in South Asia, despite challenges. The South Asian experience shows that it is critical for social policy analysis to be rooted in a firm understanding of the nature of forms of government, the way public policy institutions are shaped by these, and the impact these have on the implementation of social policies.

The post-colonial project in South Asia, with modernist ideologies and inward-oriented development, reinforced—even if unintentionally—the economic and social dualism that was established under colonialism. Like in many African countries, social policies in South Asia obtained a strongly dualistic nature, despite a strong universalistic and often rights-based approach to welfare, and notwithstanding the exceptions of Sri Lanka and Kerala in India. A wide range of specific programs have been designed and continuously refined for people below the poverty line, while people in the "unorganized sector" have remained excluded from benefits of those in the small organized sector. While health and education policies have been universal in principle, implementation has been fragmented. Globalization seems to have had relatively little direct impact, compared to the path dependence of the region's public policy institutions.

Moreover, in large parts of South Asia, deep-rooted inequalities continue to pervade government, public institutions, and the public debate. There have been many new policy initiatives, notably in India, "with renewed universal aspirations." The programs have been successful in some places, but they also have tended to leave deep institutional problems and inequalities unaddressed, and new initiatives usually imply an addition to already large numbers of programs with overlapping objectives. Electoral cycles have not helped to address institutional problems either, though public debates and movements to enhance accountability and decentralization have clear potentials to enhance the performance of public policy institutions. The big challenge for social policies in the region, in the context of continued economic transition and globalization, is for transformative forces to find strong anchors in public institutions, and to shape a more inclusive social contract.

PART THREE

CONCLUSION

9

A Normative Framework for Social Policy

This book has been an exploration of the role of social policy in improving well-being and reducing exclusion, but also in shaping the conditions for economic growth, focusing on experiences across Asia in the last 30 years. In doing so, it has employed notions of social policy regimes, freely using the work of Esping-Andersen, the framework developed by Ian Gough to describe the driving forces behind the way social policies evolve, and the work by UNRISD that has continued to stress social policies as an essential component of development. This is a very ambitious undertaking, and this book hopes to provide additional stimulus for analysis of the public policies to enhance well-being.

The challenges for such policies are enormous. At the turn of the first decade of the 21st century, the world is not only witnessing record levels of inequalities but also an economic crisis—preceded by crises of fuel and food process—that can be compared to the one in the 1930s in terms of financial losses, with great uncertainty about the impact this will have in different parts of the world, and fears of retreats into protectionism. At the same time, this is an opportunity to reignite crucial debates about appropriate policy responses. To do this across Asia, while ambitious, is very appropriate, not only because countries like China and India are rapidly becoming important global actors, but also and even more importantly because new public policies are rapidly emerging in these countries.

This concluding chapter tries to bridge the analytical framework with a practical framework for supporting social policy making. It provides proposals about how a notion of social policy as used in this book can make a difference for the development agenda in the early 21st century. It provides a framework for supporting social policy making, from normative and rights-based principles, emphasizing the need to move toward universalism while taking into account the deeply context- and path-dependent character of social policy. Its practical perspective focuses on entry points into the strengthening of integrated policy making for development and poverty reduction. It does not suggest that there is one model for social policy, or even that there is a trend toward more homogeneity in social policy making in an increasingly interconnected world, but that there is great potential for lesson learning across countries.

Responsive and Inclusive Social Policy

The social policy framework emphasized here highlights the interrelated nature of public policies, as illustrated particularly after economic crises, the need for strengthening capacity of policy making at macro level, and to embed this in an understanding of the political economy of social policy. Despite its origins in northern debates, this book has argued, a social policy framework can be of great value for international development practices and national policy making. This includes the following practical entry points.[1]

The proposed approach to integrated public policy making has implications for the frameworks used by development and national agencies. As highlighted in work on health, nutrition, and education, the long-term impact of investment calls for cost-benefit analysis across sectors, and with a time frame of decades not years. The potential beneficial impact of reducing inequality on economic growth, similarly, has important implications for the way economic investment is considered: what appears as trade-off may, in the long run and under specific conditions, constitute win-win cases. In any case, it is important for national governments and international agencies alike to coordinate across sectors, with forms of analysis taking account of cross-sectoral and long-term impacts.

[1] This builds on the practical guidance provided by Christiansen and Whyte (2008); Dani and de Haan (2008); de Haan (2007b); Devereux and Cook (2000); Hall and Midgley (2004); Moser (1992); Norton and Bird (1998).

The emphasis is on social "policy" rather than social development. This implies a need for social development advice and practice to move "upstream" from its emphasis on projects, to engage at the level of macroeconomic policy debate and public expenditure, and encourage dialogue and coordination between ministries. It should focus on capacity of institutions, as in many cases, as the African Union (2006: 7) highlights: "...public institutions for social development are inadequately governed." Many of the public institutions tend to be weak in places where they are most needed. Social policy analysis thus needs to engage with debates and policies, for example, on devolution, while continuing to emphasize the importance of national policy in shaping local processes. In the context of a diversity of providers, the role of the state as regulator, and its capacity to undertake often very complicated tasks, becomes even more important. Such a social policy approach implies critical assessment of project and targeted approaches that remain dominant in social sector approaches of international agencies and many national institutions, as well as of the charitable, patriarchal, and emergency mode in which many social services are provided. Engagement at the policy level should and can be based in a rights approach, and focus on strengthening the social contract between the state and citizens.

A social policy framework should adopt a broad perspective on the agencies involved. In communist countries, more can be done to involve civil society organizations in social policy, and to learn from complementary efforts elsewhere. In other contexts, a social policy framework should take account of a limited role played by the state, and the significant role of private efforts, for example, in health or elderly care, and of course, the contested role of markets in health provisions. The framework should, thus, also include an understanding of the role of service-providing NGOs as in Bangladesh, advocacy movements as in India, and in the context of international charity, as well as private sector agencies in delivering services. These form central parts of social policy regimes, articulating specific principles of solidarity. A social policy framework should try to crowd-in the contributions of a variety of providers, ensure incentives are compatible while avoiding stigma and dependency, and build toward universalism based on these complex realities.

Simultaneously, as highlighted in Dani and de Haan (2008a), social policy institutions themselves need to become more inclusive. Social policy and advice needs to be context specific, to region, but also groups of people, as the poor do not form a homogeneous group. Timing of social policy delivery can be critical with respect to work requirement during agricultural seasons, or for migrant groups—much experience exists to show that and how specific needs can be taken into account. Moreover, forms of delivery inevitably interact with social norms, and often shape them, particularly but not only in education. Social policy should be flexible, to be able to respond to new challenges, and be prepared for emergencies. Also, and once again highlighting the importance of a multi-sectoral approach, the compartmentalization of policies is likely to restrict the extent to which social policy can respond to particular needs. Overall, universal provisions have proven to be more efficient, while responsiveness to particular groups may assign an important role to targeted policies. Finally, and challenging in many countries, is the management of ethnic or racial diversity within delivery and policy formulation, to ensure that the interests of different racial and ethnic groups are sufficiently incorporated—new evidence on how this can be done is emerging from South Africa, Brazil, and Nepal, for example, while India provides lessons on the basis of decades of affirmative action, and China shows the role the social transformation under communist rule has played.

Thus, social policy needs to be assessed on the question of access by its users and citizens, including of vulnerable and marginalized groups like migrants. Social policy analysis implies an assessment of both the responsiveness of state institutions and citizens' voice and advocacy, based in an understanding of national principles of solidarity, of institutions, of financing needs and possibilities, and modes of delivery of services. This refers to the access of services, which implies a range of mechanisms for accountability, feedback, and participation, regarding quality and relevance. But it also refers to the access to the policy-making processes, for which there are important lessons in recent initiatives in participation in budget formulation, and indeed, though not always successfully, through PRSPs. A key challenge in this respect is the institutionalization of such mechanisms for feedback and participation, including in cross-sectoral budget decision making, and sustained reform of top-down policy processes.

On Globalization, and the Primacy of National Policies

The recent period of globalization has been the one of unprecedented economic growth and many indicators of well-being, but is has also contained many risks, as of course the 2008–09 financial crisis illustrates. China and Vietnam, and to some extent India, have been exceptionally successful in meeting the demands of global integration, and indeed shaping the most recent phase of "supercapitalism" but other countries have been far less successful. While there may not be a simple trend toward increased global inequality, parts of the world and large numbers of people have been falling behind rapidly, and have been vulnerable to the crises that have accompanied the expansion of global markets. Public policy in many cases has failed many, and it has often taken crises—like the 1997–98 East Asian crisis—to bring about more inclusive public policies.

This book was written against a background of fierce debates on globalization, though more so in India than in China, for example, but also in "old Europe," where the rise of China and India, regional integration, and international migration has led to increased nationalism. Perceptions about globalization itself are important, as they inform global politics as much as "reality." The reasons for global trends in well-being and inequalities, of course, are complex, but one of the key ones relates to public policy capacity and the conditions under which globalization can be managed and negotiated. Histories of East Asia, China, and most recently India, show very clearly the central role of public policies in managing the diverse aspects of globalization. Social policy has a key role to play in the way countries negotiate globalization. The East Asia history clearly indicates this, and arguably, India's limited social transformation also illustrates a link with a particular mode of integration in the world economy. Even before the current economic crisis, there has been no evidence of a general demise of the state—though its role has changed during two decades of neo-liberal ideology and policies. Human development is central in the integration into global markets, and while the links between inequality and growth are disputed, more equal countries do not perform worse in international markets. When countries' economies have opened up, social protection has often come to play a more important role, even if this came with a lag. Social policy reform depends on national traditions and the socio-political dynamics in which they are embedded, thus calling for good analysis and deep understanding of local politics and dynamics to inform development approaches.

National social policy making does not happen in isolation. Countries learn from each other and regional economic integration influences—as social policy does not operate independently from economic policy and trends—national social policy. The crisis in East Asia impacted upon the social policy dynamics, partly making them more inclusive and partly, more welfarist. In the case of countries subjected to adjustment, ideas put forward—and imposed—by international organizations have played a key role. The debate over social spending shows that the directions these interactions take are by no means straightforward. Social policy advice needs to be based in a good understanding of the interaction between international exchanges, including those driven by aid, and national politics and vested interests.

A social policy agenda in a globalizing world is about reform of international institutions, northern protectionist policies, etc. But it also requires reaffirmation of the primacy of national politics. With the recent emphasis on national ownership in international development, national policy capacities are taken more serious. The lessons from PRSPs indicate that in the international community much still can be done to support the strengthening of national capacity, in a way that integrates an understanding of local politics, and aims to embed national public policy capacity in progressive social policy traditions. Nation-states remain the principal political institutions, as East Asia shows in particular. An effective global social policy agenda requires stronger national policies that allow countries to integrate in global markets on a more equitable basis, and political and cultural capital that allows countries to engage in debates about global architecture. For international agencies, there does not need to be a dilemma here, and they can do more to support national dialogue and research on social policy options, and support international fora—particularly in response to the recent global financial crisis—that facilitate sharing of ideas.

Global Convergence or Social Policy Regimes?

This book has explored the question whether a notion of social policy regimes is useful to understand public policy making in the South. The answer to this is a qualified yes, with a large research agenda, and more work needed to assess such regimes, including in terms of public finance, and of course, to enrich the very short overviews presented here. The notion emphasizes the very different institutional ways in which social polices across the North have been articulated, and differences in principles of solidarities, and how these evolve in context-specific ways. Further, in the North as much as the South—despite a general trend away from universalism since the 1970s—each country combines different forms of social policies: of universalism, occupation-based and exclusive insurance, targeting, and affirmative action, and cutting across or underlying most of these is the question of the role and importance of the state, and the way in which social policies are formulated with welfarist or productivist objectives. An agenda for understanding social policies in specific countries implies a charting of these different forms of solidarities, and how these combine to provide welfare for the entire population. Globalization has altered but not eliminated these complexities.

Social policy making is not a technocratic exercise, but shaped by national traditions and the political economy of interest struggles. Understanding those national traditions and politics—including the way southern trajectories have been influenced by northern patterns, through respective colonial links—is essential for analyzing impacts of globalization on approaches to policy making. As with respect to labor market policies, the period of adjustment, while generally blamed for the creation of the safety net approach, has tended to reinforce more deeply rooted dualistic social policies. Choices for public–private (NGO, and for-profit) mix, and processes of privatization, also need to be understood in the context of interaction between national traditions and global forces. National politics have given rise to new social policies, in areas of cash transfers as well as affirmative action. As Polanyi described for Europe in the 19th century, neo-liberal trends and moves toward residual social policies continue to be contested by social forces. These contestations increasingly operate on a global scale, and the debates have intensified with the 1997 Asian and 2008 global crises, but in the end, always result in complex patterns of social policy making, a complexity that is critical to shape ways for enhancing capabilities and reducing exclusion and inequalities.

The articulation of principles of solidarities through social policy is the outcome of political contestation, heavily influenced by power relations but also histories of perceived and real disadvantages. Demographic change and economic structures, particularly of labor markets, play a key role in structuring interest groups, in turn determining the dynamics of, support for, or resistance against social policy reforms. These dynamics are context specific, much more so than the more defeatist analyses of globalization have predicted. In aid-dependent countries, donors play a key but insufficiently recognized role in the politics that drive the articulation of social policy, while in the emerging economies of East Asia, new and rapidly evolving traditions of social policy are emerging. But in both sets of circumstances, both the politics and the more technical aspects of social policy remain complex and contested.

A Cross-sectoral View of Social Policy

> In developmental contexts, social policy has typically had a multiplicity of objectives that have included equity, social inclusion, nation-building, conflict-management, human capital formation…[and] social transformation. (Mkandawire, 2005: 15)

The analysis in this book concurs strongly with Mkandawire's assessment—who emphasized the role of social policy, for example, in the context of the "late industrializers" that successfully caught up with the global economy—that social policy is about development, not just poverty eradication, and that it is thus necessarily multi-sectoral. There has been much well-articulated criticism of the residual or safety net approach to social policy, approaches to social funds, and poverty analysis that has focused on identifying the poor rather than analyzing societal relations that sustain exclusions. Available evidence suggests that the wide range of social policies and institutions play key roles in overall development paths, and the inter-linkages of economic and social policies call for a much stronger cross-sectoral focus on public policy making and analysis.

Specific policies and programs, including those categorized under the new social protection agenda, themselves perhaps rightly categorized as residual, can have enormously important functions for specific vulnerable groups. Much evidence on reasons for success is now available. The Maharashtra Employment Guarantee Scheme, for example, has a successful solution to specific problems, social funds experiences contain interesting lessons of what can and cannot work, and the new generation of cash transfers in Latin America and responses to the East Asia 1997 crisis show important successes and identify challenges. Such "residual" schemes may even positively influence more mainstream policy making and public sector provisions, by empowering people, or by setting standards which can contribute to increasing accountability, and targeted programs can have important functions within overall universalist regimes. The key point is not that these programs are important or not—they clearly can be from both pro-poor and political perspectives—or that one approach is better than the other. The main message is that the policy dialogue needs to pay more attention to the wide range and interaction of public policies, which jointly determine and are embedded in the social contract between states and their citizens, and look at targeted programs in the context of an overall universalist approach and formulate ways in which such overall universalism can be assessed.

Our simple quantitative description of state expenditure shows state revenue and expenditure as significant part of GDP in many countries. Social spending is often a substantial component, but with much spending off-budget. Public spending should be higher to achieve MDGs in many places, and the quality of such spending, in many cases, needs to be much improved. The international literature has paid too little attention to social spending, highlighted, for example, in the lack of cross-sectoral data that are internationally comparable. Patterns of public expenditure are important in a cross-sectoral focus on public policies and reforms. While calls for enhancing spending on education are important of course, in my view, they should be justified in a cross-sectoral public policy perspective, that is, one that identifies the needs and political and financial margins to allocate public finance across a range of sectors, on the basis of needs in investments in rural areas, social protection, and health.

Apart from the simple quantitative importance, social spending matters because of a double Robin Hood paradox, extending the conclusion put forward by Peter Lindert. There is less social spending where it is most needed, both because of limited state resources in poor countries and because of limited advocacy by poor people for spending that would benefit them. Moreover, existing public spending can be regressive, as some of the benefits in incidence studies as well as an overall picture of state spending in unequal countries suggest. Social spending is not just a cost, and much evidence exists about the positive impact of health, nutrition, and education on economic growth, thus requiring substantial public investments. The study by Peter Lindert, in fact, shows that social spending can be a "free lunch" and that the returns are positive, but this happens under specific conditions only, of accountability and political processes. This implies the need to strengthen mechanisms of accountability as well as improving the understanding of the politics of public policies, with social policies as a core component of strengthening the social contract.

Social Development, too, is Political

Debates about social policy, and social protection in particular, tend to have a technocratic character. It tends to be about practical solutions to important problems and needs, without much attention to the political nature of such solutions. But social policies are outcomes of historical processes of political, power, and ideological struggles, in which elite interests, agency of professionals, and concerns for nation building can be as important as the struggle of deprived groups and altruism (Hill, 1996). The large difference between OECD welfare states on the one hand, and policies in the South on the other, should not stop us from seeing social policies as historically specific and politically determined outcomes, as the differences between East and South Asia clearly illustrate.

As Mackintosh and Tibandebage (2004: 156–57) stress with respect to health, the "redistributive commitment within a health care system…is deeply influenced by the general patterns of social class and inequality in a society, and...the particular institutions of the system and the norms of behaviour established within them." Similarly, education is central to the construction of citizenship. Social programs—even small ones—are important elements in political and electoral contestation, and of political patronage (often severely regressive). As Dunham (2008: 107) argues regarding the emergence and dismantling of the Sri Lankan welfare state, a "notion that universal welfare policies can help build an inclusive society and reinforce social cohesion is...a relevant lesson that warrants more attention." International sectoral funding for social services adds a particular and insufficiently studied dimension to these politics, of altruism, self-interest as well as patronage and corruption.

At the same time, patterns of spending are a statement of public policies, and the outcome of political struggles. In India, which has relatively low overall public spending in social sectors, the increase in spending on primary education was partly the result of effective lobbying of activists. Anti-poverty schemes—such as the Maharastra Employment Guarantee Scheme and the NREG—are the outcome of political negotiation and in turn, can be grounds for advocacy on behalf of poor people. In much of Africa, donors have played an important—and contested—role in determining patterns of public spending, including regarding the protection of basic social services. In China, patterns of spending reflect the shifting power balance of ideologies around fiscal prudence and equality, as well as concerns for national stability.

Social policy making is not a technocratic exercise, nor is it determined solely by levels of economic development. It is shaped by national traditions that create path dependence, of institutions, ideas, and practices. It is the outcome of political settlements, and often parts of political projects, related to processes of nation building and the creation of social contracts or citizenship and the rights and duties of citizens. National traditions, politics, and ideologies—within a dynamic international context of competition, learning, and pressure—shape patterns of inclusion and exclusion. They contain solidarity principles, which are expressed through specific forms of private–public mix, statutory or community-based approaches, social insurance versus national service approaches, ways in which labor markets are structured, and indeed, how social objectives are matched with economic ones.

A social policy framework, thus, needs to be based in a good understanding of politics, including how international debates and norms interact with local ones. While aiming to enhance social integration and reducing conflict, analysis should assess the various interests and politics in providing social services, and how such services in turn shape state–citizen relations, create expectation and public responses, and are part of nation-building projects. It should assess, for example, the public support for programs to assist the poorest, and consider these against universal provisions which can generate broader public support. Crucially, an understanding of politics should form the basis for program that simultaneously enhances access to services, citizens' voice, and accountability.

A Rights Approach to Social Policy

Notwithstanding the quantitative nature of MDGs, which has given direction to national governments and development agencies over the last decade, the ultimate aim of development efforts is the realization of human rights: civil, political, economic, and social. The Universal Declaration of Human Rights, reaffirmed globally at Copenhagen and Copenhagen+10 summits, forms the basis of the social policy framework proposed here.

A progressive social policy framework requires a deep understanding of a rights perspective, in at least four ways. First, this considers social services as a right for its citizen, or progressive realization toward such rights. Particular modes of funding in social sectors, in project mode, altruistic, and voluntary nature, may lead to improved outcomes, but do not necessarily—if they remain charitable—strengthen state–citizen relationships. Second, a rights framework incorporates a notion of duties as well, and particularly, taxation plays a critical but undervalued role in the development of social contracts. Third, a rights agenda does not assume a state role as provider of services, but is critically important in articulating a role as regulator and as such, as final guarantor of citizens' rights. Finally, this social policy framework should focus squarely on the linkages between social policy formation and implementation, and forms of political representation, voice, and the strengthening of public institutions. Amartya Sen (1999) showed the importance of democracy to prevent famine; histories of social policies also show that effective service provision can contribute to democratization.

Social polices are embedded in and graft social contracts. Graham (2002) notes that extension of social protection and the establishment of permanent systems "ultimately requires the development of a politically sustainable social contract." Countries that have expanded publicly financed social protection in the last two decades, such as Brazil, have achieved this on the basis of a renewal of the social contract. New social policies—like extension of health insurance in Thailand and China, reforms in

Korea and Indonesia—followed crises and the perceived need by leaders to respond to public and political pressure. Developing countries often finance temporary programs with international support, thus avoiding difficult political economy choices that are necessary for longer term programs. Such choices do need to be made in the longer run, involving preparing for crises (as China did after 1997), but also enhancing accountability of services and citizens' feedback, and progressive expansion of taxation, as the core of social contracts to be developed in the long run.

As in the work of Marshall, the idea of social policies, and welfare states in particular, is intimately linked to an idea of citizens' rights. Social provisions and rights and citizenship can—and should—be mutually reinforcing. Assessing social policy needs to start from the recognition that provision of social services structures citizenship, which in practice often has reproduced patterns on inequality on the basis of gender, race, etc. These services in turn provide the grounds for contestation, over services, programs, and policies, but often implying struggles over rights and what it means to be a citizen. Recent examples captured under the title "new democratic spaces," highlight a movement toward strengthened accountability, and many of the examples have originated in countries with high inequality, like Brazil and South Africa. We described the example of Chile, and during crises we often witness emergence of "new deals," as the prototype in the US in the 1930s, and perhaps China where the 2008–09 crisis reinforced resolve to promote a "harmonious society." The current crisis provides much concern regarding the depth and duration of its global impact, particularly for the poor and vulnerable, but also provides hope that new deals—at international and national levels—may emerge.

Annexure

Selected Data on Well-being and Government Spending

	Well-being data				Public spending				
	GDP per capita	*Infant mortality per 1000*	*Access to safe water (%)*	*Gini coefficient*	*Government expenditure (% GDP)*	*Public health spending (% government expenditure)*	*Public education spending (% government expenditure)*	*Health expenditure per capita*	*Aid (% GNI)*
Argentina	11,615	14	96	0.51	18.1	14.2	13.1	484	0.05
Bangladesh	1,119	52	74	0.33	10	5.5	14.2	12	1.85
Bolivia	3,816	50	85	0.60	23.8	12.4	18.1	71	5.38
Brazil	8,673	19	90	0.57	22.6	6.7	10.9	371	0.01
Cambodia	1,569	65	41	0.42	9.8	12	14.7	28.57	7.59
Chile	12,627	8	95	0.55	25.9	13.2	18.5	396.78	0.07
China	4,501	20	77	0.47	9.6	1	13.0	81	0.05
Colombia	6,181	17	93	0.56	26	17.7	11.1	201	0.67
Cuba	–	5	91	–	–	11.7	14.2	310	–
Ghana	1,207	76	75	0.41	23.8	6.9	–	30	9.17

(*Annexure Continued*)

(Annexure Continued)

	Well-being data				Public spending				
	GDP per capita	*Infant mortality per 1000*	*Access to safe water (%)*	*Gini coefficient*	*Government expenditure (% GDP)*	*Public health spending (% government expenditure)*	*Public education spending (% government expenditure)*	*Health expenditure per capita*	*Aid (% GNI)*
Indonesia	3,348	26	77	0.39	18.4	5.1	9.0	26	0.40
Kenya	1,421	79	61	0.43	19.8	6.1	17.9	24	4.13
Korea, Rep.	22,278	5	92	0.32	23.3	10.9	16.5	973	–
Lesotho	1,395	102	79	0.63	50	18.2	29.8	69	.3.83
Malawi	678	76	73	0.39	–	16.6	24.6	19	21.39
Malaysia	12,149	10	99	0.49	23.7	7	25.2	222	0.16
Mexico	11,801	29	97	0.46	14.7	12.5	25.6	474	0.03
Central African Rep.	669	115	75	0.61	8.1	10.9	–	13	8.99
Ethiopia	617	77	22	0.30	15	10.8	17.5	6	14.66
Mozambique	716	96	43	0.47	–	12.6	19.5	14	26.23
Namibia	4,671	45	87	0.74	28	10.1	21.0	165	2.24
Nepal	968	46	90	0.47	10.9	8.4	14.9	16	5.71
Nigeria	1,562	99	48	0.44	–	3.5	–	27	11.35
Pakistan	2,288	78	91	0.31	13.5	1.5	12.32	15	1.66

Peru	6,873	21	83	0.52	17.6	8.4	17.0	125	0.55
Philippines	3,055	24	85	0.45	16.2	5.5	16.4	37	0.44
Rwanda	715	98	74	0.47	10.6	16.9	19.0	19	23.63
South Africa	8,807	56	88	0.58	31.8	9.9	17.6	437	0.29
Tanzania	964	74	62	0.35	–	12.6	–	17	14.46
Thailand	7,364	7	99	0.42	20.2	11.3	25.0	98	–0.11
Uganda	865	78	60	0.46	13.5	10	18.3	22	16.70
Venezuela	10,719	18	83	0.48	28.4	7.9	–	247	0.03
Vietnam	2,290	15	85	0.37	–	5.1	–	37	3.09
Zambia	1,220	102	58	0.51	17.7	10.7	14.8	36	14.64
Zimbabwe	–	68	81	0.50	29.5	8.9	–	21	11.70

Source: World Bank, World Development Indicators 2008, CD-Rom, Washington DC (available via ISS Library).

References

Abedian, I. and M. Biggs (eds). 1998. *Economic Globalization and Fiscal Policy*. Cape Town: Oxford University Press.

Abu Sharkh, M. and I. Gough. 2008. "Global Welfare Regimes: A Cluster Analysis," Mimeo, Stanford University.

Adelman, I. 2000. "Introduction to Redrafting the Architecture of the Global Financial System," *World Development*, 28(6): 1053–60.

Adésínà, J. 2006. "In Search of Inclusive Development: Social Policy in the Sub-Saharan African Context," Presentation at UNRISD-Sida/SAREC Workshop on Social Policy and Equality, Buenos Aires, February 21–22.

———. 2007. "Social Policy and the Quest for Inclusive Development. Research Findings from Sub-Saharan Africa," Social Policy and Development Programme Paper Number 33, UNRISD, Geneva.

———. 2010 "Rethinking the Social Protection Paradigm: Social Policy in Africa's Development," paper presented at Conference for the European Report on Development, Dakar, June 28–30.

African Development Bank. 2008. *African Development Report 2008/09. Conflict Resolution, Peace and Restructuring in Africa*. Published for the African Development Bank by Oxford University Press.

African Union. 2006. "Meeting Social Development Challenges. Social Policy Framework in Africa," Addis Ababa.

Agyepong, I.A. and S. Adjei. 2008. "Public Social Policy Development and Implementation: A Case Study of the Ghana National Health Insurance Scheme," *Health Policy and Planning*, 23(2): 150–60.

Ahmad, E., J. Drèze, J. Hills, and A. Sen (eds). 1991. *Social Security in Developing Countries*. New Delhi: UNU/Oxford University Press.

Ahuja, V., B. Bidani, F. Ferreira, and M. Walron. 1997. *Everyone's Miracle? Revisiting Poverty and Inequality in East Asia*. Washington, DC: World Bank.

Aina, T.A. 1999. "West and Central Africa: Social Policy for Reconstruction and Development," in D. Morales-Gómez (ed.), *Transnational Social Policies. The New Challenges of Globalization*, pp. 69–87. London: Earthscan.

———. 2004. "Introduction: How Do We Understand Globalization and Social Policy in Africa," in T.A. Aina, C.S.L. Chachage, and E. Anna-Yao (eds), *Globalization and Social Policy in Africa*, pp. 1–20. Senegal: CODESRIA.

Aizenman, J. and Y. Jinjarak. 2006. "Globalization and Developing Countries—a Shrinking Tax Base?" available at http://econ.ucsc.edu/faculty/jaizen/pubs/Glob_dev_countries.pdf (accessed in May 2007).

Alesina, A. and E.L. Glaeser. 2004. *Fighting Poverty in the US and Europe. A World of Difference.* Oxford: Oxford University Press.

Amorim, R. 2009. "Crisis and Development: Is a Different Path Possible," Paper presented at workshop, "Social Policy Responses to Crises," Beijing, February 23–24.

Amsden, A.H. 2007. *Escape from Empire. The Developing World's Journey through Heaven and Hell.* Cambridge, MA: MIT Press.

Andalón, M. and L.F. Lopez-Calva. 2002. "The Many Mexicos: Income Inequality and Polarization in Urban Mexico During the 90s," Paper presented at Cornell-LSE-WIDER Conference on Spatial Inequality, London, June; available at www.wider.unu.edu/conference/conference-2002-2/papers/luis-f-lopes-calva.pdf (accessed in April 2006).

Andersson, M. and C. Gunnarsson. 2004. "Egalitarianism and the Process of Modern Economic Growth: The Case of Sweden," Background Paper for World Development Report 2006; available at www.worldbank.org/socialpolicy (accessed in May 2010).

Anderson, E. and A. McKay. 2004. "Why is Inequality so High, but also so Variable, in Sub-Saharan Africa?," Mimeo, ODI, London.

Appleton, S. 2001. "User Fee Expenditure Rationalisation and Voucher Systems in Education," in G. Murasu, C. Ugaz, and G. White (eds), *Social Provision in Low-Income Countries,* pp. 157–85. Oxford: Oxford University Press.

Aryeetey, E. and M. Goldstein. 2000. "The Evolution of Social Policy," in E. Aryeetey, J. Harrigan, and M. Nissanke (eds), *Economic Reforms in Ghana. The Miracle and the Mirage,* pp. 284–303. Trenton, NJ: Africa World Press.

Aryeetey, E. and A. McKay. 2005. "Operationalizing Pro-Poor Growth. A Case Study on Ghana," Paper for the multi-donor research program, Operationalizing Pro-Poor Growth, DFID, London.

Atkinson, A.B. 1999. "Is Rising Income Inequality Inevitable? A Critique of the Transatlantic Consensus," WIDER Annual Lecture 3, Helsinki.

Atkinson, A.B. and J. Hills. 1991. "Social Security in Developed Countries: Are There Lessons for Developing Countries?," in E. Ahmad, J. Drèze, J. Hills, and A. Sen (eds), *Social Security in Developing Countries,* pp. 81–111. Oxford: UNU/Oxford University Press.

Baldacci, E., B. Clements, S. Gupta, and Q. Cui. 2004. "Social Spending, Human Capital and Growth in Developing Countries: Implications for Achieving the MDGs," IMF Working Paper 04/217; available at www.imf.org/external/pubs/ft/wp/2004/wp0417.pdf (accessed in May 2010).

———. 2008. "Social Spending, Human Capital, and Growth in Developing Countries," *World Development,* 36(8): 1317–341.

Balioumune-Lutz, M. and S. Lutz. 2004. "Rural-Urban Inequality in Africa: A Panel Study of the Effects of Trade Liberalization and Financial Deepening," ZEI Working Paper B06–2004, Bonn; available at www.zei.de/download/zei_wp/B04-06.pdf (accessed in May 2010).

Baltodano, A.P. 1999. "Social Policy and Social Order in Transnational Societies," in D. Morales-Gómez (ed.), *Transnational Social Policies. The New Challenges of Globalization,* pp. 19–42. London: Earthscan.

Banerjee, A., A. Deaton, N. Lustig, and K. Rogoff. 2006. "An Evaluation of World Bank Research, 1998–2005"; available at http://siteresources.worldbank.org/DEC/Resources/84797-1109362238001/726454-1164121166494/RESEARCH-EVALUATION-2006-Main-Report.pdf (accessed in May 2010).

Bangura, Y. 2005. "Ethnicity, Inequality, and the Public Sector: A Comparative Study," Manuscript, UNRISD; available at http://hdr.undp.org/events/forum2005/papers.cfm (accessed in May 2007).

Bardhan, P. 2007. "Inequality in India and China: Is Globalization to Blame," *Yale Global*, October 15.

Barrientos, A. 2004a. "Latin America: Towards a Liberal-Informal Welfare Regime," in I. Gough, G. Wood, with A. Barrientos, P. Bevan, P. Davis, and G. Room (eds), *Insecurity and Welfare Regimes in Asia, Africa and Latin America*, pp. 121–68. Cambridge: Cambridge University Press.

———. 2004b. "Financing Social Protection," Mimeo, Manchester, Paper commissioned by DFID, London.

———. 2008. "Cash Transfers for Older People Reduce Poverty and Inequality," in A. Bebbington, A.A. Dani, A. de Haan, and M. Walton (eds), *Institutional Pathways to Equity. Addressing Inequality Traps*, pp. 169–92. Washington DC: The World Bank.

Barrientos, A., J. Gideon, and M. Molyneux. 2008. "New Developments in Latin America's Social Policy," *Development and Change*, 39(5): 759–74.

Barrientos, A. and D. Hulme (eds). 2008. *Social Protection for the Poor and Poorest. Concepts, Policies and Politics*. Hampshire: Palgrave MacMillan.

Bastagli, F. 2009. "From Safety Net to Social Policy? The Role of Conditional Cash Transfers in Welfare State Development in Latin America," Working Paper No.60, International Policy Center for Inclusive Growth, Brasilia; available at www.ipc-undp.org/pub/IPCWorkingPaper60.pdf (accessed in May 2010).

Basu, K. 2001. "Marginalization in a Globalizing World. Some Plausible Scenarios and Suggestions," paper for the Asia and Pacific Forum on Poverty: Reforming Policies and Institutions for Poverty Reduction, Asian Development Bank, Milan, February 5–9.

Bebbington, A., A.A. Dani, A. de Haan, and M. Walton (eds). 2008. *Institutional Pathways to Equity. Addressing Inequality Traps*. Washington DC: The World Bank.

Bennett, L. 2008. "Policy Reform and Culture Change: Contesting Gender, Caste, and Ethnic Exclusion in Nepal," in A.A. Dani and A. de Haan (eds), *Inclusive States: Social Policy and Structural Inequalities*, pp. 197–224. Washington DC: The World Bank.

Berg, J. and L. Taylor. 2001. "External Liberalization, Economic Performance, and Social Policy," in L. Taylor (ed.), *External Liberalization, Economic Performance, and Social Policy*, pp. 11–55. Oxford: Oxford University Press.

Berkman, S. 2008. *The World Bank and the Gods of Lending*. Sterling, VA: Kumarian Press.

Berry, A. 2006. "A Review of Literature and Evidence on the Economic and Social Effects of Economic Integration in Latin America: Some Policy Implications," Paper presented at conference, Lives and Livelihoods, University of Guelph, May; available at www.livesandlivelihoods.org (accessed in September 2006).

Besley, T., R. Burgess, and B. Esteve-Volart. 2004. "Operationalizing Pro-Poor Growth. A Case Study on India," Paper for multi-donor research program, Operationalizing Pro-Poor Growth, DFID, London.

Besley, T., R. Burgess, and I. Rasul. 2003. "Benchmarking Government Provision of Social Safety Nets," Social Protection Discussion Paper No. 0315, World Bank, Washington DC.

Bevan, P. 2004. "The Dynamics of Africa's In/security Regimes," in I. Gough, G. Wood, with A. Barrientos, P. Bevan, P. Davis, and G. Room (eds), *Insecurity and Welfare Regimes in Asia, Africa and Latin America*, pp. 202–52. Cambridge: Cambridge University Press.

Bhagwati, J. 2005. *In Defence of Globalization*. Oxford: Oxford University Press.

Bhalla, G.S. 2008. "Access to Land in India: Contemporary Issues," Paper presented at the International Conference on Universalising Socio-Economic Security in South Asia, New Delhi, February 17–20.

Bhatia, B. and J. Drèze. 2006. "Employment Guarantee in Jharkhand: Ground Realities," *Economic and Political Weekly*, 41(29): 3198–202.

Birdsall, N. 2005. "The World is Not Flat: Inequality and Injustice in Our Global Economy," WIDER Annual Lecture 9, Helsinki.

Birdsall, N., D. Ross, and R. Sabot. 1995. "Inequality and Growth Reconsidered: Lessons from East Asia," *World Bank Economic Review*, 9(3): 477–508.

Blackden, M. and C. Bhanu. 1999. "Gender, Growth and Poverty Reduction," World Bank Technical Paper No. 429, World Bank, Washington DC.

Blackden, M., S. Canagarajah, S. Klasen, and D. Lawson. 2006. "Gender and Growth in Sub-Saharan Africa," WIDER Research Paper No. 2006/37, Helsinki.

Boix, C. 2008. "Spain: Development, Democracy and Equity," in A. Bebbington, A.A. Dani, A. de Haan, and M. Walton (eds), *Institutional Pathways to Equity. Addressing Inequality Traps*, pp. 217–44. Washington DC: The World Bank.

Booth, D., A. Grigsby, and C. Toranzo. 2006. "Politics and Poverty Reduction Strategies: Lessons from Latin American HIPCs," Working Paper 262, ODI, London.

Borraz, F. and E. López-Córdova. 2004. "Has Globalization Deepened Income Inequality in Mexico?," GTAP Resource 1455; available at www.gtap.agecon.purdue.edu/resources/download/1707.pdf (accessed in April 2006).

Bourguignon, F. and C. Morrisson. 2002. "Inequality among World Citizens: 1820–1992," *American Economic Review*, 92(4): 727–44.

Bowles, S.S. 2000. "Globalization and Economic Justice," Benjamin H. Hibbard Memorial Lecture, University of Wisconsin–Madison.

Brawley, M.R. 2003. *The Politics of Globalization. Gaining Perspective, Assessing Consequences.* Peterborough: Broadview Press.

Brett, E.A. 2003. "Participation and Accountability in Development Management," *Journal of Development Studies*, 40(2): 1–29.

Brown, G. 2005a. "Making Ethnic Citizens. The Politics and Practice of Education in Malaysia," Working Paper 23, Centre for Research on Inequality, Human Security and Ethnicity, Oxford; available at www.crise.ox.ac.uk/pubs/workingpaper23.pdf (accessed in May 2010).

———. 2005b. "The Formation and Management of Political Identities: Indonesia and Malaysia Compared," Working Paper 10, Center for Research on Inequality, Human Security and Ethnicity, Oxford; available at www.crise.ox.ac.uk/pubs/workingpaper10.pdf (accessed in May 2010).

Brown, G. and F. Stewart. 2006. "The Implications of Horizontal Inequality for Aid," CRISE Working Paper No. 36, Oxford.

Budd, E. 2004. *Democratization, Development, and the Patrimonial State in the Age of Globalization*. Maryland: Lexington Book.

Budlender, D. 2000. "The Political Economy of Women's Budgets in the South," *World Development*, 28(7): 1379–390.

———. 2003. "Gender Budgets and Beyond: Feminist Fiscal Policy in the Context of Globalisation," *Gender and Development*, 11(1): 15–24.

Burgoon, B. 2001. "Globalization and Welfare Compensation: Disentangling the Ties that Bind," *International Organisation*, 55(3): 509–52.

Buvinić, M. and J. Mazza. 2008. "Addressing Exclusion: Social Policy Perspectives from Latin America and the Caribbean," in A.A. Dani and A. de Haan (eds), *Inclusive States: Social Policy and Structural Inequalities*, pp. 123–44. Washington DC: The World Bank.

Casey, Bernard H. and R. McKinnon. 2009. "Social Pensions and Policy Learning: The Case of Southern Africa," *International Social Security Review*, 62(4): 81–102.

Cao Hongmin. n.d. "The Strategy and its Impact of Cooperation between Eastern and Western Regions in Alleviating Poverty"; available at http://www.ifpri.org/2020Chinaconference/pdf/004CaoHongmin.pdf (accessed in May 2007).

Central Bureau of Statistics (CBS) Nepal. 2006. *Resilience Amidst Conflict. As an Assessment of Poverty in Nepal, 1995–96 and 2003–04,* Government of Nepal, Kathmandu.

Chang, H.-J. 2003. *Globalisation, Economic Development and the Role of the State*. London: Zed Books.

———. 2004. "The Role of Social Policy in Economic Development: Some Theoretical Reflections and Lessons from East Asia," in T. Mkandawire (ed.), *Social Policy in a Development Context*, pp. 246–61. Basingstoke: Palgrave Macmillan.

———. 2007. *Bad Samaritans. Rich Nations, Poor Policies and the Threat to the Developing World*. London: Random House.

Chatterjee, M., R. Levine, N. Murthy, and S. Rao-Seshadri. n.d. *Sparing Lives. Better Reproductive Health for Poor Women in South Asia*. Washington DC: World Bank.

Chen, S. and M. Ravallion. 2008. "The Developing World is Poorer Than We Thought, But No Less Successful in the Fight Against Poverty," Policy Research Working Paper 4703, World Bank, Washington DC.

Chen, S., M. Ravallion, and Youjuan Wang. 2006. "Di Bao: A Guaranteed Minimum Income in China's Cities?," Policy Research Working Paper 3805, World Bank, Washington DC.

Cheru, F. 2006. "Building and Supporting PRSPs in Africa: What Has Worked Well So Far? What Needs Changing?," *Third World Quarterly*, 27(2): 355–76.

Chhachhi, A. 2008. "Ensuring Democratic Citizenship: A Gender Perspective on Contending Models of Social Protection," Paper presented at the International Conference on Universalising Socio-Economic Security in South Asia, New Delhi, February 17–20.

Chopra, M., D. Sanders, R. Shrimpton, and A. Tomkins. 2002. "Making Nutrition a Part of Social Sector Reform: Challenges and Opportunities," Draft Background Paper for the 5th Report on the World Nutrition Situation, presented in Berlin.

Christiansen, C. and S.R. Whyte. 2008. "Arenas of Child Support: Interfaces of Family, State, and Nongovernmental Organization Provisions of Social Security," in A.A. Dani and A. de Haan (eds), *Inclusive States: Social Policy and Structural Inequalities*, pp. 295–320. Washington DC: The World Bank.

Chronic Poverty Research Center. 2008. "The Chronic Poverty Report 2008–09," Manchester; available at www.chronicpoverty.org (accessed in May 2010).

Chua Beng Huat. 2005. "Welfare Developmentalism in Singapore and Malaysia," in H.-J. Kwon (ed.), *Transforming the Developmental Welfare State in East Asia*, pp. 98–117. London: Palgrave Macmillan; UNRISD.

Cichon, M. 2009. "A New Deal for People in a Global Crisis—Social Security for All: Making the Economic and Affordability Case," Presentation, New York, January.

Cichon, M., W. Scholz, A. van de Meerendonk, K. Hagemejer, F. Bertranou, and P. Plamondon. 2004. *Financing Social Protection*. Geneva: International Labour Office and International Social Security Association.

Cigno, A., F.C. Rosati, and L. Guarcello. 2002. "Does Globalisation Increase Child Labour," *World Development*, 30(9): 1579–90.

Clements, B., S. Gupta, and G. Inchauste. 2004. "Fiscal Policy for Economic Development: An Overview," in S. Gupta, B. Clements, and G. Inchauste (eds), *Helping Countries Develop. The Role of Fiscal Policy*, pp. 1–22. Washington DC: International Monetary Fund (IMF); available at www.imf.org/external/pubs/nft/2004/hcd/ch01.pdf (accessed in May 2006).

Collier, Paul. 2007. *The Bottom Billion. Why the Poorest Countries Are Failing and What Can Be Done about It?* Oxford: Oxford University Press.

Comptroller and Auditor General. 2007. "Performance Audit of Implementation of National Rural Employment Guarantee Act, 2005 (NREGA)," draft report, New Delhi; available at http://www.cag.gov.in/html/reports/civil/2008_PA11_nregacivil/introduction.pdf (accessed in May 2010).

Conway, T., A. de Haan, and A. Norton (eds). 2000. *Social Protection: New Directions of Donor Agencies*. London: DFID.

Cook, Sarah and Huck-Ju Kwon. 2007. "Economic Reform and Social Protection in East Asia"; available at http://www.unifi.it/confsp/papers/pdf/Kwon_Cook.doc (accessed in May 2010).

Cook, S. and G. White. 2001. "Alternative Approaches to Welfare Policy Analysis: New Institutional Economics, Politics, and Political Economy," in G. Mwabu, C. Ugaz, and G. White (eds), *Social Provision in Low-Income Countries. New Patterns and Emerging Trends*, pp. 26–52. Oxford: Oxford University Press; The United Nations University-World Institute for Development Economics Research (UNU-WIDER).

Cornia, G.A. 1999. "Liberalisation, Globalisation and Income Distribution," World Institute for Development Economics Research (WIDER) Working Paper No. 157, WIDER, Helsinki.

———. 2004. "Inequality, Growth, and Poverty: An Overview of Changes over the Last Two Decades," in G. A. Cornia (ed.), *Inequality, Growth, and Poverty in an Era of Liberalization and Globalization*, pp. 3–25. Oxford: Oxford University Press; The United Nations University—World Institute for Development Economics Research (UNU-WIDER).

Cornia, G.A., R. Jolly, and F. Stewart. 1987. *Adjustment with a Human Face*. Oxford: Clarendon Press.

Cornia, G.A. and L. Menchini. 2005. "The Pace and Distribution of Health Improvements During the Late 40 Years: Some Preliminary Results," UNDP–French Government Sponsored, Forum on Human Development, Paris, January.

Cornwall, A. 2004. "New Democratic Spaces? The Politics and Dynamics of Institutionalised Participation," *IDS Bulletin*, 35(2): 1–10.

Cornwall, A. and J. Gaventa. 2000. "From Users and Choosers to Makers and Shapers. Repositioning Participation in Social Policy," *IDS Bulletin*, 31(4): 50–62.

Cortés, R. 2008. "The Contemporary Social Policy Debate in Latin America," *Global Social Policy*, 8(1): 109–14.

Cox, R.H. 1998. "The Consequences of Welfare Reform: How Conceptions of Social Rights are Changing," *Journal of Social Policy*, 27(1): 1–16.

Cramer, C. 2003. "Does Inequality Cause Conflict?," *Journal of International Development*, 15(4): 397–412.

Cruces, G. 2009. "Social Policy Responses to the Crisis of 2001–2002 in Argentina," Paper presented at workshop, "Social Policy Responses to Crises," Beijing, February 23–24.

Dani, A.A. and A. de Haan. 2008a. "Social Policy in a Development Context: Structural Inequalities and Inclusive Institutions," in A.A. Dani and A. de Haan (eds), *Inclusive States: Social Policy and Structural Inequalities*, pp. 3–37. Washington DC: The World Bank.

——— (eds). 2008b. *Inclusive States: Social Policy and Structural Inequalities*. Washington DC: The World Bank.

Datt, G. and M. Ravallion. 2002. "Is India's Economic Growth Leaving the Poor Behind," Policy Research Working Paper, World Bank, Washington DC.

Davis, P. 2004. "Rethinking the Welfare Regimes Approach in the Context of Bangladesh," in I. Gough, G. Wood, with A. Barrientos, P. Bevan, P. Davis, and G. Room (eds), *Insecurity and Welfare Regimes in Asia, Africa and Latin America*, pp. 255–86. Cambridge: Cambridge University Press.

Davoodi, H.R., E.R. Tiongson, and S.S. Asawanuchit. 2003. "How Useful Are Benefit Incidence Analyses of Public Education and Health Spending," IMF Working Paper WP/03/227, IMF, Washington DC.

De Grauwe, P. and M. Polan. 2003. "Globalisation and Social Spending," CESIfo Working Paper No. 885; available at http://www.econ.kuleuven.be/ew/academic/intecon/Degrauwe/PDG-Publications_recent.htm#discussion papers (accessed in May 2010).

de Haan, A. 1997. "Migrants and their Families: Rural-Urban Labour Migration in India during the Twentieth Century," *The History of the Family. An International Quarterly*, 2(4): 481–505.

———. 1998. "Social Exclusion: An Alternative Concept for the Study of Deprivation?" *IDS Bulletin*, 29(1): 10–19.

———. 2005. "Migration, Gender, Poverty—Family as the Missing Link?" in S. Arya and A. Roy (eds), *Poverty, Gender and Migration*. New Delhi: Sage Publications.

———. 2006. "Migration in the Development Studies Literature: Has It Come Out of Marginality?," UNU-WIDER Research Paper, RP 2006/19, Helsinki.

———. 2007a. "Labelling Works: The Language and Politics of Caste and Tribe in India," in Rosalind Eyben and Joy Moncrieffe (eds), *The Power of Labelling. How People are Categorized and Why it Matters*, pp. 143–59. London: Earthscan.

———. 2007b. *Reclaiming Social Policy. Globalization, Social Exclusion and New Poverty Reduction Strategies*. Basingstoke: Palgrave MacMillan.

———. 2008. "Disparities within India's Poorest Region: Why Do the Same Institutions Work Differently in Different Places?," in A. Bebbington, A.A. Dani, A. de Haan, and M. Walton (eds), *Institutional Pathways to Equity. Addressing Inequality Traps*, pp. 103–36. Washington DC: The World Bank.

———. 2009a. "Aid: The Drama, the Fiction, and Does It Work?" ISS Working Paper 488, ISS, The Hague.

———. 2009b. "DFID and Social Exclusion. The Use and Otherwise of a Concept in International Aid," Paper for the panel on Adverse Incorporation and Social Exclusion, Conference Escaping the Poverty Trap, Washington DC, February 26–27.

———. 2009c. *How the Aid Industry Works: An Introduction to International Development*. Sterling, VA: Kumarian Press.

———. 2010a. "A Defining Moment? China's Social Policy Response to the Financial Crisis," *Journal of International Development*, 22.

———. 2010b. "The Financial Crisis and China's 'Harmonious Society," Journal of Current Chinese Affairs, 2.

———. Forthcoming 2010. "Social Integration in Europe post-2001: Social Policy Regimes under Pressure," paper for the International Sociological Association World Congress of Sociology, Gothernburg, July 11–17.

de Haan, A. and A. Dubey. 2003. "Extreme Deprivation in Remote Areas in India: Social Exclusion as Explanatory Concept," Paper for Manchester Conference on Chronic Poverty, April 7–9.

de Haan, A., A. Dubey, and G. Sabharwal. 2009. "Between Emergency Responses and Rights-Based Approaches: Addressing Poverty and Undernutrition in Eastern India," *IDS Bulletin*, 40(4): 39–44.

de Haan, A., B. Huber, and A. van den Heever. 2001. "Report of a Workshop on Integrating Social and Economic Polices," Mimeo, DFID and UNDESA.

de Haan, A. and G. Sabharwal. 2008. "South and East Asian Social Policy Experiences: Institutions and Governance in the Extension of Social Security," *Indian Journal of Human Development*, 2(1): 63–78.

de Haan, A. and M. Everest-Phillips. 2010. "Can New Aid Modalities Handle Politics?" in George Mavrotas (ed.), Foreign Aid for Development: Issues, Challenges and the New Agenda, pp. 197–221. Oxford: Oxford University Press.

de Haan, A. and S. Sen. 1999. *A Case for Labour History*. Calcutta: K.P. Bagchi.

de Haan, A., Xiaobo Zhang, and Shenggen Fan. 2010. "China's Reforms: Are There Lessons for Other countries?" in Zhang Xiaobo, Shenggen, Fan and Arjan de Haan (eds), *Narratives of Chinese Economic Reforms: How Does China Cross the River?* Singapore, New Jersey, London: World Scientific Publishing.

de Mello, L. 2002. "Public Policies and the Millennium Development Goals," *IMF Research Bulletin*, 3(4): 1–7.

de Mello, L. and E.R. Tiongson. 2003. "Income Inequality and Redistributive Government Spending," IMF Working Paper No. 03/14, IMF, Washington DC.

de Silva, S. and J.-W. Sum. 2008. "Social Funds as an Instrument of Social Protection. An Analysis of Lending Trends, Social Protection Discussion Paper. FY 2000–2007," HDNSP, World Bank, Washington DC.

Deacon, B., with M. Hulse and P. Stubbs. 1997. *Global Social Policy: International Organisations and the Future of Welfare*. London: Sage Publications.

———. 2000. "Globalization and Social Policy," UNRISD Occasional Paper 5, Geneva.

———. 2003. "Prospects for Equitable Social Provision in a Globalising World," in P. Mosley and E. Dowler (eds), *Poverty and Social Exclusion in North and South. Essays on Social Policy and Global Poverty*, pp. 17–33. London and New York: Reduction, Routledge.

———. 2004. "Globalization of the Welfare State? World Society, Transnational Social policy and 'New Welfare State'," Paper for International Conference at Hanse Institute for Advanced Studies, Delmenhorst: Germany.

———. 2005. "From 'Safety Nets' Back to 'Universal Social Provision. Is the Global Tide Turning?'," *Global Social Policy*, 5(1): 19–28.

Deaton, A. and J. Drèze. 2009. "Food and Nutrition in India: Facts and Interpretations," *Economic and Political Weekly*, 44(7): 42–65.

Department of Agriculture, South Africa. 2001. "The Strategic Plan for South African Agriculture." Available online at http://www.nda.agric.za/docs/sectorplan/sectorplanE.htm (accessed in May 2010).

Deshpande, A. and K. Newman. 2010. "Where the Path Leads: The Role of Caste in Post-University Employment Expectations," in Sukhadeo Thorat and Katherine S. Newman (eds), *Blocked by Caste. Economic Discrimination in Modern India*, pp. 88–122. New Delhi: Oxford University Press.

Dev, S.M. 2008. *Inclusive Growth in India. Agriculture, Poverty, and Human Development*. New Delhi: Oxford University Press.

Dev, S.M. and J. Mooij. 2002. "Social Sector Expenditures and Budgeting. An Analysis of Patterns and the Budget making Process in India in the 1990s," Working Paper 43, CESS, Hyderabad.

Devereux, S. and S. Cook. 2000. "Does Social Policy Meet Social Needs," *IDS Bulletin*, 31(4): 63–73.

Devereux, S. and R. Sabates-Wheeler. 2004. "Transformative Social Protection," IDS Working Paper 232, IDS, Brighton.

———. 2007. "Editorial Introduction: Debating Social Protection," *IDS Bulletin*, 38(3): 1–7.

Department for International Development (DFID). 2005. "Social Transfers and Chronic Poverty: Emerging Evidence and the Challenge Ahead," A DFID Practice Paper, DFID, London.

Dijkstra, G. 2005. "The PRSP Approach and the Illusion of Improved Aid Effectiveness: Lessons from Bolivia, Honduras and Nicaragua," *Development Policy Review*, 23(5): 443–64.

———. 2006. "Rejoinder," *Development Policy Review*, 24(4): 481–82.

Dijkstra, G. and J.K. van Donge. 2001. "What Does the Show Case Show? Evidence of and Lessons from Adjustment in Uganda," *World Development*, 29(5): 841–63.

Dollar, D. 2008. "Lesson from China for Africa," World Bank Policy Research Working Paper 4531, Washington DC.

Dollar, D. and A. Kraay. 2002. "Growth *is* Good for the Poor," *Journal of Economic Growth*, 7(3): 195–225.

Dow, J. 2003. "The Social Inclusión/Exclusión Dichotomy in Guyana and the Caribbean," Paper presented at seminar on Good Practices in Social Inclusion: A Dialogue between Europe and Latin America and the Caribbean, Milan, Italy, March 21–22.

D'Souza, E. 2008. "Globalization's Underbelly: Capital Flows and Indian Economy," *Economic and Political Weekly*, August 30, pp. 34–38; available at http://epw.in/epw/uploads/articles/12603.pdf (accessed in May 2010).

Dreher, A. 2006. "The Influence of Globalization on Taxes and Social Policy: An Empirical Analysis for OECD Countries," *European Journal of Political Economy*, 22(1): 179–201.

Drèze, J. and A.K. Sen. 1989. *Hunger and Public Action*. Oxford: Clarendon Press.

———. 1991. "Public Action for Social Security: Foundations and Strategy," in E. Ahmad, J. Drèze, J. Hills, and A. Sen (eds), *Social Security in Developing Countries*, pp. 3–40. New Delhi: UNU/Oxford University Press.

Driscoll, R. and A. Evans. 2005. "Second-Generation Poverty Reduction Strategies: New Opportunities and Emerging Issues," *Development Policy Review*, 23(1): 5–25.

Durevall, D. and F. Munshi. 2006. "Trade Liberalization and Wage Inequality: Empirical Evidence from Bangladesh," Mimeo, Department of Economics, School of Business, Economics and Law, Göteborg University.

Dutt, A.K. and J.M. Rao. 2001. "India: Globalization and its Social Discontents," in L. Taylor (ed.), *External Liberalization, Economic Performance, and Social Policy*, pp. 179–216. Oxford: Oxford University Press.

Dutta, Puja, Rinku Murgai, Martin Ravallion, and Dominique van de Walle. 2010. "Status of NREG in Bihar," presentation at the International Seminar on Poverty in Bihar: Pattern, Dimensions and Eradication Strategies, Patna, April 18–20.

Dunham, D. 2008. "Growth and Dismantling of the Welfare State in Sri Lanka," *Indian Journal of Human Development*, 2(1): 93–110.

Dunt, I. 2009. "Why I'll Never Understands Americans," August 14; available at http://www.politics.co.uk/analysis/health/comment-i-ll-never-understand-americans-$1318652.htm, (accessed in May 2010).

Echeverri-Gent, J. 1993. *The State and the Poor: Public Policy and Political Development in India and the United States*. Berkeley: University of California Press.

ECLAC. 2006. *Shaping the Future of Social Protection: Access, Financing and Solidarity*, Report of Thirty First Session of Economic Commission for Latin America and the Caribbean (ECLAC), Montevideo.

Economist. 2003. "Where's the Stick. Something has gone Wrong with Bosses Pay. The Solution has to Lie with Shareholders," *The Economist*, October 11; available at http://www.economist.com/opinion/displaystory.cfm?story_id=E1_NTNTRVG (accessed in May 2010).

Economist. 2006a. "How to Make China Even Richer. Let the Peasants Own Their Land," *The Economist*, March 25; available at http://www.economist.com/opinion/displaystory.cfm?story_id=5660833 (accessed in May 2010).

———. 2006b. "Inequality and the American Dream. The World's Most Impressive Machine Needs a Little Adjusting," *The Economist*, June 17; available at http://www.economist.com/opinion/displaystory.cfm?story_id=E1_SDVJTVV (accessed in May 2010).

———. 2007. "Rich Man, Poor Man. A Poisonous Mix of Inequality and Sluggish Wages Threatens Globalisation," *The Economist*, January 20; available at http://www.economist.com/opinion/displaystory.cfm?story_id=8554819 (accessed in May 2010).

———. 2008a. "Half-way from Rags to Riches. A Special Report on Vietnam," *The Economist*, April 26.

———. 2008b. "The Financial Crisis. What Next?" *The Economist*, September 18; available at http://www.economist.com/displayStory.cfm?story_id=E1_TNNGPTVR (accessed in May 2010).

———. 2009. "The Return of Economic Nationalism," *The Economist*, February 7; available at http://www.economist.com/printedition/displayStory.cfm?Story_ID=13061443 (accessed in May 2010).

Edhigeji, Omano. 2005. "A Democratic Developmental State in Africa? A Concept Paper," Center for Policy Studies, Johannesburg; available at http://www.rrojasdatabank.info/devstate/edigheji.pdf (accessed in May 2010).

Elson, D. 2004. "Social Policy and Macroeconomic Performance: Integrating 'the Economic' and 'the Social'," in T. Mkandawire (ed.), *Social Policy in a Development Context*, pp. 63–79. Basingstoke: Palgrave Macmillan.

Elson, D. and N. Çagatay. 2000. "The Social Content of Macro-economic Policies," *World Development*, 28(7): 1347–64.

———. 2003. "Introduction," *World Development*, 28(7): 1145–56.

Esping-Andersen, G. 1990. *The Three Worlds of Welfare Capitalism*. Cambridge: Polity.

———. 1999. *Social Foundations of Post-Industrial Economies*. Oxford: Oxford University Press.

European University Institute (EUI) and European Commission (EC). Forthcoming. "European Report on Development 2010: Promoting Resilience through Social Protection;" available at http://erd.eui.eu/erd-2010/ (accessed in July 2010).

Evans, M. and S. Harkness. 2008. "Social Protection in Vietnam and Obstacles to Progressivity," *Asian Social Work and Policy Review*, 2(1): 30–52.

Eyoh, D. and R. Sandbrook. 2003. "Pragmatic Neo-liberalism and Just Development in Africa," in A. Kohli, C. Moon, and G. Sorensen (eds), *States, Markets, and Just Growth, Development in the Twenty-first Century*, pp. 227–57. Tokyo: United Nations University Press.

Fan, S. and N. Rao. 2003. "Public Spending in Developing Countries: Trend, Determination and Impact," Discussion Paper, IFPRI, Washington DC.

Ferreira, F.H.G., J.A. Litchfield, and P.G. Leite. 2006. "The Rise and Fall of Brazilian Inequality, 1981–2004," World Bank Policy Research Working Paper 3867, World Bank, Washington DC.

Figueora, A. and M. Barrón. 2005. "Inequality, Ethnicity, and Social Disorder in Peru," CRISE Working Paper No. 8, Centre for Research on Inequality, Human Security and Ethnicity, Oxford; available at www.crise.ox.ac.uk/pubs/workingpaper8(lq).pdf (accessed in May 2010).

Forbes, K. 2000. "A Re-assessment of the Relationship between Inequality and Growth," *American Economic Review*, 90(5): 869–87.

Foster, M. 2000. "New Approaches to Development Co-operation: What Can We Learn from Experiences with Implementing Sector Wide Approaches," Working Paper 140, ODI, London.

Fosu, A.K. 2009. "Inequality and the Impact of Growth on Poverty: Comparative Evidence for Sub-Saharan Africa," Working Paper 98, Brooks World Poverty Institute.

Fraser, D. 1973. *The Evolution of the British Welfare State*. London: Palgrave MacMillan.

Fumo, C., A. de Haan, J. Holland, and N. Kanji. 2000. *Social Fund: An Effective Way to Support Local Action for Poverty Reduction?* London: DFID.

Gaiha, R. and V.S. Kulkarni. 2006. "Common Interest Groups, Village Institutions and Rural Poor in India—A Review of the District Poverty Initiatives Project," Mimeo, to appear in *Contemporary South Asia*, New Delhi.

Gasparini, L. 2004. "Poverty and Inequality in Argentina: Methodological Issues and a Literature Review," Centro de Estudios Distributivos, Laborales y Sociales, Universidad Nacional de La Plata.

Gaspart, F. and J.-P. Platteau, 2006. "The Perverse Effect of Cheap Aid Money," Paper presented at World Institute for Development Economics Research (WIDER) Conference, Helsinki, June 16–17.

Gayi, S. 1995. "Adjusting to the Social Costs of Adjustment in Ghana: Problems and Prospects," *European Journal of Development Research*, 7(2): 77–100.

Gelb, S. 2003. *Inequality in South Africa: Nature, Causes and Responses for DfID Policy Initiative on Addressing Inequality in Middle-income Countries*. Johannesburg: The Edge Institute; available at www.the-edge.org.za/publications.htm (accessed in May 2007).

Gill, I., T. Packard, and J. Yermo. 2005. *Keeping the Promise of Social Security in Latin America*. Washington DC: World Bank; Palo Alto: Stanford University Press.

Gilson, L. and D. McIntyre. 2005. "Removing User Fees for Primary Care in Africa: The Need for Careful Action," *British Medical Journal*, 331(October): 762–65.

Glaessner, Philip J., Kye W. Lee, Anna M. Sant'Anna, and Jean-Jacques de St. Antoine. 1994. "Poverty Alleviation and Social Investment Funds: The Latin American Experience," Discussion Paper No. 261, World Bank, Washington DC.

Glewwe, P., M. Gragnolati, and M. Zaman. 2000. "Who Gained from Vietnam's Boom in the 1990s? An Analysis of Poverty and Inequality Trends," World Bank Policy Research Working Paper No. 261, World Bank, Washington DC.

Glewwe, P., S. Koch, and B.L. Nguyen. 2002. "Child Nutrition, Economic Growth and the Provision of Health Care Services in Vietnam in the 1990s," World Bank Policy Research Working Paper No. 2776, World Bank, Washington DC.

Global Social Policy. 2006. "GSP Forum: The World Bank and Social Development Policy—Turning the Tide?" *Global Social Policy*, 6(3): 259–87.

Goñi, E., J.H. López, and L. Servén. 2008. "Fiscal Redistribution and Income Inequality in Latin America," Policy Research Working Paper 4487, World Bank, Washington DC.

Goudswaard, K. and K. Caminada, 2010, "The Redistributive Effect of Public and Private Social Programmes: A Cross-country Empirical Analysis," *International Social Security Review,* 63(1): 1–19.

Gough, I. 2000. "Welfare Regimes: On Adapting the Framework to Developing Countries," Global Social Policy Working Paper No. 1, Institute for International Policy Analysis (IFIPA), University of Bath.

Gough, I. 2004a. "East Asia: The Limits of Productivist Regimes," in I. Gough and G. Wood (eds), *Insecurity and Welfare Regimes in Asia, Africa and Latin America*, pp. 169–201. Cambridge: Cambridge University Press.

———. 2004b. "Welfare Regimes in Development Contexts: A Global and Regional Analysis," in I. Gough and G. Wood (eds), *Insecurity and Welfare Regimes in Asia, Africa and Latin America*, pp. 15–48. Cambridge: Cambridge University Press.

———. 2008. "European Welfare States: Explanations and Lessons for Developing Countries," in A.A. Dani and A. de Haan (eds), *Inclusive States: Social Policy and Structural Inequalities*, pp. 39–72. Washington DC: The World Bank.

Gough, I., G. Wood, with A. Barrientos, P. Bevan, P. Davis, and G. Room (eds). 2004. *Insecurity and Welfare Regimes in Asia, Africa and Latin America*. Cambridge: Cambridge University Press.

Government of Malawi. 2002. "Malawi Poverty Reduction Strategy Paper. Final Draft"; available at http://povlibrary.worldbank.org/files/Malawi_PRSP.pdf (accessed in 2004).

Graham, C. 2002. "Crafting Sustainable Social Contracts in Latin America: Political Economy, Public Attitudes, and Social Policy," Working Paper, The Brookings Institute; available at http://www.brookings.edu/es/dynamics/papers/socialcontracts/socialcontracts.pdf (accessed in May 2010).

Green, Duncan. 2008. *From Poverty to Power. How Active Citizens and Effective States Can Change the World*. Oxford: Oxfam International.

Greenspan, A. 2008. "Banks Need More Capital," *The Economist*, guest article, December 18.

Grindle, M.S. 2002. "Good Enough Governance: Poverty Reduction and Reform in Developing Countries," Mimeo, Harvard University.

Grosse, M., K. Harttgen, and S. Klasen. 2008. "Measuring Pro-poor Growth in Non-Income Dimensions," *World Development*, 36(6): 1021–47.

Guan, Xinping. 2005. "China's Social Policy: Reform and Development in the Context of Marketization and Globalization," in H. Kwon (ed.), *Transforming the Developmental Welfare State in East Asia*, pp. 231–56. London: Palgrave Macmillan; UNRISD.

Gubhaju, B. 2007. "Fertility Decline in Asia: Opportunities and Challenges," *The Japanese Journal of Population*, 5(1): 19–42.

Gustafsson, B. and D. Quheng. 2007. "Social Assistance Receipt and Its Importance for Combating Poverty in Urban China," Discussion paper 2758, IZA Bonn; available at http://www.;iza.org/

Gustafsson, B., Li Shi, and T. Sicular (eds). 2008. *Inequality and Public Policy in China*. Cambridge: Cambridge University Press.

Governance and Social Development Research Center (GSDRC). 2008. "HelpDesk Research Report, Policy Learning and Transfer," September 17; available at http://www.gsdre.org/ (accessed in July 2010).

Haddad, L. and S. Zeitlyn (eds). 2009. "Lifting the Curse: Overcoming Persistent Undernutrition in India," *IDS Bulletin*, 40(4).

Hall, A. 2007. "Social Policies in the World Bank: Paradigms and Challenges," *Global Social Policy*, 8(1): 151–75.

Hall, A. and J. Midgley. 2004. *Social Policy for Development*. London: Sage Publications.

Harriss, J. 1999. "Comparing Political Regimes across Indian States. A Preliminary Essay," *Economic and Political Weekly*, 34(48): 3367–377.

———. 2001. "Globalisation and the World's Poor: Institutions, Inequality and Justice," *Economic and Political Weekly*, 36(23): 2034–037.

Harriss, J. and N. Kohli. 2009. "Notes on the Differing 'States' of Child Undernutrition in Rural India," *IDS Bulletin*, 40(4): 9–15.

Heerink, N., M. Spoor, and Futian Qu. 2007. "Transition, Economic Policy, and Institutional Reforms in China and Vietnam," in Max Spoor, Nico Heerink, and Futian Qu (eds), *Dragons with Clay Feet? Transition, Sustainable Land Use, and Rural Environment in China and Vietnam*, pp. 11–46. Lanham, MD: Lexington Book.

Heller, P., et al. 2006. "Managing Fiscal Policy in Low Income Countries: How to Reconcile a Scaling up of Aid Flows and Debt Relief with Macroeconomic Stability," paper presented at UNU-WIDER Conference on Aid: Principles, Policies and Performance, Helsinki, June 16–17; available at http://www.hlfhealthmdgs.org/Documents/June2006Helsinki Paper.pdf (accessed in July 2010).

HelpAge International. 2003. *Non-contributory Pensions and Poverty Prevention. A Comparative Study of Brazil and South Africa*. London: Helpage.

———. 2004. "Age and Security. Summary Report. How Social Pensions Can Deliver Effective Aid to Poor Older People and their Families," London; available at www.helpage.org/Resources/Policyreports (accessed in May 2010).

———. 2007. "Social Cash Transfers for Asia. Ensuring Social Protection/Social Pensions in Old Age in the Context of Rapid Ageing"; available at www.helpage.org (accessed in May 2010).

Herbst, J. 1994. "The Dilemmas of Explaining Political Upheaval: Ghana in Comparative Perspective," in J.A. Widner (ed.), *Economic Change and Political Liberalization in Sub-Saharan Africa*, pp. 182–98. Baltimore and London: Johns Hopkins University Press.

———. 2000. *States and Power in Africa. Comparative Lessons in Authority and Control*. Princeton: Princeton University Press.

Hickey, S. 2005. "The Politics of Staying Poor: Exploring the Political Space for Poverty Reduction in Uganda," *World Development*, 33(6): 995–1009.

———. 2008. "Conceptualising the Politics of Social Protection in Africa," in A. Barrientos and D. Hulme (eds), *Social Protection for the Poor and Poorest. Concepts, Policies and Politics*, pp. 247–63. Hampshire: Palgrave MacMillan.

Hill, M. 1996. *Social Policy: A Comparative Analysis*. London: Prentice Hall.

Hillman, A. and E. Jenker. 2004. "User Payment for Basic Education in Low-Income Countries," in S. Gupta, B. Clements, and G. Inchauste (eds), *Helping Countries Develop. The Role of Fiscal Policy*, pp. 213–64. Washington DC: International Monetary Fund (IMF).

Hoekman, B. and A.L. Winters. 2005. "Trade and Employment. Stylized Facts and Research Findings," Policy Research Working Paper 3676, World Bank, Washington DC.

Holmqvist, G. 2009. "The Impact of the Financial Crisis on Africa, The Unpredictable Flows: Aid and Remittances," Nordic Africa Institute, May; available at www.nai.uu.se/FinancialCrisisAidAnd-Remittances090504b.pdf (accessed in May 2010).

Holmqvist, G. and K. Metell Cueva. 2006. "If the PRSP Experiment in Latin America is a Disappointment, What is the Alternative," *Development Policy Review*, 24(4): 477–80.

Holliday, Ian. 2000. "Productivist Welfare Capitalism: Social Policy in East Asia," *Political Studies*, 48(4): 706–23.

Holzmann, R. 2008. "Social Protection for the Poorest: The Position and Experience of the World Bank"; available at http://siteresources.worldbank.org/EXTSOCIALPROTECTION/Resources/SPforPoorest_8Feb08_Eng.pdf (accessed in May 2010).

Holzmann, R. and R. Hinz. 2005. *Old Age Income Support in the 21st Century. An International Perspective on Pension Systems and Reform.* Washington DC: World Bank.

Hopenhayn, Martin. 2008. "Recognition and Distribution: Equity and Justice Policies for Disadvantaged Groups in Latin America," in A.A. Dani and A. de Haan (eds), *Inclusive States: Social Policy and Structural Inequalities*, pp. 145–74. Washington DC: The World Bank.

Hort, S.E.O. and S. Kuhnle. 2000. "The Coming of East and South-East Asian Welfare States," *Journal of European Social Policy*, 10(2): 162–84.

Huang Jing. 2009. "Social Security Crucial to Higher Consumption," *China Daily*, January 15, p. 8.

Hussain, A. n.d. "Social Welfare in China in the Context of Three Transition," Asia Research Centre, LSE, London.

Hujo, K. 2008. "Background Note for UNRISD Research Project on 'Financing Social Policy,'" Mimeo, UNRISD, Geneva.

Hutton, W. 2007. *The Writing on the Wall: China and the West in the 21st Century.* Brown: Little.

Ibrahim, J. 2006. "Affirmative Action. Nigeria," Policy Brief 15, Inter-Regional Inequality Facility; available at http://www.odi.org.uk/inter-regional_inequality/papers/Policy% 20 Brief%2015%20-%20 Nigeria.pdf (accessed in September 2007).

International Monetary Fund (IMF). 2000. "Globalization: Threat or Opportunity? An IMF Issues Brief," available at http://www.imf.org/external/np/exr/ib/2000/041200to.htm (accessed in May 2010).

———. 2006. *Vietnam: Poverty Reduction Strategy Paper—Annual Progress Report.* IMF Country Report No. 06/70, http://www.imf.org/external/pubs/ft/scr/2006/cr0670.pdf (accessed in May 2010).

International Monetary Fund (IMF), Independent Evaluation Office. 2003. "Fiscal Adjustment in IMF supported Programs," IMF, Washington DC; available at http://www.imf.org/external/np/ieo/2003/fis/pdf/all.pdf (accessed in May 2010).

IMF and World Bank. 2005. "PRS Review: Balancing Accountabilities and Scaling Up Results," World Bank, Washington DC; available at http://siteresources.worldbank.org/INTPRS1/Resources/PRSP-Review/2005_Review_Final.pdf (accessed in May 2010).

International Social Security Association (ISSA). 2008. "Dynamic Social Security for Africa: An Agenda for Development." Available online at http://www.issa.int/aiss/Resources/ISSA-Publications/Dynamic-Social-Security-for-Africa-An-Agenda-for-Development (accessed in May 2010).

Jalan, J. and M. Ravallion. 1999. "Income Gains to the Poor from Workfare. Estimates from Argentina's Trabajar Program," Policy Research Working Paper 2149, World Bank, Washington DC.

James, K.S. 2008. "Economic Change and Health Status in India: New Evidence," Paper presented at the International Conference on Universalising Socio-Economic Security in South Asia, New Delhi, February 17–20.

Jenkins, R. 2003. "Globalisation and Employment: Working for the Poor?" *Insights*, June; available at www.id21.org (accessed in 2005).

Jenkins, C. and L. Thomas. 2004. "The Changing Nature of Inequality in South Africa," in G.A. Cornia (ed.), *Inequality, Growth, and Poverty in an Era of Liberalization and Globalization*, pp. 376–404. Oxford: Oxford University Press; The United Nations University-World Institute for Development Economics Research (UNU-WIDER).

Jingzhong, Ye, James Murray, and Wang Yihuan. 2005. *Left-behind Children in Rural China: Impact Study of Rural Labour Migration on Left-behind Children in Mid-west China.* Beijing: Social Sciences Academic Press.

Johanssen, L. and K.H. Pedersen. 2008, "The Responsive State: Openness and Inclusion in the Policy Process," in A.A. Dani and A. de Haan (eds), *Inclusive States: Social Policy and Structural Inequalities*, pp. 97–120. Washington DC: The World Bank.

Jomo, K.S. and R. von Arnim. 2008. "Trade Liberalisation for Development? Who Gains? Who Loses?," *Economic and Political Weekly*; available at www.epw.org.in (accessed on November 29, 2008).

Joshi, A. 2005. "Do Rights Work? Law, Activism and the Employment Guarantee Scheme, IDS Sussex"; available at http://www.ids.ac.uk/gdr/cfs/drc-pubs/summaries/summary%2013%20-Joshi-EGS-DoRightsWork.pdf (accessed in May 2010).

Joshi, S. 2006. "Impact of Economic Reforms on Social Sector Expenditure in India," *Economic and Political Weekly*, 41(4): 358–65.

Kabeer, N. 2004. "Imagining 'the Social': Social Policy Analysis for the Poor in Poor Countries," IDS Working Paper 191, IDS, Brighton.

Kabeer, N., S. Mahmud, and Tran Thi Van Anh. 2003. "The Poverty Impacts of Female Employment," *Insights*, June; available at www.id21.org (accessed in 2005).

Kakwani, N., H.H. Son, and R. Hinz. 2006. "Poverty, Old-age and Social Pensions in Kenya," Working Paper 26, International Poverty Center, Brasilia; available at http://www.undp-povertycentre.org/pub/IPCWorkingPaper24.pdf (accessed in July 2010).

Kanbur, R. 2001. "Economic Policy, Distribution and Poverty: The Nature of Disagreements"; available at http://www.kanbur.aem.cornell.edu/papers/Disagreements.pdf (accessed in May 2010).

——— (ed.). 2003. *Q-Squared. Qualitative and Quantitative Methods of Poverty Appraisal.* Delhi: Permanent Black.

———. 2007. "What's Social Policy Got to Do with Economic Growth?," *Indian Journal of Human Development*, 1(1): 3–19.

Kanbur, R. and X. Zhang. 2004. "Fifty Years of Regional Inequality in China. A Journey through Central Planning, Reform and Openness," World Institute for Development Economics Research (WIDER) Discussion Paper 2004/50, WIDER, Helsinki.

Kapur, D., P. Mukhopadhyay, and A. Subramanian. 2008. "More on Direct Cash Transfers," *Economic and Political Weekly*, November 22; available at www.epw.org.in (accessed in May 2010).

Kaul, I. and P. Conceição (eds). 2006. *The New Public Finance. Responding to Global Challenges.* Oxford: Oxford University Press; UNDP.

Kearny, A.T. and Foreign Policy. 2004. "Measuring Globalization," *Foreign Policy*, March/April, pp. 54–69.

Kerr, J. and C. Sweetman. 2003. "Editorial," *Gender and Development*, 11(1): 3–12.

Khanna, P. 2008. *The Second World. How Emerging Powers are Redefining Global Competition in the Twenty-first Century*. London: Penguin Books.

Khoo Boo Teik. 2004. "Managing Ethnic Relations in Post-Crisis Malaysia and Indonesia. Lessons from the New Economic Policy?" Identities, Conflict and Cohesion Programme Paper No. 6, UNRISD, Geneva.

Killick, T. 1999. "Making Adjustment Work for the Poor," ODI Poverty Briefing No. 5, Overseas Development Institute, London.

———. 2005. "Policy Autonomy and the History of British Aid to Africa," *Development Policy Review*, 23(6): 665–81.

Klasen, S. 1999. "Does Gender Inequality Reduce Growth and Development? Evidence from Cross-Country Regressions," World Bank Policy Research Report Working Paper No. 7, World Bank, Washington DC.

Klasen, S. 2005. "Pro-Poor Growth and Gender. What Can We Learn from the Literature and the OPPG Case Studies?," Unpublished Paper for the multi-donor research program, Operationalizing Pro-Poor Growth.

Klump, R. and T. Bonschab. 2005. "Operationalizing Pro-Poor Growth: A Case Study on Vietnam," Paper for joint-donor research program, Operationalizing Pro-Poor Growth, DFID, London.

Krugman, P. 2009. *The Return of Depression Economics and the Crisis of 2008*. New York: W.W. Norton & Company.

Kulunde Manda, D. 2003. "Incentive Structure and Efficiency in the Kenyan Civil Service," in Kayizzi-Mugerwa (ed.), *Reforming Africa's Institutions. Ownership, Incentives, and Capabilities*, pp. 149–69. Japan: UNU/WIDER, United Nations University Press.

Kumar, S. 2001. "Study of Political Systems and Voting Behaviour of the Poor in Orissa," Report for DFID-India, Delhi.

Kundu, A. 2009. 'Exclusionary Urbanisation in Asia: A Macro Overview', *Economic and Political Weekly*, November 28, pp. 48–58.

Kwon, Huck-ju (ed.). 2005a. *Transforming the Developmental Welfare State in East Asia*. London: Palgrave Macmillan; UNRISD.

———. 2005b. "An Overview of the Study: The Developmental Welfare State and Policy Reforms in East Asia," in H. Kwon (ed.), *Transforming the Developmental Welfare State in East Asia*, pp. 1–23. London: Palgrave Macmillan; UNRISD.

———. 2005c. "Reform of the Developmental Welfare State in Korea: Advocacy Coalitions and Health Politics," in H. Kwon (ed.), *Transforming the Developmental Welfare State in East Asia*, pp. 27–49. London: Palgrave Macmillan; UNRISD.

———. 2008. "The Reform of the Developmental Welfare State in East Asia," Mimeo, Seoul National University.

Lancaster, C. 2008. *George Bush's Foreign Aid: Transformation* or *Chaos?* Washington DC: Center for Global Development.

Lanjouw, Peter and Rinku Murgai. 2008. "Poverty Decline, Agricultural Wages, and Non-farm Employment Rural India 1983–2004," Policy Research Working Paper 4858, World Bank, Washington DC.

Lavalette, M. and A. Pratt (eds). 1997. *Social Policy: A Conceptual and Theoretical Introduction*. London: Sage.

Lee, E.W.Y. 2005. "The Politics of Welfare Developmentalism in Hong Kong," in H. Kwon (ed.), *Transforming the Developmental Welfare State in East Asia*, pp. 118–39. London: Palgrave Macmillan; UNRISD.

Leonard, M. 2008. *What Does China Think?* London: Fourth Estate.

Lindert, P.H. 2004. *Growing Public: Social Spending and Economic Growth since the Eighteenth Century* (2 Vols). Cambridge: Cambridge University Press.

Lofgren, H. and S. Robinson. 2004. "Public Spending, Growth, and Poverty Alleviation in Sub-Saharan Africa: A Dynamic General Equilibrium Analysis," Paper prepared for presentation at the conference on Growth, Poverty Reduction and Human Development in Africa, Centre for the Study of African Economies, University of Oxford, March 21–22, revised May 21.

London, J. 2009. "Welfare Regimes in the Wake of State Socialism: Vietnam, China, and the Market-Leninist Welfare Regime," Paper prepared for the conference on Asian Social Protection Conference in Comparative Perspective, Singapore, January 7–9.

Lopez, H. 2004. "Pro Growth, Pro Poor. Is There a Trade Off?" Paper for the Pro-Poor Growth Program, World Bank, Washington DC.

Lucero, J.A. 2008. "Indigenous Political Voice and the Struggle for Recognition in Ecuador and Bolivia," in A.Bebbington, A.A. Dani, A. de Haan, and M. Walton (eds), *Institutional Pathways to Equity. Addressing Inequality Traps*, pp. 139–68. Washington DC: The World Bank.

Lula da Silva, Luiz Inácio. 2009. "The Future of Human Beings is What Matters," *The Financial Times*, March 10.

Lundberg, M. and L. Squire. 1999. "The Simultaneous Evolution of Growth and Inequality," Mimeo, World Bank, Washington DC.

Luo Xiaopeng. 2007. "Cognitive Ability of Collectivity and the Choice of Reformation Path—Thinking of Two-way Price Reformation Process in Theory," in Zhang, Fam, and de Haan (eds), *Narratives of Chinese Economic Reforms: How Does China Cross the River?* Singapore, New Jersey, London: World Scientific Publishing.

Mackintosh, M. and P. Tibandebage. 2004. "Inequality and Redistribution in Health Care: Analytical Issues for Developmental Social Policy," in T. Mkandawire (ed.), *Social Policy in a Development Context*, pp. 143–74. Basingstoke: Palgrave Macmillan.

Mamdani, M. 2001. *When Victims Become Killers. Colonialism, Nativism, and the Genocide in Rwanda*. Princeton: Princeton University Press.

———. 2005. "Political Violence and the Dilemma of Citizenship in Post Colonial Africa," Paper for the conference, "New Frontiers of Social Policy," Arusha; available at www.worldbank.org/socialpolicy (accessed in May 2007).

———. 2008. "Lessons of Zimbabwe"; available at www.pambazuka.org (accessed in December 3, 2008).

Mander, H. 2004. *The Ripped Chest. Public Policy and Poor People in India*. Bangalore: Books for Change.

Manji, F. 2000. "Social Policy and Rights in Africa: From Social Contract to Loss of Self-Determination," *IDS Bulletin*, 31(4): 11–20.

Manor, James. 2005. "Introduction," *IDS Bulletin*, 36(3): 1–7.

Marshall, T.H. 1950. *Citizenship and Social Class*. London: Cambridge University Press.

Martin, R. and A. Seguro-Ubiergo. 2004. *Fiscal Discipline and Social Spending in IMF-Supported Programs (1)*, pp. 249–70. Monografías: Hacienda Pública Española; available at http://129.3.20.41/eps/pe/papers/0504/0504012.pdf (accessed in May 2010).

Mason, M. 1997. *Development and Disorder. A History of the Third World since 1945*. Hanover and London: University Press of New England.

Medrano, P., C. Sanhueza, and D. Contreras. 2006. *Inequality in Latin America: A Synthesis of Recent Research on the Levels, Trends, Effects and Determinants of Inequality in its Different Dimensions*. London: ODI, Inter-Regional Inequality Facility.

Mehrotra, S. and E. Delamonica. 2007. *Eliminating Human Poverty. Macroeconomic & Social Policies for Equitable Growth*. London: Zed Books.

Mehta, Aasha Kapur and Andrew Shepherd (eds). 2006. *Chronic Poverty and Development Policy in India*. New Delhi: Sage.

Mesa-Lago, C. 1997. "Social Welfare Reform in the Context of Political-Economic Liberalization: Latin American Cases," *World Development*, 25(4): 497–517.

Meschi, E. and M. Vivarelli. 2009. "Trade and Income Inequality in Developing Countries," *World Development*, 37(2): 287–302.

Milanovic, B. 1999. "Do More Unequal Countries Redistribute More? Does the Median Voter Hypothesis Hold?," Mimeo, World Bank, Development Research Group, Washington DC; available at http://siteresources.worldbank.org/INTPGI/Resources/13263_do_more_unequal_countries_redistribute_more.pdf (accessed in May 2010).

Milanovic, B. 2003. "The Two faces of Globalization: Against Globalization as We Know It," *World Development*, 31(4): 667–83.

———. 2005. *Worlds Apart: Measuring International and Global Inequality*. Princeton, NJ: Princeton University Press.

Mishra, R. 1999. *Globalization and the Welfare State*. Cheltenham: Edward Elgar.

Mitchener, K. 2009. "Experience from the Great Depression," Paper presented at the workshop, "Social Policy Responses to Economic Crises," Beijing, February 23–24.

Mkandawire, T. 2000. *Social Policy in a Development Context*. Geneva: UNRISD.

Mkandawire, T. (ed.). 2004. *Social Policy in a Development Context*. Basingstoke: Palgrave Macmillan.

———. 2005. "Targeting and Universalism in Poverty Reduction," Working Paper No. 23, UNRISD, Geneva.

Mommsen, W.J., in collaboration with W. Mock (ed.). 1981. *The Emergence of the Welfare State in Britain and Germany. 1850–1950*. London: Croom Helm.

Moncrieffe, J. 2008. "Beneath the Categories: Power Relations and Inequalities in Uganda," in A. Bebbington A.A. Dani, A. de Haan, and M. Walton (eds), *Institutional Pathways to Equity. Addressing Inequality Traps*, pp. 73–102. Washington DC: The World Bank.

Motonishi, T. 2003. "Why Has Income Inequality in Thailand Increased? An Analysis using 1975–1998 Surveys," ADB ERD Working Paper No. 43, Asian Development Bank, Manila, available at http://www.adb.org/Documents/ERD/Working_Papers/wp043.pdf (accessed in May 2010).

Moore, M. 2000. "States, Social Policies and Globalisations: Arguing on the Right Terrain?" *IDS Bulletin*, 31(4): 21–31.

Morales-Gómez, D. (ed.). 1999. *Transnational Social Policies. The New Challenges of Globalization*. London: Earthscan.

Moreno-Dodson, B. 2008. "Assessing the Impact of Public Spending on Growth. An Empirical Analysis for Seven Fast Growing Countries," Policy Research Working Paper 4663, World Bank, Washington DC.

Moser, C. 1992. "From Residual Welfare to Compensatory Measures: The Changing Agenda of Social Policy in Developing Countries," Silver Jubilee Paper 6, IDS Sussex, Brighton.

Moyo, Dambisa. 2009. *Dead Aid. Why Aid is Not Working and How There is Another Way for Africa*. London: Penguin Books.

Musgrove, P., R. Zeramdini, and G. Carrin. 2002. "Basic Patterns in National Health Expenditure," *Bulletin of the World Health Organization*, 80(2): 134–46.

Munck, R. 2005. *Globalization and Social Exclusion. A Transformationalist Perspective*. Bloomfield: Kumarian Press.

Myrdal, Gunnar. 1973. "Equity and Growth," *World Development*, 1(11): 43–47.

Nayyar, D. (ed.). 2002. *Governing Globalization. Issues and Institutions*. New Delhi: Oxford University Press.

Nel, P. 2003. "Income Inequality, Economic Growth, and Political Instability in Sub-Saharan Africa," *Journal of Modern African Studies*, 41(4): 611–39.

———. 2006. "The Return of Inequality. Review Article," *Third World Quarterly*, 27(4): 689–706.

Nielsen, I., C. Nyland, R. Smyth, and C. Zhu. 2005. "Marketization and Perceptions of Social Protection in China's Cities," *World Development*, 33(11): 1759–81.

Nissanke, M. and E. Thorbecke. 2005. "Channels and Policy Debate in the Globalization-Inequality-Poverty Nexus," WIDER Discussion Paper No. 2005/08.

Norton, A. and B. Bird. 1998. *Social Development Issues in Sector Wide Approaches*. London: DFID.

Norton, A. and D. Elson. 2002. *What's Behind the Budget? Politics, Rights and Accountability in the Budget Process*. London: ODI.

OECD and World Bank. 2009. "Pensions at a Glance: Asia/Pacific"; available at http://www.oecd.org/dataoecd/33/53/41966940.pdf (accessed in May 2010).

Ohno, K. 2003a. "The Role of Government in Promoting Industrialization under Globalization: The East Asian Experience," Paper based on presentation at workshop on Capacity Enhancement, Yangon; available at http://www.grips.ac.jp/vietnam/KOarchives/doc/EP15_Role.pdf (accessed in May 2010).

———. 2003b. "The Transferability of the East Asian Development Experience," presentation at UNCTAD Expert Group Meeting on "New Trade and Development Strategies in Least Developed Countries," Geneva; available at http://www.grips.ac.jp/forum/englishpg/EngGDFweb/EngGDFweb/pdf_e01/unctad1.pdf. (accessed in May 2010).

Okojie, C. and A. Shimeles. 2006. "Inequality in Africa: A Synthesis of Recent Research on the Levels, Trends, Effects and Determinants of Inequality in its Different Dimensions," Inter-Regional Inequality Facility, ODI, London.

Osei-Hwedie, K. and Arnon Bar-on. 1999. "Sub-Saharan Africa. Community-Driven Social Policies," in D. Morales-Gómez (ed.), *Transnational Social Policies. The New Challenges of Globalization*, pp. 89–115. London: Earthscan.

Owusu, F. 2003. "Pragmatism and the Gradual Shift from Dependency to Neoliberalism: The World Bank, African Leaders and Development Policy in Africa," *World Development*, 31(10): 1655–72.

Palma, J. and R. Urzúa. 2005. "Anti-poverty Policies and Citizenry: The Chile Solidario Experience," MOST Policy Papers 12, UNESCO; available at http://unesdoc.unesco.org/images/0014/001402/140240e.pdf (accessed in May 2010).

Paternostro, S., E.R. Tiongson, and A. Rajaram. 2005. "How Does the Composition of Public Spending Matter?" Policy Research Working Paper 3555, World Bank, Washington D.C.

Pattillo, C., S. Gupta, and K. Carey. 2005. "Sustaining Growth Accelerations and Pro-Poor Growth in Africa," IMF Working Paper WP/05/195; available at http://www.imf.org/external/pubs/ft/wp/2005/wp05195.pdf (accessed in May 2010).

Payne, R.J. and J.R. Nassar. 2006. *Politics and Culture in the Developing World. The Impact of Globalization*. New York: Pearson Longman.

Peden, G.C. 1991. *British Economic and Social Policy. Lloyd George and Margaret Thatcher*. New York: Philip Allan (1st edition 1985).

Pierson, C. 2004. "Late Industrializers and the Development of the Welfare State," UNRISD Social Policy and Development Paper No. 16, Geneva; available at www.unrisd.org (accessed in May 2010).

Piven, F.F. and R.A. Cloward. 1972. *Regulating the Poor. The Functions of Public Welfare*. London: Tavistock Publications.

Poku, N.K. 2002. "Poverty, Debt, and Africa's HIV/AIDS Crisis," *International Affairs*, 78(3): 531–46.

Poku, N.K. and A. Whiteside. 2002. "Global Health and the Politics of Governance: An Introduction," *Third World Quarterly*, 23(2): 191–95.

Polanyi, K. 1968 (original 1944). *The Great Transformation*. Boston: Beacon Press, 9th printing.

Pritchett, L. 1995. "Divergence, Big Time," Policy Research Working Paper 1522, World Bank, Washington DC.

Rajaraman, Indira and Darshy Sinha. 2007. "Tracking Functional Devolution by States to Panchayats," working paper, National Institute of Public Finance and Policy, New Delhi; available at www.nipfp.org.in/working_paper/wp_2007_48.pdf (accessed in May 2010).

Ravallion, M. 2001. "Growth, Inequality and Poverty: Looking Beyond Averages," *World Development*, 29(11): 1803–15.

———. 2003a. "The Debate on Globalization, Poverty and Inequality: Why Measurement Matters," World Bank Policy Research Working Paper 3038, World Bank, Washington DC.

———. 2003b. "Targeted Transfers in Poor Countries: Revisiting the Tradeoffs and Policy Options," Social Protection Discussion Paper No. 0314, World Bank, Washington DC.

———. 2004. "Competing Concepts of Inequality in the Globalization Debate," Policy Research Working Paper 3243, World Bank, Washington DC.

———. 2007. "Are There Any Lessons for Africa from China's Success Against Poverty," Policy Research Working Paper, World Bank, Washington DC.

———. 2009. "A Comparative Perspective on Poverty Reduction in Brazil, China and India," Policy Research Working Paper 5080, World Bank, Washington DC.

Ravallion, M. and S. Chen. 2004. "China's (Uneven) Progress Against Poverty," Policy Research Working Paper 3408, World Bank, Washington DC.

Recondo, D. 2008. "Local Participatory Democracy in Latin America: Lessons from Mexico and Colombia," in A.A. Dani and A. de Haan (eds), *Inclusive States: Social Policy and Structural Inequalities*, pp. 175–96. Washington DC: The World Bank.

Reich, R. 2008. *Supercapitalism. The Battle for Democracy in an Age of Big Business*. Cambridge: Icon Press.

Resnick, D. and R. Birner. 2006. "Does Good Governance Contribute to Pro-Poor Growth?: A Review of the Evidence from Cross-Country Studies," DSGD Discussion Paper No. 30, IFPRI, Washington DC; available at http://www.ifpri.org/publication/does-good-governance-contribute-pro-poor-growth (accessed in May 2010).

Reulecke, J. 1981. "English Social Policy around the Middle of the Nineteenth Century as Seen by German Social Reformers," in Mommsen (ed.), *The Emergence of the Welfare State in Britain and Germany. 1850–1950*, pp. 9–31. London: Croom Helm.

Richter, K. 2006. "Thailand's Growth Path: From Recovery to Prosperity," Policy Research Working Paper 3912, World Bank, Washington DC.

Robb, C. 2003. "Poverty and Social Impact Analysis—Linking Macroeconomic Policies to Poverty Outcomes: Summary of Early Experiences," Working Paper 03/43, IMF, Washington DC.

Rodrik, D. 1998. "Why Do Open Economies Have Bigger Governments?" *Journal of Political Economy*, 106(November): 997–1032.

———(ed.). 2003. *In Search of Prosperity: Analytical Narratives on Economic Growth*. Princeton, NJ: Princeton University Press.

Rodrik, D. and A. Subramanian. 2004. "From Hindu Growth to Productivity Surge: The Mystery of the Indian Growth Transition," IMG Working Paper 04/77; available at http://www.imf.org/external/pubs/ft/wp/2004/wp0477.pdf (accessed in May 2010).

Ross, M.L. 2008. "Mineral Wealth, Conflict and Equitable Development," in A. Bebbington, A. Dani, A. de Haan, and M. Walton (eds), *Institutional Pathways to Equity. Addressing Inequality Traps*, pp. 193–216. Washington DC: The World Bank.

Rothgang, H., H. Obinger, and S. Leibfried. 2006. "The State and its Welfare State: How do Welfare State Changes Affect the Make-up of the Nation State?" *Social policy and Administration*, 40(3): 250–66.

Rozelle, S., Linxiu Zhang, and Jikun Huang. 2000. "China's War on Poverty," Working Paper No. 60, Center for Research on Economic Development and Policy Reform, Stanford University.

Rudra, N. 2002. "Globalization and the Decline of the Welfare State in Less-Developed Countries," *International Organization*, 56(2): 441–45.

Sabates-Wheeler, R. 2008. "Asset Inequality and Agricultural Growth. How are Patterns of Asset Inequality Established and Reproduced?" in A. Bebbington, A.A. Dani, A. de Haan, and M. Walton (eds), *Institutional Pathways to Equity. Addressing Inequality Traps*, pp. 45–72. Washington DC: The World Bank.

Sabharwal, G. 2008. "From Targeted to Universal Social Protection: Vietnam's Reality," Department for International Development (DFID); available at www.eldis.org (accessed in May 2010).

Sachs, J. 2005. *The End of Poverty. How We Can Make it Happen in Our Lifetime*. London: Penguin Books.

Saith, A. 2008a. "China and India: The Institutional Roots of Differential Performance," *Development and Change*, 39(5): 723–57.

———. 2008b. "Towards Universalizing Socio-economic Security: Strategic Elements of a Policy Framework," *Indian Journal of Human Development*, 2(1): 9–38.

Sala-I-Martin, X. 2002. "The World Distribution of Income (Estimated from Individual Country Distribution)," NBER Working Paper No. w8933; available at www.nber.org/papers/w8933 (accessed in May 2010).

Sathyamala, C. 2008. "Public Health Policies in India," Paper presented at the International Conference on Universalising Socio-Economic Security in South Asia, New Delhi, February 17–20.

Schady, N. 2005. "Do Macroeconomic Crises affect Schooling and Child Health? Evidence from Peru"; available at www.worldbank.org/data/dataquery.html (accessed in December 2005).

Schmidt, V.H. Forthcoming. "Convergence With a Twist: East Asian Welfare Capitalism in Comparative Perspective," in Lian Kwen Fee and Tong Chee Kiong (eds), *Social Policy in Postindustrial Singapore*, pp. 309–31. Leiden: Brill. Available at http://profile.nus.edu.sg/fass/socvhs/ (accessed in May 2010).

Schubert, B. 2005. "The Pilot Social Cash Transfer Scheme. Kalomo District, Zambia," Paper presented at CPRC conference, "Social Protection for Chronic Poverty"; available at http://www.sed.manchester.ac.uk/research/events/conferences/documents/Social%20Protection%20Papers/Schubert.pdf (accessed in May 2010).

Schultz, T. 2002. "Why Governments Should Invest More to Educate Girls," *World Development*, 30(2): 207–25.

Sen, A. 1982. *Choice, Welfare and Measurement*. Oxford: Blackwell.

———. 1999. *Development as Freedom*. New York: Knopf.

Sen, Gong. 2009. "Current Crisis and Efforts of Development Transformation in China," Presentation at International Seminar on Financial Crisis and Global Development, ISS, The Hague, October.

Shariff, A., P. Ghosh, and S.K. Mondal. 2001. *State Adjusted Public Expenditures on Social Sector and Poverty Alleviation Programs in the Light of Budget 2001*. New Delhi: National Council of Applied Economic Research.

Shiva, V. 2005. "Two Myths That Keep the World Poor"; available at info.interactivist.net (accessed in November 2005).

Siebrits, F.K. 1998. "Government Spending in an International Perspective," in Abedian and Biggs (eds), *Economic Globalization and Fiscal Policy*, pp. 305–36. Cape Town: Oxford University Press.

Silver, H. 1994. *Social Exclusion and Social Solidarity: Three Paradigms*, IILS Discussion Papers No 69, Geneva.

Smeeding, T.M. 2005. "Public Policy, Economic Inequality, and Poverty. The United States in Comparative Perspective," *Social Science Quarterly*, 86(1): 955–83.

Smith, R.M. 2008. "Social Security as Developmental Institution? Extending the Solar Case for the Relative Efficacy of Poor Relief Provisions under the Old English Poor Law," Working Paper 56, Brooks World Poverty Institute, University of Manchester.

Song Li. 2009. "China's Fiscal Policy Responses to the Current International Financial Crisis (in Chinese)," Paper presented at the workshop, "Social Policy Responses to Economic Crises," Beijing, February 23–24.

Spence, J.D. 2002 (original 1969). *To Change China. Western Advisers in China*. New York: Penguin Books.

Standing, Guy. 2008. "Reviving Egalitarianism in the Global Transformation: Building Occupational Security," *Indian Journal of Human Development*, 2(1): 39–62.

Stern, N. 2002. "Dynamic Development: Innovation and Inclusion," Munich Lectures in Economics, Munich, November 19.

Stewart, F. 2006. "Do we Need a New 'Great Transformation?' Is One Likely?" The United Nations University-World Institute for Development Economics Research (UNU-WIDER) Research Paper 2006/36, WIDER, Helsinki; available at www.wider.unu.edu/publications/publications.htm (accessed in May 2007).

Stiglitz, J.E. 2002. *Globalization and its Discontents*. New Delhi: Penguin Books.

Subbarao, Kalanidhi. 2003. "Systematic Shocks and Social Protection: Role and Effectiveness of Public Works Programs," Social Protection Discussion Paper Series No. 03020, World Bank, Washington DC.

Sundaram, K. and S.D. Tendulkar. 2003. "Poverty among Social and Economic Groups in India in the Nineteen Nineties," CDE Working Paper 118, Delhi School of Economics, Delhi.

Sutcliffe, B. 2007. "Postscript to the Article 'World Inequality and Globalization' (Oxford Review of Economic Policy, Spring 2004)"; available at http://siteresources.worldbank.org/INTDECINEQ/Resources/PSBSutcliffe.pdf (accessed in September 2008).

Suwannarat, G. 2003. "Southeast Asia: Learning from Crisis," in S. Cook, N. Kabeer, and G. Suwannarat (eds), *Social Protection in Asia, Ford Foundation*, pp. 200–60. New Delhi: Har-Anand Publications.

Swaminathan, M. 2008. "PDS: Challenges of Universalisation," Paper presented at the International Conference on Universalising Socio-Economic Security in South Asia, New Delhi, February 17–20.

Tangcharoensathien, V., W. Teokul, and L. Chanwongpaisarn. 2005. "Challenges of Implementing Universal Health Care in Thailand," in H-j. Kwon (ed.), *Transforming the Developmental Welfare State in East Asia*, pp. 257–82. London: Palgrave Macmillan; UNRISD.

Tanzi, V. 2000. "Globalization and the Future of Social Protection," IMF Working Paper 00/12, IMF, Washington DC.

Taylor, L. 2001. "Outcomes of External Liberalization and Policy Implications," in L. Taylor (ed.), *External Liberalization, Economic Performance, and Social Policy*, pp. 1–10. Oxford: Oxford University Press.

Taylor, M. 2006. "From National Development to 'Growth With Equity': Nation-building in Chile, 1950–2000," *Third World Quarterly*, 27(1): 69–84.

Taylor-Gooby, P. 2005. "Is the Future American? Or, Can Left Politics Preserve European Welfare States from Erosion through Growing 'Racial' Diversity?" *Journal of Social Policy*, 34(4): 661–72.

Tendler, J. 2004. "Why Social Policy is Condemned to a Residual Category of Safety Nets and What to Do about It," in T. Mkandawire (ed.), *Social Policy in a Development Context*, pp. 119–42. Basingstoke: Palgrave Macmillan.

Teokul, W. 2009. "Thailand: Applying 1997's Lessons to the Current Global Financial Crisis," Paper presented at workshop on "Social Policy Responses to Crises," Beijing, February 23–24.

Therborn, G. 2004. *Between Sex and Power. Family in the World, 1900–2000*. London: Routledge.

Thobani, M. 1983 "Charging User Fees for Social Services. The Case of Education in Malawi," World Bank Staff Working Paper 572, World Bank, Washington DC.

Tilly, C. 1998. *Durable Inequality*. Berkeley, CA: University of California Press.

Timmer, P. 2004. "Operationalizing Pro-Poor Growth. A Case Study on Indonesia," Paper for the multi-donor research program, Operationalizing Pro-Poor Growth, DFID, London.

Townsend, P. 2004. "From Universalism to Safety Nets: The Rise and Fall of Keynesian Influence on Social Development," in T. Mkandawire (ed.), *Social Policy in a Development Context*, pp. 37–62. Basingstoke: Palgrave Macmillan.

Turk, C. and C. Shanks. 2003. "Refining Policy with the Poor: Local Consultations on the Draft Comprehensive Poverty Reduction and Growth Strategy in Vietnam," World Bank Research Working Paper No. 2968, World Bank, Washington DC.

Tzannatos, Z. 1998. "Women and Labor Market Changes in the Global Economy: Growth Helps, Inequality Hurt and Public Policy Matters," SP Discussion Paper 20051, World Bank, Washington DC.

United Nations Conference on Trade and Development (UNCTAD). 2009. "Lower FDI Flows to and from Developed Countries Reshape Global FDI Patterns," press release, UNCTAD/PRESS/PR/2009/049; available at http://www.paiz.gov.pl/files/?id_plik=11535 (accessed in May 2010).

UNDESA (United Nations Department of Economic and Social Affairs), Isabel Ortiz. 2007. "Social Policy," National Development Strategies, Policy Notes, UN, New York.

UNDP. 1999. *Human Development Report 1999: Globalization with a Human Face*. New York: United Nations Development Program (UNDP).

———. 2005. *Human Development Report 2005: International Trade and Security in an Unequal World*. New York: United Nations Development Program (UNDP).

———. 2007. *Human Development Report 2007–08: Fighting Climate Change. Human Solidarity in a Divided World*. Hampshire: Palgrave Macmillan.

———. 2009a. "Human Development Indicators", available at http://hdr.undp.org/en/ (accessed in May 2010).

———. 2009b. *Human Development Report 2009: Overcoming Barriers. Human Mobility and Development*. New York: United Nations Development Program (UNDP).

UN Economic and Social Commission for Western Asia (UN–ESCWA). 2008. "Integrated Social Policy Report II: From Concept to Practice"; available at http://www.escwa.un.org/information/publications/edit/upload/sdd-08-3-e.pdf (accessed in May 2010).

United Nations International Children's Fund (UNICEF). 2008. "UNICEF Regional Policy Makers' Symposium on Social Protection in South Asia," Synthesis Report, Kathmandu, August.

UNRISD. 2006. "Transformative Social Policy: Lessons from UNRISD Research," Research and Policy Brief 5, UNRISD, Geneva.

USAID. 2005. "Pro-Poor Economic Growth. A Review of Recent Literature," produced for review by United States Agency for International Development (USAID); prepared by

Development Alternatives and the Boston Institute for Developing Economies; available at http://www.povertyfrontiers.org/ev.php?ID=1535_201&ID2=DO_TOPIC (accessed in May 2010).

Van Agtmael, A. 2007. *The Emerging Markets Century. How a New Breed of World-Class Companies is Overtaking the World.* New York: Free Press.

Van der Hoeven, R. 2000. *Into the Twenty-first Century: Assessing Social and Political Concerns.* Geneva: ILO.

Van der Hoeven, R. and M. Lübker. Forthcoming. "Financial Globalization and Labour Markets in Developing Countries," in P. Goulart and M. Murshed (eds), *South–South Globalization.*

Van Ginneken, W. 2003. "Extending Social Security: Policies for Developing Countries," *International Labour Review*, 142(3): 277–93.

———. 2010. "Social Security Coverage Extension: A Review of Recent Evidence," *International Social Security Review*, 63(1): 57–76.

Vermeend, W. 2008. *De Krediet Crisis (en hoe we er sterker uit kunnen komen)* [The Credit Crisis (and how we can emerge stronger from it)]. Amsterdam: Lebowski.

Vos, Rob. 2009. "After Us The Deluge? Current Economic Prospects and the Future of Globalization," Presentation at ISS, The Hague, October 29.

Vyasulu, V. 2008. "The Case against Health Insurance," *Economic and Political Weekly*, September 27, pp. 15–17; available at http://epw.in/epw/uploads/articles/12690.pdf (accessed in May 2010).

Walby, S. 2003. "The Myth of the Nation-State: Theorising Society and Polities in a Global Area," *Sociology*, 37(3): 529–46.

Wan, G. (ed.). 2008. *Inequality and Growth in Modern China.* UNU-WIDER Studies in Development Economics. Oxford: Oxford University Press.

Watkins, K. 1998. *Economic Growth with Equity: Lessons from East Asia.* Oxford: Oxfam Insight Publications.

———. 2001. "Cost Recovery and Equity in the Health Sector: The Case of Zimbabwe," in G. Mwabu, C. Ugaz, and G. White (eds), *Social Provision in Low-Income Countries. New Patterns and Emerging Trends*, pp. 186–210. Oxford: UNU/WIDER and Oxford University Press.

Weeks, J. 2009. "Global Crisis and Africa—Responses, Lessons Learnt and the Way Forward," Paper at the conference, The Global Financial Crisis and Countercyclical Fiscal Policy, Freetown, August 12–13.

Wei, Shang-Jin and Yi Wu. 2001. "Globalization and Inequality: Evidence from Within China," NBER Working Paper No. 8611.

Wetenschappelijke Raad voor het Regeringsbeleid. 2006. *De Verzorgingsstaat Herwogen. Over Verzorgen, Verzekeren, Verheffen en Verbinden* (The Reweighted welfare. About Care, Insurance, Rising and Joining). Amsterdam: Amsterdam University Press.

Winters, A., N. McCulloch, and X. Cirera. 2001. *Trade Liberalisation and Poverty: A Handbook.* London: Centre for Economic Policy Research.

Wolf, E. 1982. *Europe and the People without History.* Berkeley: University of California Press.

Wolf, M. 2004. *Why Globalization Works. The Case for the Global Market Economy.* New Haven and London: Yale University Press.

———. 2008. *Fixing Global Finance.* Baltimore: Johns Hopkins University Press.

Wong, Edward. 2009. 'China Announces Subsidies for Health Care', *The New York Times*, January 21; available at http://www.nytimes.com/2009/01/22/world/asia/22beijing.html (accessed in May 2010).

Wood, G. 2003. "Governance and the Common Man: Embedding Social Policy in the Search for Security," in P. Mosley and E. Dowler (eds), *Poverty and Social Exclusion in North and South. Essays on Social Policy and Global Poverty Reduction*, pp. 83–121. London and New York: Routledge.

World Bank. 1990. *World Development Report 1990: Poverty*. Washington DC: World Bank.

———. 1994. *Averting the Old Age Crisis: Policies to Protect the Old and Promote Growth*. New York: Oxford University Press.

———. 1997. *Sharing Rising Incomes. China 2020. Disparities in China*. World Bank: Washington DC.

———. 2000. *World Development Report 2000–2001: Attacking Poverty*. Washington DC: World Bank.

———. 2003a. *Inequality in Latin America and the Caribbean: Breaking with History?* Washington DC: World Bank.

———. 2003b. *World Development Indicators 2003*. Washington DC: World Bank.

———. 2005. *Equity and Development, World Development Report 2006*. Oxford: Oxford University Press. *World Development Indicators 2010*. Washington DC: World Bank. Available at http://data.worldbank.org/sites/default/files/wdi/complete.pdf (accessed in July 2010).

———. 2007. *World Development Indicators 2007*. Washington DC: World Bank.

———. 2008. *World Development Indicators 2008*. Washington DC: World Bank; available at http://siteresources.worldbank.org/DATASTATISTICS/Resources/WDI08supplement 1216.pdf (accessed in May 2010).

———. 2009. "Youth and Employment in Africa. The Potential, the Problem, the Promise," Africa Development Indicators 2008/09, World Bank, Washington DC.

———. 2010. *World Development Indicators 2010*. Washington DC: World Bank. Available at http://data.worldbank.org/sites/default/files/wdi/complete.pdf (accessed in July 2010).

World Bank and DFID. 2006. *Unequal Citizens: Gender, Caste and Ethnic Exclusion in Nepal (GSEA)*. Kathmandu: Department for International Development (DFID) and World Bank.

World Bank, Kenya. 2009. "Project Appraisal Document. Cash Transfers for Orphans and Vulnerable Children Project," World Bank, Africa Region; available at www.worldbank.org (accessed in May 2010).

World Bank, South Asia Region. 2003. "India. Sustaining Reform, Reducing Poverty," Report No. 25797-In, World Bank, Washington DC.

World Commission on the Social Dimension of Globalization. 2004. "A Fair Globalization: Creating Opportunities for All," ILO, Geneva; available at http://www.ilo.org/fairglobalization/lang—en/index.htm (accessed in May 2010).

World Health Organization (WHO). 2001. "Health in PRSPs," WHO submission to World Bank/IMF Review of PRSPS, mimeo, Washington DC.

Wu, X. and M. Ramesh. 2009. "Health Care Reforms in Developing Asia: Propositions and Realities," *Development and Change*, 40(3): 531–49.

Yang Tuan (ed.). 2003. *Social Policy in China*. Beijing: The Social Policy Research Centre, Chinese Academy of Social Sciences.

Yeates, N. 2001. *Globalization and Social Policy*. London: Sage.

Yi, I. and B.H. Lee. 2005. "Development Strategies and Unemployment Policies in Korea," in H. Kwon (ed.), *Transforming the Developmental Welfare State in East Asia*, pp. 143–69. London: Palgrave Macmillan; UNRISD.

You, J.-I. and J.-H. Lee. 2001. "South Korea: Economic and Social Consequences of Globalization," in L. Taylor (ed.), *External Liberalization, Economic Performance, and Social Policy*, pp. 283–315. Oxford: Oxford University Press.

Yueh, Linda. 2008. "The Relationship between Law and Economic Growth in China," presentation at Department for International Development (DFID) Seminar series, Beijing, October 24.

Yusof, Z.A. 2006. "Affirmative Action. Malaysia," Policy Brief 13, Inter-Regional Inequality Facility; available at www.odi.org.uk/inter-regional_inequality (accessed in May 2007).

Zakaria, F. 1994. "Culture is Destiny; A Conversation with Lee Kuan Yew," *Foreign Affairs*, 73(2): 109–26.

Zhang, Wenjuan and Tang Dan. 2008. *The New Rural Social Pension and Insurance Programme of Baoji City, Shaanxi Province, China*. Chiang Mai: HelpAge International.

Zhang, Xiaobo and Shenggen Fan. 2007. "Fiscal Decentralization, Non-farm Development, and Spatial Inequality in Rural China," in Max Spoor, Nico Heerink, and Futian Qu (eds), *Dragons with Clay Feet? Transition, Sustainable Land Use, and Rural Environment in China and Vietnam*, pp. 71–81. Lanham, MD: Lexington Book.

Zhang, Xiaobo, Shenggen Fan and A. de Haan, (eds). 2010. *Narratives of Chinese Economic Reforms: How Does China Cross the River?* Singapore, New Jersey, London: World Scientific Publishing.

Zhang, Xiaobo and R. Kanbur. 2003. "Spatial Inequality in Education and Health Care in China"; available at http://www.arts.cornell.edu/poverty/kanbur/ChinaSocialInequality.pdf (accessed in May 2010).

Zhang, Xiulan, Hu Xiaojiang, and Miguel A. Salazar. 2007. "The Role of Family in Social Protection: Evidence from China"; available at http://www.unifi.it/confsp/papers/pdf/Zhang_Xiaojiang_Salazar.doc (accessed in May 2010).

Zhou, Hong. 2004. "EU Social Policy Studies in China," *Asia Europe Journal*, Vol. 2: 415–27.

Zhou, Y.R. 2008. "Review Essay: Economic Reform, Neoliberal Globalization and Social Policy: Restructuring the Relationship between the State, the Market and Citizens in China," *Global Social Policy*, 8(1): 115–28.

Index

About the Author

Arjan de Haan is Senior Lecturer at the Institute of Social Studies, Erasmus University, The Hague, where he is the Convenor of the MA specialization in Population, Poverty and Social Development. Before joining the ISS in 2009 he worked for the UK Department for International Development (DFID), including three years in India and most recently three years in China. His publications include *Reclaiming Social Policy* (2007), *How the Aid Industry Works* (2009), and edited volumes with Ben Rogaly on *Labour Mobility and Rural Society* (2002) and with Xiaobo Zhang and Shenggen Fan on *Narratives of Chinese Economic Reforms* (2010).